*The American
Immigration Collection*

Americans
in
Process

A Settlement Study

ROBERT A. WOODS, EDITOR

Arno Press *and The New York Times*

NEW YORK 1970

Reprint Edition 1970 by Arno Press Inc.

LC# 78-129419
ISBN 0-405-00573-3

The American Immigration Collection—Series II
ISBN for complete set 0-405-00543-1

Manufactured in the United States of America

AMERICANS IN
PROCESS

AMERICANS IN PROCESS

A SETTLEMENT STUDY

BY

RESIDENTS AND ASSOCIATES OF THE
SOUTH END HOUSE

EDITED BY
ROBERT A. WOODS
HEAD OF THE HOUSE

NORTH AND WEST ENDS
BOSTON

BOSTON AND NEW YORK
HOUGHTON, MIFFLIN AND COMPANY
The Riverside Press, Cambridge
1903

PREFACE

THE study of North and West End life which makes up the present volume had its beginning in an investigation of South End conditions, the results of which were published four years ago in the book "The City Wilderness." It was found that much valuable material sought out for the South End study was equally available for the North and West Ends. The direct advantage of such a presentment has been apparent in the South End. The task of each agency for local improvement has been made more distinct. By laying out the large exhaustive measure of the local community's possibilities and needs, a stronger union of forces has been secured. It was felt that a similar study of the North and West Ends would be of service to the scheme of social improvement in those districts.

In the practical work of the South End House, as its plan broadens, it is found essential that the forces existing in these other two downtown working-class districts should be understood and, so far

as possible, dealt with.   There is a gradual drift
of population, including all the different nationalities, from the northern to the southern border of
the business section of the city.   In its local work,
the House is constantly compelled to take account
of this movement of population and the causes
which produce it.   In certain large undertakings
toward social improvement, covering the city in
their scope, but having special concern for the
three downtown tenement-house sections, residents
of the House have been called into service.   This
service is partly in connection with voluntary organizations and partly under the municipality.
Certain special enactments, in the enforcement of
which the residents of the House are much interested, have an almost exclusive bearing upon
these three districts.   In efforts toward the further
development of such legislation, knowledge of the
facts as found in all three districts is needed by
the advocate of the cause of any one of them.
A peculiar stimulus to the present investigation
has come through the hindrance offered at City
Hall by a certain mysterious political power in
the West End to a great project of popular betterment for which the residents of the South End
House, among others, have long worked and will
continue to work until its success is assured.

The South End study had its best use, perhaps, in aiding thoughtful people throughout Boston and its suburbs to discern the vital relation which exists between that district and the local communities in which the prosperous classes reside. It is hoped that the present volume may further aid in making clear the responsibilities in which resourceful citizens stand for the great immigrant populations which are close at the city's heart.

In Boston, as in other large cities, municipal and social reform are much embarrassed by the lack of any kindling realization, even in the minds of sagacious, disinterested persons, of the actual, present-day truth with regard to the urban community in the thick of which the drama of their active life is set. The indifference of the so-called good citizen is largely because his best effort to produce a mental picture of his city in its essential human aspects results in something altogether vague, scattered, out-of-date. Many of the efforts toward better things reflect this lack of mental furnishing in being piecemeal, casual and beside the mark.

The purpose of this volume, as of its predecessor, is to contribute toward building up a contemporary conception of the city, as the groundwork of a type of municipal and social improvement

which shall be accurate in its adaptation to detailed facts and statesmanlike in its grasp of large
forces and total situations. It seems to the writers
that such a conception may best be gained by the
analysis of affairs in one after another of the
congested districts of the city, presenting those
districts in their measure of separateness and in-
dividuality as against the remainder of the city,
while showing, not in the language of exhortation
but in terms of ascertained reality, the complex
connections which bring these districts and the other
sections of the city into a living *ensemble*.

The writers have, with one or two exceptions,
had long familiarity with persons and affairs in
the North and West Ends. The present study
has been progressing during the time since the
volume dealing with the South End was issued.
Of course the writers do not have so intimate a
knowledge of the life of these districts as of the
section of the city in which most of them have for
years lived and worked; but some of them have resided during considerable periods amid the situation covered by the present investigation. One
contributor, Miss Beale, has for some ten years
had unusual opportunities of close acquaintance
with the inner life of the Jewish and Italian
colonies.

The resources of observation and experience possessed by many whose field of work lies largely or entirely in these districts have been freely placed at our service, and have been largely drawn upon. To all the local agents of the Associated Charities, and to all the leading philanthropic workers in both districts, we are much indebted. The public school teachers, particularly Mr. L. H. Dutton and Miss Ellen Sawtelle, have done much to forward one of the most important parts of our inquiry. We have had much assistance from clergymen and other church workers; especially we wish to thánk the Rev. Reuben Kidner, of St. Andrew's Church, for his constant aid and encouragement. For many valuable suggestions as to the social history of the North End, we are indebted to the late Henry B. Mackintosh, son of Peter Mackintosh, master of the Hancock School in the early part of the last century. The records and special knowledge of various public officials and bureaus have been put at our service, — the Police Department at the central office and the local stations, the Board of Health, the Board of Assessors, the State Factory Inspectors, the State Bureau of Statistics of Labor, the Inspector of Immigration for Boston.

The editor has again had the general assistance

of his colleague in the direction of the South End House, Mr. William I. Cole. Mrs. William L. Rutan, an associate in the work of the settlement during the past ten years, beside making her contributions to the text, has assisted with the proofreading and prepared the index. Several residents of the House have helped with the collection of statistics and other data for some of the chapters, chiefly Messrs. Fred E. Haynes, Rufus E. Miles, Roswell F. Phelps and Everett W. Goodhue.

While the study was in its early stages the writers received valuable suggestions from two books, both written by men now or formerly connected with Toynbee Hall and therefore from a point of view particularly suited to the present purpose. These books are " Italy To-Day," by Bolton King and Thomas Okey (Scribners), and " The Jew in London," by C. Russell and H. S. Lewis (Crowell).

The double-page maps, which are brought down to the time of publication, are intended accurately to indicate preponderating conditions in each block. In the nationality map, where there is a double strip of color, it is to be understood that no single nationality is in a majority in the block, but that two nationalities are represented in proportions of from thirty to fifty per cent. each. In the map showing industrial grades, a type of block is shown here which does not exist at the South End, — one in which the unskilled and the clerks are somewhat equally represented, while skilled workmen are hardly found. This state of things, which goes with the Jewish tendency to leap over the skilled labor stage in their haste to become shopkeepers, is marked by a new mixed color. In preparing the maps, the same detailed methods have been followed as those explained in the preface of " The City Wilderness." The district maps cover nearly the whole of two wards and a small portion of a third. The North End is substantially identical with Ward 6, so far as population is concerned. The West End maps cover practically all of Ward 8, with a narrow strip of Ward 11.

In a few instances reference is made to " The City Wilderness " for a somewhat fuller treatment of topics which naturally called for greater emphasis in that volume than in this. In one or two cases some repetition seemed advisable. The two books are essentially independent. It is the earnest hope of the writers, however, having proceeded thus far, that these may be fitted together with the results of further investigations into a comprehensive exposition of social conditions in Boston at the beginning of the twentieth century.

CONTENTS

MAPS

AMERICANS IN PROCESS

CHAPTER I

METES AND BOUNDS

FROM Boston Common two blocks to the north begins a wedge-shaped open space, in whose extreme angle commercial respectability fades away into freak shows, burlesque theatres, palm gardens, and the like. Scollay Square has so many radiating outlets to all corners of heaven that it might have afforded the original suggestion of Boston's somewhat outworn municipal epithet. One street dips and then runs on as straight as these old streets ever run, into the heart of the North End. Another, having begun its winding course on the city side among great office buildings, loses itself in the square, but takes up the thread again at an unexpected point among the dubious resorts, as a West End thoroughfare. A third street is one of the approaches to the North Union Station. The station, with its broad stretch of tracks and the stream of traffic to and from it, all flanked by thoroughfares to Charlestown and East Cambridge, sets off the North and West Ends distinctly from each other. At night, however, after the streets leading to the station become comparatively deserted, the districts are united by two steady processions jostling each other as they slowly move back and forth, — shoppers, theatre-goers, callers, strollers.

The North End is less than half a mile in any of its dimensions. It is a "tight little island," hemmed in by continuous and ever-encroaching currents of commercial activity. The station thoroughfares lead to the markets. The markets extend to the docks. The docks reach around from the markets to the railroads again.

The West End, beginning at the North Station, — with whose traffic it is more concerned than the North End, — has another curving water front as a boundary. On the south, Beacon Hill makes an effectual barrier. The West End population is allowed, however, to take possession of the bleak northeast slope. It is also beginning to make its way by force around the foot of the hill on either side.

The interior frame of the North End is that of one main highway to the East Boston ferry, with

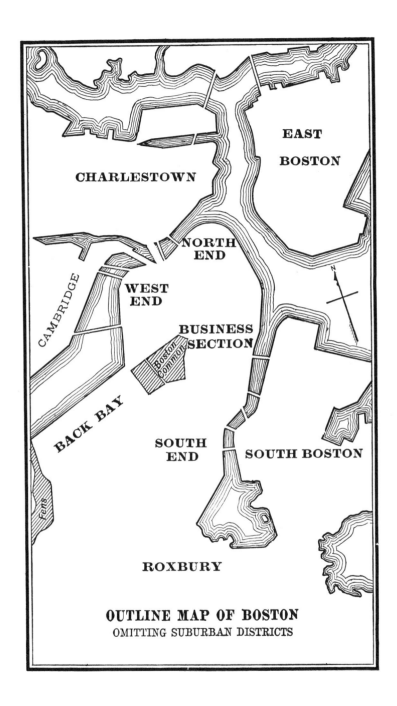

CHARLESTOWN

EAST
BOSTON

NORTH
END

WEST
END

CAMBRIDGE

BUSINESS
SECTION

Boston
Common

BACK BAY

Fens

SOUTH
END

SOUTH BOSTON

ROXBURY

OUTLINE MAP OF BOSTON
OMITTING SUBURBAN DISTRICTS

a tributary street running on either side of it. The thoroughfare, Hanover Street, is cosmopolitan. Salem Street, toward the water, selected as a place of peaceful abode by Hebraist Puritans, is now, in the whirligig of time, turned over to the Hebrews themselves. North Street, on the side toward the markets, is, as it were, an Alpine pass through cold-storage warehouses into " Little Italy." These three arteries of travel open the way to a network of cross-streets, passageways and blind alleys.

The West End has two squares serving as ganglia for its communication, one with the business section of the city, the other with the North Station. Beyond these squares go thoroughfares converging toward the West Boston Bridge to Cambridgeport. Most of the streets auxiliary to these are not so narrow nor so close together as the corresponding communicating ways of the North End. The situation in the West End is one of contrasts, — places as dark and noisome as any in the North End; frequent rows of houses retaining an air of comfort and respectability such as has almost wholly passed from the North End. Often these contrasts represent the degenerate and progressive extremes of life among the remnant of the former possessors of both districts, the Irish.

The North and West Ends do not have the

advantage of being central and pivotal in their accessibility to the whole city, as the South End has.[1] They stand curiously aloof, so far as social contact and intercommunication are concerned. The North End, shut in between the business section and the water, has no nearer neighbor for resident population — excluding the West End itself — than Charlestown and East Boston. The West End is almost as completely isolated. It touches other resident population only at the confines of the Beacon Hill quarter; and this is the one point where any of the struggling people of these districts have the semblance of neighborly contact with prosperous and responsible Boston citizens. As the inhabitants of this part of the West End are chiefly negroes, it is to be feared that the only relation resulting from the propinquity is a constrained political one, and mutually corrupting at that.

Indeed, as so often happens, contact produces a recoil, — the black belt shuts off the West End from view to a considerable extent. On the other hand, the very distinctness of the North End as a community in itself constitutes part of the attraction which it holds for the imagination. It is true, of course, that the history of the West End as a

[1] *The City Wilderness*, p. 4.

poor district is somewhat recent, while the North End has for generations been Boston's classic land of poverty. To this day, though other parts of the city can show worse neighborhoods, economically and morally, it is difficult for the elderly Boston citizen to set any distressing occurrence associated with the life of the poor in other scenes than those of the North End.

The North End combines in curious fashion the atmosphere belonging to distinct foreign colonies with that of many of the special historic associations and mementos of old Boston. Its Revolutionary landmarks make it a source of pride to all intelligent citizens of Boston. There are few days in the year when some group of visitors in the city do not find their way to these interesting spots. They can hardly return through the North End throng without some anxious query as to the part which the most recent recruits will take in the American people's future history. Such coming and going also serves to give the immigrant some intimation of the better standards which mark the country of his adoption.

The West End is more modern; and being so near to the heart of the city contains a number of the institutions that are inseparable from the movement of a great city's life. Some of these suggest care about its wreckage and tragedy, — the Charity Building, the Wayfarers' Lodge, several great hospitals, the county jail, the morgue. The public dignity of the community is present in the State House and the Court House, both of which reach back to the edge of this district. Naturally these different institutions bring a large number of responsible citizens back and forth in the West End, and contribute toward the existence of a human touch between it and more favored parts of the city.

Even the indifferent among the rich are compelled on occasion to have a glimpse of the North and West End Lazarus. The way to Europe, if one sail from Boston, lies through the North End. The way to the North Shore and its summer charms lies through the West End. Before embarking on train or ship, with all their wafting suggestion, there comes to many that challenge of responsibility for the common good, which is the very life of democracy, and without which, as recent solemn warnings have assured us, our great cities will rush to industrial and moral disaster.

This feeling of responsibility, so far as Boston is concerned, has to a large extent been infused into the Boston mind as the result of half a century of endeavor directed toward meeting the needs of the particular districts of the city which are under review in this volume. The constant change and growth of the problem as a result of successive tidal waves of immigration has made it impossible for the methods of the past to keep pace with the needs which they sought to remedy. Nevertheless, there was developed in these districts, before the days of scientific charity or preventive philanthropy, that keen social compunction out of whose very failures those maturer developments have arisen.

Fifteen years ago the organization of charity began to ripen into forms of action designed to shut off some of the need of relief in the individual and family life, and lift the people, especially the young, to the level of fair opportunities of industry and happiness. But a final overwhelming incursion of helpless, inarticulate foreigners swept in upon the North End, and in less degree upon the West End, necessarily postponing the larger growth of personal philanthropy, and precipitating sanitary, industrial and moral problems so threatening that it became necessary to call upon the State for new and unprecedented forms of legislative action.

The crowding of buildings upon land, and of human beings into buildings, became extreme and unendurable. There was much determined action on the part of the Board of Health, under the reassuring spur of an even more determined public sentiment. It was found, however, that the powers of the Board were insufficient. In London, the sanitary authorities had been granted power not merely to vacate but to destroy objectionable habitations, and certain great single areas had been demolished. New York had, so far as legislation goes, followed in the footsteps of England, but there had been as yet no satisfactory enforcement of the law. In Boston this most advanced form of legislation against the slum has for five years now been enforced with increasing grasp and effectiveness.

The new immigrant population introduced a system of home industry tending quickly to degrade family life and to depress greatly the wage standard of our people. Through adequate legislation, systematically administered, Boston has conducted an original experiment of the highest importance to the whole civilized world, resulting in the practical abolition of that worst pest of city industry, the sweating system.

At the same time, without special legislation, but by the direct pressure of public sentiment upon the police authorities, a telling blow has been dealt at the different established headquarters of those degrading forms of prostitution which, in New York particularly, have grown to be the most serious threat of congested tenement life. By these searching reforms directed almost exclusively at conditions in the North and West Ends, the two districts have had some of the most unyielding factors eliminated bodily from their social equation. As a result, voluntary public service, through which the whole of both districts is kept under general moral surveillance and, in lesser degree, under influences of a personally inspiring and upbuilding sort, finds itself in a wholly new stage of incentive and opportunity. It is an even greater source of encouragement that the developments of private philanthropy seem likely to be far outdistanced by the ministry of social opportunity on the part of the municipality.

The growth of communities of Continental immigrants in Boston was at first of the nature of a calamity to the city. The main action of the community as a whole was brought to bear, and the calamitous stage was erelong safely passed. Boston has contrived to erect dikes against its quota of the deluge of tenement-house evils with which New York and, in a different way, Chicago are still overwhelmed. Some years must still elapse before the two great metropolitan cities, with their appalling difficulties, shall have come into a calm and steady era of reconstruction such as Boston has already reached. Meanwhile, the situation outlined in these chapters may more or less closely represent the problem of alien life which confronts the average large city in the United States. It is true that no city in the country has the recuperative resources, in proportion to its size, that are available in the matured community existence of Boston. It is, however, one of the chief distinctions of present-day American life in general that there is so great a variety of effort, municipal, commercial, philanthropic, for the advancement of general human well-being among all our urban populations.

CHAPTER II

UNTIL the year 1630, the tract of New England soil that was to become the town of Boston lay a rough and almost uncultivated stretch of perhaps six hundred acres, uninhabited save for a solitary English farmer whose name is preserved at the northern and southern extremes of his ancient squatter's claim in Blackstone Street and Blackstone Square. The territory was known by the Indians as Shawmut, and was in form a peninsula, connected with the mainland upon the south by a narrow neck. With broken, irregular outline, it extended into the harbor in a general northerly direction, terminating at the northeast and northwest in promontories at the points where the Charles and the Mystic empty into the bay. The fields sloping back from these promontories were the sections known to-day as the North and West Ends of Boston, and were separated at that time by a deep tidal inlet, covered with water at high tide, but at ebb presenting a dreary surface of mud flats, in extent about equal to the present Boston Common.

These extremes of the city are often referred to as its oldest parts.   In reality the western pastures lay almost untouched for a century, while the eastern extremity as a building site was only the second thought of the colonists.   The latter lay due north from the narrow neck, directly across the bay from Charlestown.   In a letter sent back to England by a young girl, one of the first boat-load of immigrants to land at Shawmut, is a description of the locality.   " A place very uneven," Ann Pollard writes, " abounding in small hollows and swamps covered with blueberries and other low bushes."   Between the low northern tract, which these words seem to fit, and the higher lands to the south lay an almost impassable marsh, now marked by Blackstone Street, and it is to this feature that the district owes its earliest name, " The Island of North Boston."   Over the marsh's narrowest breadth, a distance of about eight hundred feet, the waters of the inlet upon the west and those of a deep indentation known as the Great Cove upon the east mingled at high tide and cut off the land to the north from the main body of the peninsula.   Except for an elevation of fifty feet close by the shore, now known as

Copp's Hill, upon which the girl may have stood as she framed her description, Shawmut's northern acres were low and would easily come within her range. Looking beyond them to the south across the waters of the Great Cove on her left, she might see Fort Hill, to-day but a memory brought to mind by the name Fort Hill Square. Beyond the waters of the tidal inlet on her right, soon to be transformed into the Mill Pond, rose the three long since diminished heads of Beacon Hill, the tri-mountain from which Boston gained her second name, preserved in Tremont Street.

The company of English Puritans who purchased the territory just described landed at a point on the coast near the present Charles River Bridge in the fall of 1630, and crossed the marsh, establishing their first homes in the neighborhood of Spring Lane. For a year or more, the chief business of their town government was the allotment of land. Only a very few assignments were made in the western pastures, but in consequence of the business possibilities suggested by the harbor frontage, shore allotments in the northern acres soon came to be looked upon as desirable. Although the low interior of the district probably did not appeal to the settlers at once as a site for homes, it was not long before its advantages were discovered. Its nearness to what soon showed themselves to be future business parts of the town, the coast line and Dock Square, gradually caused it to find favor in the eyes of the artisans, with their long hours of labor and their frequent habit of combining home and shop. Between the first place of settlement and the point upon the coast nearest the opposite village of Charlestown a track was naturally worn to the ferry, and along this road and to either side of it sprang up the humble homes of cobbler, carpenter, candle-maker, cooper, and biscuit baker, — low cottages with shops attached, and in many cases with land at the back sloping down to a wharf. In a few years the main outlines of the old North End were those that may be seen to-day, a district but three streets wide, — Hanover, Salem, and North streets, — with Hanover Street, then as now, the middle and main thoroughfare, " The Way leading to the Ferry." Salem and North streets followed the coast line; and east and west from the highway ran connecting lanes, their crooked outlines, which more than two hundred years of travel have not made straight, taking shape according to the caprice of the home-builders.

The first poor cottages that lined these quiet, country roads were no proof of the energy and ingenuity of their owners. The colony's scanty records afford occasional impressive glimpses of the determination that made the hamlet a town, and many of the efforts most important to the general welfare centred at the North End. A nineteenth century historian has exclaimed concerning Boston, " No other great city of the world has undergone such changes at the hands of man ; not a trace of its original outline remains." The beginning of this remarkable transformation may be traced to the measures taken to supply the early demand for mill facilities. Across the tidal inlet that separated the North End from the remote western pastures ran a ridge of land where Causeway Street now lies, that had been used by the Indians as a footpath over the flats. This ridge suggested a dam with the possibilities of water-power, and in a few years from the time of settlement the acres of useless, offensive flats had been transformed into a Mill Pond supplying power for tidal grist-mills, for years the chief mills of the town. A company of men who soon leased the Mill Pond privileges drained the marsh, digging a deep trench at the narrowest point and bridging it. The canal thus formed connected the Mill Pond and the Great Cove, and was known for a century and a half as the Mill Creek.

Such changes as these, rapidly increasing as they did both the accessibility and the business importance of the North End, resulted in the district's becoming before the end of the century the most densely populated part of the town, — a character it has never lost. In the burying-ground on Copp's Hill it is said that more than half of the inhabitants of the town during its first century were buried. That the population was fairly prosperous as well as numerous may be inferred from the building of the Second Church in 1650, the meeting-house of the famous Mathers on North Square. As the North End grew, this square became the centre of the district, both as a residential quarter and a place of public assembly. The town pump was there, and one of the earliest market-places, and after the building of the church the residences of the most influential parishioners clustered about it or were built in the adjoining streets. The successive generations of Mathers all lived near the church, and men like Holyoke, the soap-boiler, father of the future Harvard president, plied their trades in the cottages round about.

For the first half century, the North End continued a growing, flourishing community. From what we may gather, that earliest society had

a certain ideal character despite its grim defects.
The settlers were largely artisans, but they were
artisans of unusual quality and intense religious
convictions, whose chief ambition was to make
homes and establish an ideal state, where " magistrate and minister walked hande in hande, dis-
countenancing and punishing sin in whomsoever,
and standing for the praise of them that do well."
The homesteads of very few can be positively
located, though here and there the memory of a
man's residence and a glimpse of character survives in the name of his property or the record
of some public act. Thomas Marshall — keeper
of the first ferry " from Mylne Point to Charlestown," which lay at the foot of Black Horse
Lane, later Prince Street — frequently appears in
the old records. " Ferryman, shoemaker, selectman, land-owner, and deacon," he may be regarded
as a representative citizen. His home and garden were on " The Highway leading from the
Orange Tavern to the Ferry; " and in 1652,
moved by an idea that was perhaps shrewd as
well as generous, he gave the town a roading
across his land to shorten the distance to the
drawbridge over the Mill Creek, just as Marshall
Street now offers a short-cut from Union to Hanover Street.

This gift of a short-cut suggests also another story, that of the growth that had gone on at either side of the creek, too rapidly to be a substantial one. Stores and dwellings were of poor, slight character, structures designed to meet a hasty need, and of inflammable material. A growth of this kind could not be long uninterrupted, and between 1676 and 1679 the catastrophe inevitable in a thickly settled community of such a sort took place. Great fires swept the northern end of the town; the first, north of the creek, consuming the church on North Square and many dwellings roundabout; the second, starting in Dock Square and spreading until eighty dwelling-houses, seventy warehouses, and several vessels lying in dock were burned.

As nearly as it may be defined, the conflagrations of the last quarter of the century mark the close of the first period of Boston life, the distinctly Puritan period. The rebuilding of the northern part of the town was accomplished by a people entering upon very different conditions from those affecting the men who first struck their spades into the rocky soil of the blueberry pastures. Growing prosperity and a rapidly increasing population united with the change from colonial to crown government that came in 1685 to bring about

marked alterations both in habits and ideals.
English governors with their families and a train
of servants and employees introduced a social
life long distinct and alien from that of the Puritans, but none the less exerting a powerful and
subtle influence. If Thomas Marshall, shoemaker
and selectman, was representative of the first
period, John Hull, merchant and mint-master,
was as surely a type of the second. He, too,
lived north of the Mill Creek, where a street
still testifies to his position in the community;
and it was in his home on Sheafe Street that the
first mint was set up. It is John Hull who
said of Endicott, "He died poor, as most of
our rulers do, having more attended the public
than their own private interests." Hull's virtues
were after another order. He did not die poor.
"He rendered fairly to the public, and in return
he took his own."

With the appointment of Sir William Phips in
1692, the story of North End life becomes more
varied. Governor Phips had been a North End
boy, apprentice to a ship-carpenter, and upon his
return to Boston, enriched and titled, after many
years of absence, he built a " fair dwelling " near
his boyhood's haunts. It may have been the
mansion house of Sir William and Lady Phips,

on the corner of Charter Street, that first
turned the tide of fashion across the Mill Creek;
for at the beginning of the new century the sober
streets of the North End were here and there relieved by the gay attire and free demeanor of men
to whom court life was a familiar experience; and
mingling with the gossip of the North Church
parish spread rumors of the doings of fashionable
dames who were making the best of a temporary
exile from English society.

The buildings that sprang up after the great
fire expressed both increasing prosperity and these
changing social conditions. The flames had destroyed the hovels, and the new houses of brick
and cement suggested hospitality, and had a comfort and a beauty of their own. Many of the better
sort were built with overhanging stories and clustered gables. These devices at once gave an
imposing appearance and helped out the limited
space of the building lot, and between each and its
neighbor there was only room enough for "the
privilege of eaves-dripping." This is but one of
the many indications that the district was growing
crowded. Early in the century building companies
began to form, cutting new roads through such
meadows as yet remained, and laying them out in
house lots, narrow at the front but affording long

gardens at the back ; and by 1708, when the first formal list of streets was made, there were found to be as many streets, lanes, and alleys around Dock Square and northward as in all the rest of the town. If the North End at this time is to be thought of as the centre of population and business, the South End, stretching from Milk Street out toward the Neck, held, perhaps, the suburban part of the town, while the West End still offered opportunity for residents who preferred isolation or homes partaking of the nature of farms. The last was a section triangular in shape, and it had at the beginning of the seventeenth century but two roads cut through its pastures, — Sudbury Street, connecting it with the business centre, and Cambridge Street. Beyond were fields and pastures, which were coming to be called " The New Fields," as the eyes of the citizens turned speculatively toward them. What is now Bowdoin Square was known as Bowling Green, and fell away in a grassy slope to the Mill Pond. On a small eminence on Cambridge Street stood a windmill. At the point of the triangle were copper works, and in various parts of the fields were most of the ropewalks of the town, long, narrow sheds, sometimes over seven hundred feet in length, where rope and twine of all sorts were spun. The ropewalks became an important industry in Boston, as many as sixty spinning at one time. Even at this early date there was great demand for their products both from vessels rigged for foreign service and from fishing and coasting craft demanding rougher sort of cordage. The district was very sparsely peopled, containing only an occasional farm and the dwellings of the proprietors of those little manufacturing enterprises that demanded the stretch of ground the New Fields afforded. The land was in the hands of a few men whose names are handed down in the streets cut later on through their pastures. Phillips, Leverett, Lynde and Staniford, Chambers and Russell, were large property holders, while the Rev. James Allen at the beginning of the eighteenth century owned a far larger part of the territory of Boston than was ever held by any one individual save Blackstone, the pioneer.

The history of the district is simply one of changing and increasing proprietors and their building enterprises, and can be almost completely traced up to the time of the Revolution in the names of its streets. This last may be said also of the North End, except for the difference that there is between its characteristics and those of the West End. The latter is the story of individual citizens of an established community; while the history of the North End, as told by the varying names of its streets, is a tale of a town's inception and hard-won development. In the early Puritan times, the titles given the streets of the latter district are mostly of a cumbrous, descriptive character, as "The street leading up to the house of Sir William Phips, Knight." In Garden Court Street there still lingers a pleasant flavor of the descriptive custom; but most of the old names that survive chronicle events rather than characteristics, and show the difference between the simple expedients of a hamlet and the exacting demands of a growing town. The more formal and permanent names of streets appear in the complete list already mentioned as having been made in 1708. At that time Black Horse Lane ceased to be called after the tavern at its head and was known as Prince Street, while Fleet Street became the recognized title of Scarlet's Wharf Lane.

The year 1700 may be said to mark about the middle of a half century in which New England life was in a transition state. "The Pilgrims had gone out," wrote Sewall, "and the large men had not come in." Intellectually this was Boston's dark age. The fervor of the religious life that animated the first settlers was going, and the records of the churches show petty and revolting altercations. It was its mercantile importance, constantly increasing, that saved the social character of the town. So important a seaport could not be neglected by the mother country. The supervision of the colony's affairs demanded the services of clever governors ; the business openings offered by growing trade brought good blood from the old world to seek a younger son's uncertain fortunes in the new; and many of the incoming merchants and crown officials chose their dwellings north of the creek. Before the century had completed its first quarter the sober, church-going North End was well started upon its bravest period, and for fifty years was to be known as the court end of the town. The pronounced change from exclusive Puritanism was plainly manifested by the building of Christ Church on Salem Street in 1723. Its congregation, without doubt, was mainly made up of the families of the new English merchants and the crown officials, and the demand for its existence shows the considerable size of the new society, as the style of the edifice the wealth of its members.

North Square continued to be the social centre, and it represented both phases of life at their best. Side by side with the modest, substantial houses that were the homes of the attendants of the

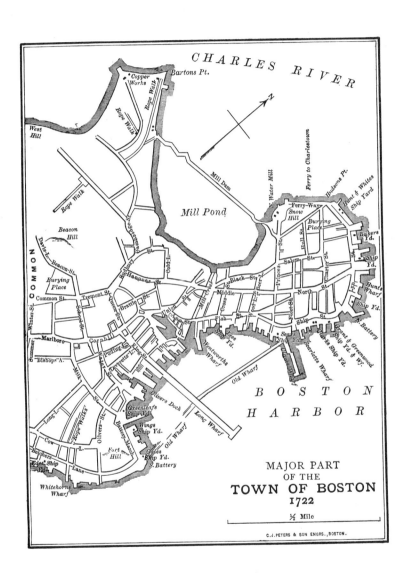

MAJOR PART
OF THE
TOWN OF BOSTON
1722

½ Mile

C.J. PETERS & SON ENGRS., BOSTON.

church of the Mathers stood two mansions around the memory of which are gathered tales of splendor and ceremony in little accord with the traditions of the Puritans. One of these, Governor Hutchinson's home, is inseparably connected with the Stamp Act troubles, for in 1765 it was sacked by the infuriated mob, its owner barely escaping with his life ; while around the house of Sir Harry Frankland linger not only tales of the young Port collector's luxurious tastes, but also the strange romance of Agnes Surriage, his peasant ward of Marblehead. These houses have long since disappeared, and the one landmark now remaining upon the square, in the low wooden house of Paul Revere, is a reminder of a very different life and spirit. The age-long drama of the Roundhead and the Cavalier was being enacted in New England as truly as it had been in the old. While a mimic London society gives color to the fifty years preceding the Revolution, a deeper, stronger life was developing among the plain people, which was doubtless broadened and rendered more effective in its final outbreak by the forced contact with the fashionable world. Names and phrases, well-worn to-day, were used then for the first time with no thought that they were to prove the imperishable catchwords of a great nation's politics. " Samuel

Adams and twenty others," writes an old historian,
"used to meet and make a *caucus*." This is the
first time this word is seen; and from the fact
that the meetings referred to were held in a part
of Boston where the ship business was carried on,
etymologists have agreed that *caucus* is a corruption of *calkers*, *meeting* being understood. A
few years later, upon Washington's birthday,
William Cooper uttered the famous words, " The
spirit of the times; " and on June seventeenth of
the same year, 1774, there was coined in Boston the
phrase " Continental Congress," when a term was
required to show American union as opposed to
the English king and Parliament. Boston was becoming more than a colonial town, and the little
North End held within its narrow breadth not only
governing forces from an old world, but also the
germs of a young republic.

The days of Winthrop and Endicott, Sewall and
Hull, were gone, but young men were being born
and bred in Boston in whose greatness posterity
has had even more reason to believe. Franklin
had left his father's home at the corner of Hanover and Union streets before 1725, preferring
to seek his fortune in another line than that of
his inherited trade of soap-boiling and candle-
making; but Adams and Hancock and Revere

and Otis lived or worked at the North End during the middle years of the century, suavely and
shrewdly conducting their business by day, while
nightly they foregathered at the Green Dragon or
the Salutation Inn, maturing plans of which the
results were to help on the birth of a nation.

This, however, was but an undercurrent for years,
scarcely disturbing the calm surface of Boston's
steady material development. North of the Mill
Creek the streets grew crowded with dwellings, all
of brick after 1711, when the law forbade the further use of wood. Side gardens became too valuable for their owners to keep, and houses elbowed
each other in their effort for frontage, or actually
united in blocks. Another church had been erected,
" seventeen substantial mechanics " forming a new
society ; and on the site of the Eliot School of
to-day had been established a "Latin Grammar
School " for boys. Every sort of business flourished along the water line and about the Town
Dock. In 1724 sixteen master ship-carpenters of
the Thames were complaining to the King that
their trade was being injured and their workmen
were emigrating on account of the New England
competition ; and six of the shipyards that were
proving such formidable rivals to the mother country lay just at the base of Copp's Hill. The great

gift of Faneuil Hall, made to the town by Peter
Faneuil in 1740, established the gateway to the
North End for the remainder of the century as
the business heart of Boston.

With this growth of business came increased
population and constant demand for building lots
having frontage upon thoroughfares.   Under such
need the West End, during the second quarter of
the eighteenth century, grew rapidly to be a community by itself.   Leverett Street was cut through
in 1730, forming a second highway to Cambridge,
and by 1733 all the older thoroughfares had been
laid out and named.   The beginning of a local
social life is seen in the establishment of the West
Church in 1736.   This church was put up on
Lynde Street, opposite Cambridge Street, and from
the day of its establishment throughout the century
and a half of its existence it continued to represent
in both pulpit and parish a most substantial type
of Boston life, both social and intellectual.   Cotton
Hill, where crown officials formed an exclusive
society, and the Bowling Green were the only
centres of wealth in the westerly part of the
town.   The other streets were built up gradually
with modest, comfortable homes, with comparatively little business encroachment except the small
shops and the increasing number of ropewalks,

though these last fled before the homes instead of the usual reverse result.

In spite of court end traditions, of which the novelists make the most, and the alleged splendors of Cotton Hill, the pre-revolutionary life of Boston seems strangely simple. John Frizell, a wealthy merchant who lived on Garden Court the first quarter of the eighteenth century, and who owned much land in the neighborhood, was the first man in Boston to keep a carriage, and the first stable in the town was his on Moon Street. By 1768, the number of people to keep carriages was only twenty-two, and even at the end of the century they numbered but one hundred and forty-five. Few houses were spacious enough to admit of large functions, and festivities of any size were held in one or two halls that could be hired for such occasions at the North End. Aside from the official life and a small group of large merchants, the prosperity of the town was represented by master mechanics and tradesmen. Toward the end of the century six of the wealthiest men of the town were bakers, three of whom, John White, Edward Edes, and Deacon Tudor, lived at the North End. At the time of the siege of Boston, the baker, Ebenezer Torrey, removed to Sudbury, and died leaving an estate of $100,000.

When the discontent of half a century culminated in the uncontrollable outbreak that became the War of Independence, the North End was the scene of exciting preliminary action, and the vantage ground from which the first decisive battle was watched. There seems to be no doubt that the plain people, joined by a scattering few of the wealthier class, formed the nucleus of Boston's patriotic party. Paul Revere, the versatile North Square goldsmith, has left on record, " In the fall of 1774 and winter of 1775, I was one of upwards thirty, chiefly mechanics, who formed themselves into a committee for the purpose of watching the British soldiers and gaining every intelligence of the movements of the Tories."

These days, in which the North End reached the height of its historic fame, were in their very nature the beginning of its decadence. When General Howe left Boston, on the eighth of March, 1776, he took with him nearly one thousand of the residents of the town. Such wealthy and important families as the North End had held were among these refugees ; and in the period of reconstruction that followed the war, the little Island of North Boston, though continuing to be the most populous district of the town, and containing within its narrow confines one third of the whole number of inhabitants on the peninsula, did not again attract people of means and ideas of luxurious living. Its streets were narrow and crooked, its houses small and too thickly crowded to admit of new buildings. The tide of fashion turned westward and up the slopes of the trimountain; and even the Puritan type, as it prospered and rebuilt, found the North End unsuited to its broadening tastes. Previous to the Evacuation, the largest congregation in the town had been that of the New North Church on Hanover Street. Its subsequent decay is typical of the change in the whole district. In 1775, many of its members retired to the country, and upon their return to Boston did not renew their connection with the church. Says an old chronicler, " The young gentlemen who have married wives in other parts of the town have found it difficult to persuade them to become so ungenteel as to attend worship at the North End. Even the clergymen have abandoned that part of the town. There are six large congregations to the northward of the canal, and only one of their ministers resides there." Hanover and Salem streets and their lanes were left to folk of busy lives and limited means who still prized the advantages of homes near the centre of trade ; and until the middle of the century they held a constantly decreasing number of thrifty mechanics and small merchants, with occasional families of means and culture who clung to their old homes.

The loss in population which Boston sustained after the war had been made up by a new element coming into the city to take advantage of the fresh commercial openings. This consisted of wealthy country families, largely from Essex County, who quickly took a prominent part in both the business and public life of the town. Splendid mansions were built, exceeding anything that Boston had seen before in the way of homes; many on Fort Hill, some on Beacon Hill, and others on the Bowling Green, which in 1788 received its new name. It was at that time the seat of spacious old-time mansion houses, with beautiful grounds and fine trees, and most of the householders were well-known men. By the beginning of the century, Bowdoin Square was the most important social centre at the West End, and it was almost the only spot at the time where any large number of wealthy or distinguished families built.

By 1775 the cross streets in the vicinity of the square had most of them the outlines of to-day. Further west the greater part of the area was in its primitive condition of pastures, with the pest-house and the Province hospital located upon Grove

Street by reason of the remoteness of the locality. In 1784 the whole West End held one meeting-house and about one hundred and seventy dwellings, and it was looked upon as rather a remote district, although it was regarded favorably as a pleasant and healthy one on account of its shelter from the east winds. From the beginning of the nineteenth century, its growth was rapid in every direction. In thirty years it had outwardly much the appearance of to-day, and socially the character that it was to preserve for half a century. To the west and north, streets were quickly put through, and by 1804 Pinckney and Hancock and Myrtle streets were crowned with pleasant homes. In that year the child population had become sufficiently large and democratic to demand a public school, and the Mayhew School was erected on the corner of Chardon and Hawkins streets.

The social development of the West End was for many years in inverse ratio to the decay of the North End. Just as the former reached its best development, the latter, about 1850, was yielding up its last traces of the old American life. Its changes, however, after the first great loss of wealth in 1775, were gradual ones. Names still spoken in Boston are associated with the decadent period of the old court end. Hanover Street,

though abounding in small stores, held a good
many substantial families up to 1840.   On Sheafe
Street, Lyman Beecher and his famous family
made their home ; and it is this street, with its old
gardens at the back, which was the last to suc-
cumb to the pressure of the immigrants.   Its final
surrender was dramatically sudden, according to
the district's historian.   Nine families who ate
Thanksgiving dinner on Sheafe Street one year
were partaking of it the next at the South End.
North Street, long doubtful in character, sunk still
further in degradation, and gradually infected its
neighbors.   One by one the quiet streets were
encroached upon by the two fatal enemies of home
life, the tenement and retail business; until for
fifty years the North End has been simply a
synonym for the first sheltering place of hordes of
immigrants fleeing from oppressive conditions of
the old world ; one race after another successively
settling, prospering, and moving on.

As of old, North Square is the centre of a social
life ; but over the doors of houses where once
stood the homes of English carpenters, coopers,
and candle-makers, hang Italian patronymics ; and
the quiet triangle resounds to the chatter of a
people to whom the tongue of Holyoke and Mather
is almost as strange as the famous Puritans' names.

As of old, the district is but three streets wide. The pressure of business buildings erected on the new land keeps the tenements within the old outlines prescribed by the waters of the long-forgotten Pond, Creek, and Cove. The North End is no longer an island, no longer even a peninsula; acres of made land connect its area with that of the West End, the promontory so many centuries divided from it by the tide-water and the Mill Pond. At the beginning of the last century, the Mill Pond was filled in; in 1828 the water was cut off from the Mill Creek; and in 1868 came the final obliterations of the island's early outlines, when the shore of the Great Cove was dredged and the Cove made solid land by the transference to its bed of the earth that had once formed Fort Hill. Boston's original distinguishing features, a historian observes, were its hills and coves; but in the course of years " its coves have swallowed up its hills."

This development of the old district's possibilities had its effect upon the character of the neighboring West End, though the change was so gradual as to be hardly perceptible at any one time. For many years the district altered very little outwardly, the vacant lots on the slopes of the hill filling up with tall, narrow houses overflowing with

family life. Regular blocks were the exception,
as householders were establishing their own homes
for the most part, and each built after his own
fancy so far as limited space would permit. The
occasional wooden house of the first of the century
gave up its garden to the square-cornered brick
wedge that followed it as a model dwelling, and
both were overshadowed later on by the four-story
swell front that gained in favor after 1850. The
important changes henceforth were the gradual,
imperceptible ones incidental to the pressure from
behind of business and immigration.

As Bowdoin Square earliest became a social
centre, so it first felt these encroachments which
advanced quickly after the work of filling in
the Mill Pond began. The square's existence as
a fashionable quarter covered perhaps fifty years.
Within that period its character changed from
country homes to suburban estates ; these later
giving way to city blocks of stone and brick, some
of which still survive transformed into buildings
for public use. After 1875, changes came rapidly,
and old inhabitants began to look back upon a
time when society was unmixed with the dreaded
" foreign element."

During most of the nineteenth century, the
West End was a district splendidly representative

of Anglo-Saxon American life. Upon the summit
of Beacon Hill were the finest residences of the
city, rapidly increasing in number after the com-
pletion of the State House in 1798; and upon the
streets just behind the State House to the east,
Hancock, Temple, and Bowdoin streets, lived some
of the most distinguished men in Boston's history.
In sharp contrast, close by, on the slope of the
hill, stood miserable huts tenanted by the most
disreputable people of the city. At the end of
Joy Street and straggling northward was a colony
of negroes living in extreme squalor. Except for
the portions occupied by these extremes of society,
the West End was a comfortable, fairly well-to-do
community, abundantly supplied with churches and
public schools. It was cut off from the rest of
residential Boston by the Common and business
sections, and preserved the distinct local feeling
and characteristics of a small town. Allen and
McLean streets held the homes of the most privi-
leged; Chambers, Staniford, Lynde, and part of
Leverett streets were inhabited by the fairly well-
to-do; and the narrow houses on the steep hillside
streets were owned or rented by thrifty, ambitious
American families but one generation from the
farm. The population was comparatively free
from foreigners, and the public schools were filled

with the children of typical New England homes, whose heads represented the substantial business life of the city, in all its grades. The English High School for boys was located at the west end of Pinckney Street. It was founded for the purpose of giving to boys who did not care for college training a good English and business preparation, and the knowledge of the French language. When a High School for girls was projected, the best district in the city for the experiment was considered to be that of the Bowdoin School on Myrtle Street. Except upon the summit of the hill, the life was mostly the simple, democratic one expressed by the public schools; and so stable was the population that sometimes three generations of the same family received their elementary education in the same grammar school.

The first enemy of the home life of the West End was not the one that earliest attacked the older district. It was the outcome, not of foreign immigration, but of increase in native population drawn in by the growth of the city's trade. Boarding-houses, and not tenements, here put the homes to flight. Lads from sixteen to twenty-five, leaving the farm for the larger opportunities of the city, demanded shelter. Widows and spinsters of the West End opened their doors, thankful for this new means of bread-winning at a time when needlework and teaching were the only occupations for American women. The boarding-house life of the middle of the century is held often in pleasant and grateful remembrance by gray-haired business merchants ; and literary circles, that the reading world has come to think of with affection, existed within these narrow boarding-houses on some of the hilly streets of the West End. Their less worthy successors, the lodging-houses, still mark the advance of irresistible forces that are at last pushing all the earlier types of American life entirely outside of the confines of old Boston.

CHAPTER III

THE INVADING HOST

THE North End, for its present inhabitants, has representatives of twenty-five different nationalities. Irish, Jews, and Italians are the large factors in the population, together making up four fifths of the whole. In 1895, the total population of the North End was 23,800. The census of 1900 shows that this number has grown to 28,000.

The West End has had a later development than the North End, and shows a less variety of nationalities. Its population has never been of so foreign a character as that of the North End, although a large Jewish influx has poured into its streets during the past few years, and has changed the complexion of the entire district. At the present time, the West End may be divided, by a line running through Green and Allen streets, into two distinct sections. The section north of this line is similar to the North End in the character of its inhabitants, while the southern section resembles the South End. The total population of

the West End in 1895 was 28,000, nearly one half
of which was made up of Jews and Irish. In 1900,
the total population was approximately 34,500,
and the proportion of Jews was greatly increased.[1]
The homogeneous character of Boston's population was first seriously disturbed by the Irish
famine of 1846. For fifteen years before that
date a fairly steady immigration of Irish, English,
British-Americans, and Germans had made the
foreign-born inhabitants of the North End number
about one third of a total population of 20,000.
Immigration into Boston for ten years following
the Irish famine was so preponderatingly Irish
that other nationalities may be practically disre-
garded. The growth of the Irish during those ten
years, including their children born in this country, was over 100 per cent. Already, in 1850, the
Irish formed about one half of the population of

---

[1] The census of 1900 brings out the interesting fact that, for
the city as a whole, the older nationalities — the Irish, English,
Scotch, and Germans — have decreased slightly since 1895. The
British-Americans and Swedes have made steady increase, and
the Italians and Jews have grown with astonishing rapidity. The
Italians have grown from 7900 to 13,738, making an increase of
74 per cent. in five years : the Russians have grown from 11,979
to 14,995, or 25 per cent.; and the Poles from 1221 to 3832, or
214 per cent. The greater part of this increase of Italians and
Jews has been in the two districts under consideration.

23,000 in the North End, while the **Americans** numbered only 9200. Still, the Irish were closely packed away on the back streets, so that the general effect was Anglo-Saxon rather than Celtic.[1] By 1855 the Irish had grown to 14,000, and the total population to 26,000. Fortunately for the health of the inhabitants, the North End has never contained a larger population than this. The Irish inhabitants continued to increase slowly up to 1880. Since that time, with the advent of other nationalities, they have rapidly diminished. In 1895 they numbered 6800. The Americans, meantime, have dwindled to insignificant proportions. In 1895 only about 1500 persons remained whose parents were born in the United States, and half this number were children of parents born outside Massachusetts. It requires diligent search to find any Boston family still clinging to its old home, in the midst of this motley mixture of races. In the West End, the Irish never had so great a preponderance as in the North End. In 1850 they formed about one fifth of a total population of 20,518, and in 1855 they formed a little less than one fourth of a population of

[1] A city census of 1850 gives the nationalities by streets, making possible an exact comparison between that period and the present.

23,500. A steady increase until 1880 brought their numbers up to 10,000, which gave them a lead of 3600 over the American residents. Before another census was taken the tide had turned, just as it had in the North End, and the decrease has continued up to the present. In 1895, the Irish, numbering 7200, were the leading nationality in the West End. During the past seven years, however, the Jews have displaced them so rapidly that the Irish probably no longer hold first place. A larger number of Americans live in the West End than in the North End. In 1895, 4800 resided there, though to a large extent they belong to the lodging-house class and do not represent American family life.

The advent of the Irish brought about the first in a series of racial shiftings in the North and West Ends. About 1880 there came a marked change in the character of immigration. Since then, so rapid a transformation has been produced that even old inhabitants, daily witnesses of the scene, have been startled at times. In 1880, less than 1000 Italians lived in the North End, and only 125 in the West End. In the whole of both districts, only a few hundred Jews were to be found, and most of those were Germans. The Russians were outnumbered even by the Poles. In the present situation one can trace but little resemblance to that of 1880. The story of immigration into Boston for the last twenty years is for the most part an influx of Jews and Italians followed by more Jews and Italians. According to the census of 1895, the number of Italians in the North End had reached 7700. The Russians and Poles, who, roughly speaking, form the Jewish population, numbered 6200, all but 400 of these being Russians. Although it has been a popular belief that a greater mass of Jews than of any other subdivision of humanity will collect in a given space, a longer acquaintance with the Italians has forced one to abandon this idea. When the North End reached the point of human saturation, the less persistent material — that is, the Jews and the Irish — found its way to neighboring places, leaving the Italians in possession. In the West End, in 1895, there were 6300 Jews and only 1100 Italians, and migration to this section from the North End continues to be more largely Jewish than Italian. At present, immigration from Ireland is just about sufficient to keep up the number of Irish homes in these districts. The excited, venturesome immigration of the fifties has now given place to a calm and confident arrival in response to invitations of relatives or friends.

Besides the Irish, Jews, and Italians, some of the less important nationalities deserve mention. About 800 Portuguese were living in the North End in 1895; but removals to the suburbs have since thinned them out. British and British-Americans to the number of 1200 are scattered throughout the North End. In the West End, they are more numerous, as they centre in lodging-house districts. Some 1400 British and 2000 British-Americans are to be found in the West End, chiefly in the southern part of the district. About 3000 negroes also occupy a fairly well-defined area around Phillips Street in the West End.

A number of more temporary residents make themselves conspicuous in both districts. Sea-faring transients of many nationalities find harbor from the dangers of the deep in sailors' boarding and lodging houses, which are not without their own peculiar perils. At any given time perhaps one hundred sailors may be found in the district; but the number varies. They go on a coasting voyage of from four to six weeks, and stay ashore till their wages are spent. This does not take long; for the recreation of the majority of them includes some sort of dissipation. Besides these regular sailor inhabitants, a number of sailors from the steamships spend their leisure in the city while living aboard their vessels. A larger number of tramps also seem to live in the cheap lodging-houses of the North End than in other parts of the city. They cling to the outskirts of the district, and ask for a drink or for a cent to get across the ferry. No tramp was ever yet on the right side of a ferry.

The causes of the enormous influx of Jews and southern Italians during recent years are exceptional, and deserve consideration. In the south of Italy emigration is confined chiefly to the peasants from the mountain districts, where the civilization of the coast regions has not penetrated, but where the tax-gatherer never fails to appear. The natural poverty of the country would be in itself a sufficient cause of emigration; for artisans' wages are less in Italy than in Germany, and farm-hands receive barely enough to maintain life, their wages not infrequently falling below twenty cents a day. [1] But the unbearable part of Italian poverty lies in the vicious system of taxation, which seems to be specially arranged to oppress the poor. "Progressive taxation topsy-turvy," some one calls it, for it has been estimated that fifty-four per cent. of the taxes are paid by the poor and working classes.[2]

[1] See *Italy To-day*, by Bolton King and Thomas Okey, p. 126.
[2] Ibid., p. 138.

The small farmer is perhaps most seriously affected. The land tax alone takes from twenty to twenty-five per cent. of the net profits of the farm, and in addition to it he must pay income tax, succession duty, and communal cattle tax, beside the various indirect taxes which bear heavily upon the necessaries of life.[1] Not infrequently the profits of a farm are entirely absorbed by taxes, and improvements are not undertaken through fear of increased assessment.

Poverty in Italy is also intimately associated with over-population. The birth-rate is high; in fact, for all of Europe, the excess of births over deaths is greater only in Germany, Great Britain, and the Scandinavian countries; and parts of Italy are among the most densely peopled districts of Europe. One third too many laborers in the Po valley is the estimate of one writer.[2] This surplus population is, of course, a serious impediment to the economic progress of the lower classes ; but the high birth-rate, especially marked among the very poor, seems to show that the over-population is rather the result of utter hopelessness arising out of economic conditions than the cause of those conditions. At any rate economic conditions and the surplus population together make Italy a coun-

[1] Ibid., p. 140.   [2] Ibid., p. 311.

try to get away from; and the stories of a returned emigrant or the persuasiveness of a steamship agent will be enough to start a considerable exodus. Sometimes the renting or selling of a farm will provide the funds for passage money, but many who are unable to raise a sufficient amount are assisted by friends in America. It will be easily understood, therefore, that they have little money to exhibit upon their arrival in this country.

The emigration of Jews from Russia has been indirectly necessitated by the repressive action of the Russian government. The real cause of the trouble lies in the long and bitter contest which has gone on in that country between Jew and Gentile. At last many of the Gentiles, finding themselves undermined by the subtle Jewish methods, organized riots and destroyed the property of those who, they felt, had undone them. The " May Laws " of 1882, following the anti-Semitic riots, revoked certain privileges which had been accorded to the Jews since 1865, and required the enforcement of previous laws restricting the residence of most Jews to fifteen provinces in the western part of Russia known as the Jewish Pale of Settlement; and it furthermore prohibited their residing in the country districts. Those decrees have been enforced with varying degrees of severity in the different districts; but the result has been to overcrowd the towns of the Pale and to deprive a large number of the Jews of even the bare means of livelihood. It has been through the benevolence of Baron de Hirsch that thousands who had no means of their own were enabled to reach America. Now, however, the influence of the administrators of his great trust is exerted to turn the tide of immigration toward the Argentine Republic.

To Jewish sympathizers the action of the Czar has seemed an uncalled-for persecution, an outrage against humanity. It has indeed involved much barbarous severity and a vast amount of undeserved suffering. It was not, however, as is often supposed, the outcome of mere meaningless hatred. The case of the Russian is summed up simply in the old story of the money-lending Jew. From the Russian point of view, the matter was an urgent one, and the remedy was thought to be, under the circumstances, a great piece of statesmanship. The Russian peasant was, of course, no match for the Jew in the instinct for sharp practice in trade. Even hedged in by a multitude of restrictions, the Jews have become an economic power in Russia — too often a grasping and relentless power. If they had perfect freedom, they would erelong control the material resources of the country. But such a triumph of a narrow and specialized economic instinct is a form of survival to which the Czar is inalterably opposed. He stands as the protector of his hundred million Russian subjects, and feels that the Jew must not be allowed to outwit them and hinder their natural economic development.

The American sequel to these and similar passages in the history of Europe during the past century has to do with imparting distinctive American qualities to the individual immigrant type, and with bringing about a degree of common feeling among these diverse ethnic types in their immediate relations one with another. Both these ends may possibly be attained by the same means, but not necessarily. It is easy to see that two nationalities may readily adopt American ideals and standards of life and yet not conform to each other. They may never be wrought into social unity. The Americanizing process is — up to a certain point — the less difficult of accomplishment. American ideals in time usually appeal to persons who have sufficient enterprise to emigrate, although extreme isolation is likely to thwart such a tendency. To obtain complete social unity, there must be concrete common interests sufficient to insure active coöperation between the members of the different racial groups. All this means more than naturalization and casting a vote. To appreciate the difficulty properly involves an inquiry into every phase of social life; though only some of the most important tendencies, as seen in Boston's chief immigrant districts, can be noted here.

A disturbed balance of the sexes is the inevitable result of any great movement of population. A significant characteristic of the North End lies in the abnormal excess of males over females, which, according to the census of 1895, amounts to 1500, two thirds of this excess being attributed to the Italians. This number, however, is doubtless too small; for the census was taken in the spring of the year, when the Italians begin to get work outside the city. It is pretty certain that a much larger number of single men than is indicated by the census returns resides in the Italian quarter during the greater part of the year, and the actual number is still further augmented by transients, who are always a considerable factor in a colony of this size. Each nationality has some excess of males over females, with the exception of the Irish, British-Americans, and Portuguese. The excess of females in these cases is insignificant, save with the Irish, where it amounts to over 200.

These facts mean a distinct majority of men in the tenement houses, with a slight preponderance of women in the lodging-houses.

To the disproportion of the sexes in the tenements, a large degree of overcrowding and the crime resulting therefrom may be directly traced. A considerable, though a decreasing, proportion of Italians are temporary residents in this country, and they occupy provisional quarters. Their purpose is to save money, and they do it by maintaining the most niggardly kind of existence. Families having small tenements sublet rooms to them for their accommodation. Eight, ten, and sometimes more men will occupy a single room. For the room, a fire, and perhaps some slight services in mending, each lodger pays twenty-five or thirty cents a week. A scant amount of cheap food takes a dollar more. But this small expense for necessaries is sometimes supplemented by a large liquor bill. A number of men living together in idleness makes card-playing and beer-drinking common and, for them, expensive modes of recreation; and in this kind of life may be found the cause of most of the serious crime of the North End. Being an excitable race, the Italians resort to knives and pistols in quarrels over cards or from jealousies arising from the relationship of the sexes.

But overcrowding among the Italians is not confined to single men. Many Italian families live in very congested fashion. The tenement-house census of Boston, taken in 1891, presented some very significant figures as to this point. At a time when there was a much smaller number of Italians than at present, two precincts, occupied chiefly by Italians, contained 154 families who were occupying only one room each; and 459 families, or more than one half the inhabitants of the precincts, were living on an average with more than two persons to a room. Even families who could well afford comfortable tenements often show no inclination to give up their insanitary dwellings. But many of the Italians are beginning to seek something better. They are now, in considerable numbers, moving into the more desirable tenements to the west of Hanover Street; and some families, especially of the second generation, are taking a more significant step in detaching themselves from the colony and settling amid pleasanter surroundings. Meanwhile many new additions are being made to the colony, as the result of the establishment of a direct line of steamers between Boston and the Mediterranean.

Jewish abodes in the North End are only a little less crowded than those of the Italians, but it is the crowding due to large families, not to numbers of adults. As the Jews become more wealthy, or in other words, as time passes, they do not proportionately enlarge their quarters. Still having the herding instinct of the ghetto, the overcrowding of their rooms occurs to them as an easy method of thrift. The uncleanly ways of the ghetto thus continue to find a pretext.

But neither cramped quarters nor the absorption of business affairs destroys Jewish home and family life. Married life is the normal state of the Jews, and they uniformly have large families. Their children are nurtured and trained with affectionate care. There is noticeable attachment between the two generations, even outside the family circle. A mutual regard and confidence exists between old and young, such as is seldom found among other nationalities. Jewish boys associate freely with their elders, and the relationship is so natural as to show neither presumption on the one side nor patronage on the other. Small children may be seen tagging along after the patriarchs, who give a friendly welcome to their advances. And the freedom engenders in the young a respect for their elders, which is lacking among those nationalities in which the two generations are seldom united in free social intercourse. It is one of the sad and disappointing aspects of life for the older members of the Jewish community that, as time goes by, the language and customs of the new country become a serious barrier between their children and themselves. Jewish women are tenderly cared for as mothers, though, true to ancient traditions, the men are superior in all things. Strangely enough, considering their family life, matrimonial alliances occasionally come to be business transactions, and professional matchmakers are not infrequently resorted to. In such cases trading ability is more valued in the spouse than domestic traits.

The Negroes in the West End are not, on the whole, in a congested district, although instances where lodgers are crowded in with a family are not unknown among them. Such a practice is at best conducive neither to health nor to morality; but it is especially deleterious to the Negroes, for any indiscriminate mingling of the sexes serves only to increase their natural tendency to immorality. Most of the tenements occupied by Negroes are poor, though they are generally kept clean. Single men among them are lodged in much less desirable quarters than white men who are receiving the same wages. Signs of prosperity take the shape of decorations of the person.

Economy in home comforts and lavishness in outward display is often a characteristic of the poorer classes, but it is carried to its last extreme by the Negroes.

The Irish of the North End, for the most part, do not représent the best qualities of their race. A small minority are of the more progressive kind. Such families remain on account of owning real estate, or because the young men have political interests; but the majority are of the less enterprising, who have not shown the ability to rise, — for the Irish in the North End are not recent immigrants. Many, it must be feared, have joined the ranks of the permanently poor. But, being older residents, and speaking the English language, they stand to the later immigrants as the native type, unfortunately not always to the profit of the American reputation. The Irish in the West End are, in general, more intelligent and prosperous, and resemble more nearly those in the South End. They have made progress in every way, and by their remarkable race trait of adaptability they have conformed in a great degree to American ways.

The lodging-house population in the West End differs but little from that in the South End. Rows of brick houses with non-committal fronts shelter a population of all shades of character and interests. The men belong to the clerk and artisan classes, and are chiefly Americans, British-Americans, and Irish. They represent a class which is trying to maintain its social position under conditions which are no longer favorable. By postponing marriage they succeed in keeping up an appearance of their old standard in an atmosphere which is careless of the individual, and in which the individual becomes careless of himself, because he has no strong guiding or restraining attachments. Lodging-house life is at best temporary and forms a poor substitute for the home. But even that takes the greater part of the lodgers' wages, and too often normal home life is never realized. Comparatively few marry later in life. Temporary unions are often the expedients of insufficient resources, and tend to become a sort of recognized institution. Numbers of the lodging-house class are simply being sacrificed industrially and morally because of their inability to conform to a lowered scale of living.

Among the different nationalities the Jews are perhaps making the most rapid progress ; and this is not in material resources alone, for the advantages of an education are not ignored. Jewish children are among the brightest in the schools, and they study with a seriousness which is foreign to their Irish and Italian mates. High school and even college attracts a large number of those whose means permit. To most of the poorer Jews, however, the desire for an education simply does not arise before the all-important question of making a living, and getting on. Boys go to school in order to get a license to sell papers; while both parents devote their whole energy to increasing the family resources.

The Italians have not been as successful as the Jews in gaining financial headway, but their progress has been sufficiently encouraging. They are developing into skilled workmen following a variety of useful and productive callings. It is these specialized workmen who form the more permanent and desirable part of the North End colony. A small number of better educated Italians have not on the whole proved to be a very desirable class. They sometimes have more education than honesty, and manage to live as parasites on their inexperienced countrymen. At the other extreme, the illiterate are a handicap to progress in the Italian colony. Next to the Portuguese and Spaniards, the Italians are the most illiterate of any nationality in western Europe. Comparatively few of the southern peasants can read and write their own language. This is doubtless one reason why they are so backward about learning English, although the nature of their occupations makes English less essential to them than to the Jews. It ought to be said that the cause of illiteracy in their own country is not so much a disregard of education on the part of the people as it is the absence of a persistent and rational policy on the part of the government.

Among the Portuguese, poverty is an altogether too common characteristic. While this poverty does not amount to complete pauperism, assistance from charitable societies is very common. The most successful among this nationality are small tradesmen and artisans. Sea-faring Portuguese form a small part of the North End colony. Not a few families are dependent upon the labor of women, and their lot is a hard one. Yet in the matter of clean homes, the Portuguese stand in striking and happy contrast with the Jews. Portuguese of the first generation keep to themselves pretty closely. Their quarrels and their immoralities are not complained of, and consequently are little noticed. Children of both sexes, however, desire to get away from the confinement of the home and work in factories. Thus in the second generation the isolation of the Portuguese is overcome.

The Negroes are acted upon by conflicting forces. On the one hand, they are ambitious, imitative, and anxious to appear like other people ; on the other hand, certain animal propensities and the intoxication of Northern freedom are continual impediments to their progress, and tend to widen the breach between them and those white people whom they wish to resemble. As the better class of Negroes are leaving the West End, those that remain are coming more and more to represent undesirable types, such as are found in the lower part of the South End.   A large majority of the Negroes are poor, and they are improving their condition very slowly.   All except the oldest are possessed of at least the rudiments of an education.   They are proud of all achievements in this line, for it makes them more like other people.   The acquisition of knowledge, however, though easy for the little children, becomes arduous after a few years, and many drop out before they have finished the grammar school course.   Perhaps their assistance is needed for the support of the family, but the children themselves say they do not get marks high enough, and they do not like to go to school. Notwithstanding the Negroes' desire for assimilation, color remains an almost insuperable obstacle to them.   Occasional marriages occur between colored men and white women, but they are of little avail in breaking down the barrier. Such couples are usually absorbed by the Negro race, although if they belong to the more educated class they enter into natural relationships with neither race.

In regard to identification of interest and feeling among the different ethnic groups there are, aside from the Negro problem, many encouraging features. On the whole, of course, progress in this direction is slow. Irish immigrants during the early part of the century were a desirable class, and coming in smaller numbers they assimilated with native Americans pretty readily. Later the assisted immigration that followed the Irish famine brought an inferior type, and the influx into the North End was also too sudden. The Americans gradually moved to other parts of the city, and left the Irish in control. The religious question was the chief cause of ill feeling between these two races, and was the great hindrance to easy assimilation.

When the Italians and Jews became noticeable factors in the North End, they were received with little tolerance by the Irish, who were then " old inhabitants." They were unwelcome interlopers, and became subjects of petty persecution. Direct

molestations have ceased, but there is little intercourse between the groups.

Less friction is noticeable in the schools than
anywhere else, although a schoolboy's honor seldom
extends beyond the limits of his own kind. In
social clubs, which are more personal affairs, the
nationalities seldom mix. The Jews and Italians
get along with each other better than either does
with the Irish. The dignity of Irish lads is
somewhat compromised by associating intimately
with Jewish or Italian boys, and their wit makes
them schoolboy leaders. One Irish club voted an
Italian boy a member because he was a " good
fellow," and then upon further consideration voted
him out again because he was an Italian. They
feared that companionship with him would open
the way to companionship with other Italian boys.
Jewish boys in the same way would not vote an
Irish boy into their clubs, and an Irish boy would
not on his life be voted in. The seriousness that
pervades a Jewish boys' club is depressing to the
Irish spirit. This is aptly illustrated by the remark of a twelve-year old member who, becoming
disgusted with an endless debate over parliamen-
tary procedure, exclaimed, " I can't idle away my
wastin' hours. If you want me to belong to this
club you must do something." Social and philan-

thropic institutions find it better to work with a single nationality, or at least to keep the nationalities separate as far as possible.

Political activities bring about association among the different nationalities, and in this the Irish manage to overcome their exclusiveness. The Irishman regards politics as a separate department of life. It is an end in itself, and is undertaken for its own sake. To be sure, he hopes by its means to be able to gain a living, but that is the stake of a game which has a fascination all its own. The political interest of the Irish people is shown not only in the large proportion of Irish voters, but also in the greater activity of those voters. They are not merely the most easily organized of any nationality, but they are the most capable organizers. According to their own account, this political capacity is the result of the struggle for independence in Ireland.

Oppression of the Jew has resulted in his being gravely deficient in civic sense. Business is his great concern, and politics is wholly subsidiary to it. First interested in politics through his business associations, business interests still influence his vote. Although the percentage of Jewish voters is hardly more than half as large as that of the Irish, considering their short residence they make a very creditable showing. They are kept from becoming organizers, however, by the mutual jealousies of their leaders. Consequently the Irish step in and attempt a task which proves a strain even to their ingenuity. In fact, the Jew is a thorn in the flesh to the Irish politician. The Irishman does not court the Jew because he loves him so, but because he wishes to convince his much doubting brother that, although they may differ socially and religiously and may be rivals in business, it is entirely possible to be friends in the party camp. At first the Jews so imperfectly understood the political game that they formed educational clubs to influence their people to become naturalized, without regard to the party affiliations of the prospective citizens. Such conduct is incomprehensible to Irish politicians; yet it was several years before they could teach the Jews the art of naturalizing only such a person as would support the party. Even now, they assert, the Jews have not the constancy to follow the lead of those true friends who have aided them to become citizens of the United States.

The Italians are much more docile. Although they have taken little real interest in public affairs, they are ready to follow the lead of others and become American citizens. But most of the Italians are not eligible for citizenship, and the law has been strained somewhat for their benefit. As the law confers the right of citizenship upon minors with the father's naturalization, Italians are often able to recollect, upon second thought, that they do fulfill the proper conditions for the special privilege. Notwithstanding this liberal possibility, a smaller percentage of Italians than of any other nationality possesses the franchise, though a marked increase of Italian names on the local voting lists has recently been made.

The English and British-Americans assimilate politically less easily than might be expected, considering their high percentage of literacy and the similarity of their institutions with our own. This very similarity, however, awakens a feeling of rivalry which is not evident among other nationalities. While immigrants from continental Europe come here with a kind of preconceived belief in the perfection of American institutions, English subjects have a distinct feeling that their own are superior, and are loath to become citizens of a country which they have adopted merely for economic reasons. British Provincials are seen at the polls less frequently than the native English, but this may be partly for the reason that a large number of them are only temporary residents here.

The Portuguese show almost as small a proportion of voters as the Italians. They have the advantage of a somewhat longer residence in this country than the Italians, but on the other hand they are the most illiterate of all our foreign inhabitants.

The Negroes, like the Jews, show the lack of a tradition of citizenship. They ignore their opportunities in political life. If they were in any sense an organized body, possessed of a fraction of Irish sagacity, they would be a more powerful and respected people in public life.

Intermarriage among nationalities, as a rule, affords important indications of the fading of race distinctions. Measured by this standard, the English and British-Americans assimilate most readily of all, not excepting the Irish. Both nationalities have entered into alliances pretty freely with the Irish and Americans, as well as with other races. The Irish, owing partly to the large excess of females, have intermarried with almost all the nationalities, but much more commonly with the English-speaking people. Other nationalities residing in these districts have thus far made comparatively few outside marriage ties. Italians, particularly the men, are beginning to form unions with the Irish and Portuguese, even difference of language not forming an insuperable obstacle. A case in point is that of an Italian who married a Portuguese girl when neither could understand the language of the other. Such unions have their inconveniences; and they must be especially disadvantageous to the Portuguese, for their tongues are their most common weapon of defense. Marriages between Jews and Gentiles are not unknown, still they are infrequent enough to occasion comment whenever they occur. The most frequent cases are those in which Jewish men take Irish or American wives, although occasionally Jewish women marry outside the faith. On the whole, the sentiment is quite strong against the unions of Jews and Gentiles, and such unions are too exceptional to be cited as evidence of any present Jewish tendency toward affiliation with other ethnic groups.

The separateness of the Jew has always been a favorite theme, yet something might be said on the other side. They are not so compact a mass as is often supposed. Jews from different countries differ not a little from each other. The Russians are the most pronounced type, and are probably the most conservative of all. The Germans are more liberal, and give support to the reformed sect. A few who come to this country after living in

England bear a characteristic impress in their speech, and even seem to have caught a certain sturdy quality from the English environment.[1] Both the German and the English Jews consider the Russians much inferior, while the Russians are shocked at the irreligious deportment of their more progressive brethren. The isolation of this peculiar people, originating in their religion, is preserved by ever-present reminders in all their scheme of life that they are Jews. It is possible, however, that under the dissipating force of freedom the Jews will lose much of their aloofness ; some of their peculiar traits will disappear, and others will be modified. They are beginning to enter a larger number of occupations, and are coming into friendly relations with outsiders in business and in politics. They drink beer like their neighbors, and sometimes sell it. They are less particular about their Jewish diet, and an increasing number are observing less rigorously many of the religious ceremonies they formerly kept so strictly. As to their separateness in religion, the very term Christian has been to

---

[1] English Jews are said to have a nearer resemblance to their Christian countrymen than to the members of their own race who have recently poured into London from Russia. See *The Jew in London*, Russell and Lewis, p. 24.

them so long a synonym for persecution, that the aversion which they have felt toward the Christian religion cannot be wondered at. Many of them, however, are coming to have a curious way of omitting and ignoring the hated term as applied to Gentile friends.

On the whole, it may be said that the racial elements in the North and West Ends are reluctant to mingle with each other, but tend slowly to conform to American ideals. In the development of American patriotic feeling, two of the chief types leave little to be desired. No nationality can show more loyal Americans among its numbers than the Irish. Their hatred of the English, which they say is born in the blood, has made them love their adopted country the more. Although they always retain tender memories of their native land, the freedom with which they have gained access to American life has made their assimilation thorough and their loyalty complete. Among the Italians enthusiasm for their own country is always shown by fitting observance of their national holidays ; still the American flag always receives equal attention with their own in the decorations. The children, both in school and in the boys' and girls' clubs, learn American traditions and come to love American freedom.

There is sufficient ground for anxiety in the case of each of the racial groups in these districts. The residuum of the Irish are in danger of the extreme forms of degradation. It is unfortunate that the Italians are allowed to live in a way which tends to dwarf their simple virtues, and which offers fertile soil for the growth of crime. The Jews in their very process of conformity are losing some of their most desirable qualities. Virtue by tradition is failing to withstand the seductive clamor of the city's temptations. The Negroes, condemned to conditions which do not tend to elevate the race, too easily accept their lot. Through the social preference among them for personal service as against independent labor, they relinquish the last possibility of associating with the whites upon the same plane, and open wider the way to industrial and moral shiftlessness. In general, the danger of the situation in the North and West Ends is that a considerable proportion of the newcomers, instead of finding here opportunities of preparation for a more normal life, will be overcome by their own numbers and their isolated situation, and will settle back, accepting present conditions as their permanent lot.

CHAPTER IV

THE first important sanitary problem to be faced in the development of a city is that of the drainage. At the outset no special provision is made other than the utilization, in the simplest manner, of some neighboring stream or body of water. In Paris, as late as 1750, open ditches had served all purposes of drainage. At that time the little stream into which many of these ditches emptied their foul waters was covered over, chiefly in order to make more building space. Up to a comparatively recent period, the canals of Amsterdam were stagnant sewers. Hamburg's sewerage was carried into the Elbe and, until the cholera epidemic of 1892, allowed to float back with the tide, polluting the water supply. The tendency of both European and American cities has been to adopt the cheapest, most temporary measure in sanitation until forced by epidemics to a provision both more costly and more adequate.

In Boston, as late as the second decade of the

nineteenth century, there was an open sewer crossing the centre of the city. Mill Creek, the outlet of the old Mill Pond, received the drainage of the higher ground of the North End, and with the increase of population became the first important public nuisance to be corrected by the town government. Private drainage was unregulated. Each householder was at liberty to construct his own system and to dig ditches in the street at his own pleasure.

Following the problem of drainage comes the problem of a pure water supply. Here again cities have usually waited to be forced by epidemics into proper sanitary provisions. At first public wells were sufficient. These were supplanted by private wells. Then, as the possibilities of pollution from bad drainage became understood, water was brought from the nearest and most convenient course. With recent years the sources have been more carefully selected and guarded and the water filtered.

The cleaning of the streets has been a matter of slower development. Not yet is the problem satisfactorily solved, although great improvement is manifest in the past ten years. And perhaps the most important sanitary problem of all, the proper housing of the people, has waited until the present century, with its enormous advance in urban population, to receive adequate recognition.

Previous to the year 1800, Boston had few sanitary regulations. The frequent epidemics came and went without teaching their lessons. There is record of at least twelve visitations of smallpox in the seventeenth and eighteenth centuries. In 1722, of the 4549 inhabitants living north of Mill Creek, 2596 were victims of this disease and 281 died. The first Board of Health was established in 1799 by act of the legislature. To this board was given the power to enter forcibly any building or vessel, examine into all causes of sickness and all nuisances, " and the same to destroy, remove or prevent, as the case may require." [1]

With the incorporation of the town as a city in 1822, and the advent of Mayor Josiah Quincy in the following year, came the beginning of a thorough and adequate treatment of sanitary problems. A uniform system of drainage was established under a municipal " superintendent of common sewers." Steps were taken to insure a permanent and pure water supply, owned by the city and under its control. The Board of Health gave place to a single health commissioner, responsible to the mayor and aldermen. After five

[1] Shaw, *History of Boston*, p. 154.

years of vigorous effort and struggle in the courts, the right of the city to exercise complete juris-diction in sanitary matters was established per-manently.

Mayor Quincy paid especial attention to the problem of street cleaning. Previously the respon-sibility had been divided between the householders and the Board of Health, much of the work was done by private contract, and the results were very unsatisfactory. The mayor determined on an effective object lesson. He secured an outfit of carts and horses, expended $1400, and removed three thousand tons of dirt from the city streets at one cleaning. The result convinced the city of the need of permanent municipal control. The falling of the death rate of 1827 below the rate of any previous year, even below that of any city of equal population on record, was the crown-ing tribute to the effectiveness of the administra-tion.

In order that the housing problem of later days may be understood, it is necessary that its roots in sanitary conditions should be made clear. Bad drainage, impure water, and unclean streets gave rise to epidemics; these epidemics were most violent in overcrowded and improperly drained and ventilated houses. The attention drawn to such houses, usually inhabited by the poorest of the people, developed a more comprehensive study of housing conditions and an effort to remedy the defects. Some of the evils of bad housing have come only with the later growth of the cities, and could not have been foreseen. But the problem as a whole would never have become so serious had the people of Boston persisted in living up to the light which was given them in the early years of the nineteenth century.

There are four well-defined periods in the history of the sanitary and housing problems of the North and West Ends. These may be designated as the period of epidemics, until the last outbreak of smallpox in 1872 ; the period of constructive effort, from the clearing away of Fort Hill in 1867 to 1889; the period of detailed investigation, from 1889 to 1897 ; and the present period, with its enlarged municipal powers, beginning in 1898.

As early as 1678 the Reverend Thomas Thacher put forth a broadside entitled " A Brief Rule to guide the Common People of New England how to order themselves and theirs in the Small Pocks, or Measles." It remained for another clergyman, the Reverend Joseph Tuckerman, minister at large from 1826, and founder of the Benevolent Fra-

ternity of Churches, to cry out against the overcrowded and miserable tenements and the inhabited
cellars.   When the smallpox appeared in 1824,
and the Asiatic cholera for the first time in 1832,
the city was already aware of the local causes that
aided the spread of the contagion.   Many years
passed, however, before those causes were remedied.
Fifty thousand dollars were appropriated to stay
the first attack of cholera, and a general fast day
appointed.   But the overcrowding and filth remained.

The census of 1845 gave the city a total population of 114,366.   Wards 5 and 6, in the West
End, had the fewest inhabitants to a house
(8.4); while Ward 2, the eastern part of the
North End, and Ward 8, the eastern part of
the Fort Hill district, near by, had 17.79 and 19.15,
respectively.   The average for the city was 10.57.
" Less than one third of the houses in the city and
none of the houses in the North End took aque-
duct water; and many houses were not connected
with the city sewerage system." [1]

These facts made it easy to predict the territory
which would be most afflicted by the next epidemic.
In 1848 one of the city physicians published a
statement which ought to have aroused the city.

[1] Bushee, *Growth of the Population of Boston.*

He said : " The dwellings of the poor are mostly filthy, often from neglect on the part of the landlords, who get large rents and do not provide suitable drains, privies, yards, etc. Municipal regulation is far from effective. We need a health commissioner who should be dictator and turn out any excess of population from houses and streets."

In spite of these warnings conditions were not improved, and in 1849 the Asiatic cholera raged for the second time. According to the report of a " Committee on Internal Health " made after the epidemic had run its course, those sections of the city nearest sea-level, the least perfect in drainage, the worst ventilated, and the most crowded and filthy, were the most afflicted. Especial mention is made of the Fort Hill neighborhood, which is called the worst spot in the city. A nest of miserable tenements at the corner of Stillman and Endicott streets was described as " filled to overflowing with a most vicious and miserable population." In the rear of 136 Hanover Street there were twelve deaths in two days out of 50 inhabitants. Altogether there were about 114 deaths in the North End and 66 in the West End during the four months of the disease. The whole number of deaths throughout the city was 611.

In connection with the report there is a vivid description of the cellar dwellings, 586 of which were then occupied, usually sheltering from five to fifteen persons in each. The police had reported one cellar as the sleeping apartment of thirty-nine persons. "In another," wrote the city physician, "the tide had risen so high that it was necessary to approach the bedside of a patient by means of a plank which was laid from one stool to another; while the dead body of an infant was actually sailing about the room in its coffin. Many of the inhabited cellars are inundated by the back-water of the drains during high tides; and being entirely below the level of the sidewalks, they are almost entirely without light and ventilation. But far from being considered a hardship, a residence in them is considered preferable to loftier apartments. They are said to be cooler in summer and warmer in winter, and consequently command higher rents." [1]

Five years later, cholera appeared for the third time. Keith's Alley and the Fort Hill district were the centres of its greatest virulence. An attempt was made by the Board of Health, namely, the mayor and aldermen, who had dispossessed the single health commissioner in 1850,

[1] *Report of the Committee on Internal Health*, Boston, 1849.

to remedy matters by vacating the most obnoxious buildings. The tenants did not choose to be ejected, and there were many contests between them and the police in the effort to enforce sanitary measures. As a result, such measures were not thoroughly enforced.

The period of epidemics culminated with the fearful outbreak of smallpox in 1872. There was no suitable hospital for contagious diseases. The city officials charged three dollars for fumigating one room and five dollars for a tenement. As a result, the most needy houses were neglected: 738 persons died of the epidemic in 1872, and 302 in 1873, out of a total of 3700 cases. It was made clear that the sanitary administration of the city was inadequate. Although the mayor and aldermen called upon an unpaid advisory board of physicians for aid in times of epidemic, they often took offense at advice; and the physicians, finding that the measures they recommended were not carried out, refused to serve. Mayor Gaston led the movement for a separate Board of Health, independent of politics and composed of qualified men. In 1873, under the pressure of the smallpox epidemic, the City Council was obliged to yield its opposition, and such a board was established.

The period of constructive effort in sanitation and housing began with the removal of Fort Hill. The territory now bounded by Pearl, Milk, and Broad streets was cut down an average of twenty-five feet, the highest point being fifty feet above the present level. Although commercial reasons, such as the demand of business upon the district and the need of soil for the filling in of Albany Street, were the chief reasons for the improvement, yet the fact that for over twenty years Fort Hill had been pointed out as the most overcrowded and unsanitary spot in the city undoubtedly weighed heavily in favor of its removal. The work was begun in October, 1866, and finished in July, 1872, at a cost of $1,575,000.

Previous to this time very little had been done in the way of improved tenement-house construction. Dr. Tuckerman had advocated building suburban houses, thinking that by getting many of the poor out of the overcrowded districts it would be comparatively easy to care for those that remained. On the other hand, a committee appointed at a public meeting on June 12, 1846, to consider the expediency of providing better tenements for the poor, reported that the poor would not go out of the city, and that it was quite practicable to build sanitary tenement houses in the city which

would yield a fair return on the investment.
Beyond a few sporadic attempts with single houses,
nothing seems to have resulted from either of these
suggestions until 1871. In that year the Boston
Coöperative Building Company was organized with
a capital of $200,000. Its object was to provide
homes at moderate rates : first, by building new
tenements ; second, by cleaning and remodeling old tenements ; and third, by erecting small
houses in the country to be sold on monthly install-
ments. It was probably expected that the third
of these three methods of improving housing conditions would be the most successful. This has
not proved to be the case; but the first two
methods have been carried out with excellent
results. Three estates owned by the company in
the North and West Ends, including old houses
remodeled as well as new houses especially constructed, provide accommodations for eighty-four
families, at a weekly rental varying from seventy-
seven to eighty-five cents per room. In 1900 the
net profit of one of these estates, based on the
present valuation, amounted to seven per cent., and
of another eight per cent. The company has paid
to its stockholders annual dividends ranging from
three to seven per cent. in all but five or six years
of its existence. The present rate is five per cent.

Another form of constructive effort is illustrated in the work of Mrs. Alice N. Lincoln, who has leased and managed various large tenement houses in the West End. One of the most important of these houses was taken in 1879, thoroughly cleaned and ventilated, and rented to the poorer class of tenants. By careful supervision, the house still continues to yield a fair return over expenses. Similar results have been achieved in other private enterprises.

State legislation, at first in 1868 copied from a New York law of the previous year and later re-modeled, gave the new Board of Health ample power to regulate sanitary conditions. In 1885 was passed the act in relation to the preservation of health in buildings in the city of Boston, com-monly called the " Boston Health Act," and sub-stantially in force at the present time. It expli-citly prescribes all that is necessary in the matter of cleanliness and drainage, the removal of refuse, the care and ventilation of rooms and passages. It also regulates overcrowding and the habitation of cellars.

But notwithstanding better machinery and strin-gent legislation, the slums of the city multiplied from year to year. Not yet had the remedies been sufficiently radical. The effort to clean up un-

wholesome spots did not prevent evil conditions
from constantly recurring. The time had come
for a more thorough study of bad housing with a
view to prevention. Boston entered in 1889 upon
the period of investigation, and during the following nine years much light was thrown on its housing problem.

The first thorough investigation, apart from the
somewhat superficial and sensational revelations
of occasional newspaper articles, was undertaken
in 1889 by Professor Dwight Porter of the Institute of Technology. With the aid of half a dozen
students he conducted a careful inspection of 910
houses in six different wards, containing a population of about 12,000 persons. He found overcrowding in 203 tenement houses, and made especial note
of the condition of the Italians in the North End.
Bad drainage and unclean water-closets were found
to be very common. Special recommendations of
the report were: the widening of the narrowest
streets, the tearing down of rear buildings, the increase of the number of sanitary inspectors, the
doing away with all unventilated sleeping-rooms,
the individual trapping of all sink pipes, the vigorous supervision of all plumbing by the Board of
Health, the designation of the number of occupants
to be allowed in each house, the establishment of

open squares in tenement-house districts, the restriction of the proportion of a lot to be covered by a tenement house, and the prohibition of the occupancy of cellars. It is an encouraging fact that nearly all of these recommendations have since been incorporated in state and city laws.

Following this report, in two years came the elaborate annual reports of the Massachusetts Bureau of Statistics of Labor for 1891 and 1892, made under the direction of Mr. H. G. Wadlin. They gave the number of families living in rented tenements in the city of Boston, the rentals paid, the number of rooms occupied, the sanitary condition of these tenements, and other similar data. This investigation was ordered by the legislature, and came at a time when public sentiment was awakening to the questions involved. Some of the facts brought out concerning the North and West Ends were of striking interest.

The average number of people to a house varied from 17.81 in the precinct bounded by North Street, North Square, Prince and Hanover streets to 8.65 in the district between Chambers, Poplar, Spring, Allen, Blossom, and Parkman streets. Overcrowding was especially noted in old Ward 6, comprising the northern and eastern portion of the North End. Here 259 families were reported as living in one-room tenements, with an average of 2.67 persons to a family, and 1154 families in two-room tenements, with an average of 3.74 to a family. The corresponding figures for the whole city were found to be an average of 1.96 per family for the 1053 families in one-room tenements and 2.87 per family for the 5695 families in two-room tenements.

Outside sanitary conditions — the cleanliness and size of neighboring spaces, the exposure of the house to the sun, and the drainage of the surrounding district — were distinguished from inside sanitary conditions, such as light, ventilation, cleanliness of water-closets and cellars. Every house was classified in respect to both outside and inside sanitary conditions as either " excellent," " good," " fair," " poor," or " bad." The following statistics concerning the houses classed as " bad " in the North and West Ends revealed a situation that needed vigorous remedy : —

	North End.	West End.
Whole number of families	4942	4435
Number with bad outside conditions	199	157
Number with bad inside conditions	129	88
Number with all conditions bad	52	84

The specific location of nearly all the houses with bad inside conditions, an evil which, as Mr. Wadlin said, rests primarily upon the landlord, was as follows : On Battery Street, ten houses; Charter Street, fourteen ; Crescent Place, fourteen ; Merrimac Street, thirty ; Norman Street, fifteen ; North Street, sixteen ; North Margin Street, fifteen ; South Margin Street, fifty-one ; Cusson Place, eight.

Although the report did not disclose housing conditions as bad in proportion as those in New York City, yet it was clearly an indictment, and established the fact that the tenement houses of Boston had been too much neglected. The fact that 522 families were found in the city living in wholly bad sanitary conditions both outside and inside showed that the municipal authority to vacate unsanitary dwellings had not been sufficiently exercised. In fact, the official reports of the Board of Health reveal this ; for in 1891 only eleven houses were actually vacated ; in 1892 none at all ; in 1893 twenty-one ; and in 1894 twenty-six.

Public sentiment revealed itself in the formation in 1892 of the Better Dwellings Society for the purpose of aiding " in improving the sanitary condition of Boston, and especially of its tenement houses." For two years this society did good service in gathering and publishing lists of unsanitary tenement houses and private alleys. As a result of a hearing granted to the society by the Board of Health, a considerable number of the worst houses, many of them in the North End, were ordered vacated.

The City Council felt the pressure of public sentiment, and in 1895 and 1896 appointed committees to report on the improvement of the tenement houses. The first of these committees went so far as to say that " In the North End the tenement houses are to-day a serious menace to public health." But no adequate remedies were suggested, and the superficial character of the report showed that the situation was not taken seriously. The report of the second committee was even less satisfactory.

Private enterprise proved more efficient. In 1898 an investigation made for the Tenement House Committee of the Twentieth Century Club by Mr. H. K. Estabrook was in some respects the most effective for good results of all that had been undertaken. Several hundred houses in many parts of the city were visited, and sixty-eight of the most typical selected for description. A pamphlet was published giving drawings of the ground plans of many of these houses, with an account of their bad drainage, uncleanliness, and general condition when visited.

This report [1] attracted much attention, and was extensively copied in the public press.   It revealed in an authoritative manner a situation which demanded official action.   Public sentiment was aroused by the report.   The municipal authorities recognized that the time had come for a more radical treatment of the slum problem.   At a public hearing, granted by the Board of Health in June, 1898, to a considerable number of citizens who petitioned to have the slums that had been mentioned in Mr. Estabrook's report, as well as others, effectively dealt with, Mayor Quincy appeared in person and told the members of the board that he would support an active crusade on their part.

This was the beginning of the fourth period of enlarged municipal activity.   Preparation had been made not only in the investigations of the previous twenty years, but especially in the new power to demolish unsanitary buildings, granted to the Board of Health by the legislature of 1897.   The origin of this act of the legislature is to be found in the English " Housing of the Working Classes " Act of 1890.   Previous to that year there had been much accomplished in English cities in the clearing of slum areas; but it had always been necessary

[1] Estabrook, *Some Slums in Boston*, 1898.

for the municipality to buy the unsanitary property at exorbitant prices. The Act of 1890 remedied this defect and made it possible for local authorities to take such property by compulsory purchase, paying no more than a fair market value, less the amount necessary to put the property in good sanitary condition. A similar law was passed by the New York Assembly in 1895. With the new Massachusetts law of 1897 behind them, and the aroused public sentiment sustaining them, the health authorities proceeded to order demolished many of the worst buildings in the city. During the four years since the passage of the law, over 150 dwelling-houses and 80 stables have been torn down. So far no damages have been paid, and not until the summer of 1901 did an expropriated property owner carry his case into the courts. By condemning only the worst buildings, the Board of Health has not yet found anything due the owners on account of the buildings, after deducting from their market value the expense of tearing them down.

The result of clearing away or remodeling old and unsanitary buildings has usually been a permanent improvement. This may be illustrated by three examples typical of the changes which are taking place in the crowded sections of the city.

The first method is that of opening up a playground or park where there has been a nest of overcrowded and miserable houses. A good illustration of this is the playground between North Bennett and Prince streets, adjoining the Paul Revere School. In this space, now permanently cleared, were formerly twenty-five or more houses, nearly all of which had become unfit for habitation. A number of small alleys ran into this area from the streets mentioned; otherwise almost the whole of the ground was covered. This undertaking involved the purchase of 11,384 square feet of land in addition to the schoolhouse site. Another instance was the clearing of the area north of the Copp's Hill burying-ground for the present Copp's Hill Terrace and North End Park. Here seven acres have been made available for purposes of rest and recreation.

The second type of improvement is shown in the replacing of a group of unsanitary houses by a single tenement house or a tenement-house block. This is well illustrated on Fleet Street, between North and Hanover, where there was formerly a cluster of ten wooden and brick houses on either side of Clifford Place and the adjoining alley. Mr. Estabrook, in 1898, described the houses on Clifford Place as follows: " In none of the houses is there

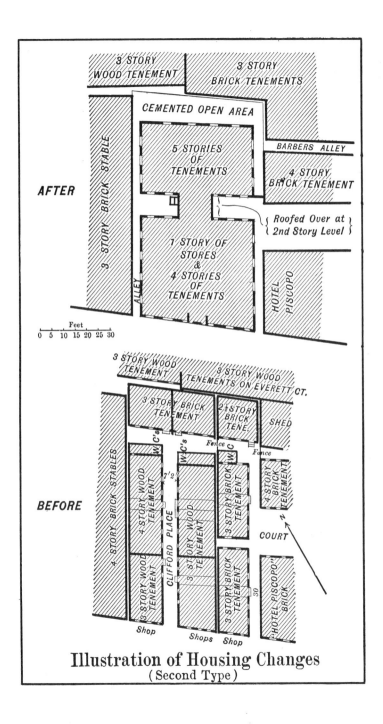

AFTER

3 STORY WOOD TENEMENT

3 STORY BRICK TENEMENTS

CEMENTED OPEN AREA

3 STORY BRICK STABLE

5 STORIES OF TENEMENTS

BARBERS ALLEY

4 STORY BRICK TENEMENT

{ Roofed Over at 2nd Story Level }

ALLEY

1 STORY OF STORES & 4 STORIES OF TENEMENTS

HOTEL PISCOPO

Feet
0 5 10 15 20 25 30

BEFORE

3 STORY WOOD TENEMENT

3 STORY WOOD TENEMENTS ON EVERETT CT.

3 STORY BRICK TENEMENT

2½ STORY BRICK TENE.

SHED

4 STORY BRICK STABLES

W.C's

W.C's

W.C

Fence

Fence

4 STORY WOOD TENEMENT

7'2"

CLIFFORD PLACE

3 STORY WOOD TENEMENT

3 STORY BRICK TENEMENT

4 STORY BRICK TENEMENT

COURT

N

3 STORY WOOD TENEMENT

3 STORY BRICK TENEMENT

30

"HOTEL PISCOPO" BRICK

Shop

Shops Shop

Illustration of Housing Changes
(Second Type)

any thorough ventilation; air shafts were not thought of when these houses were built. Though the sun shines into some rooms on the top floors, all the lower rooms are very dark. From cellar to roof, each house is very dirty and battered. In many rooms pieces of the ceiling have already fallen, and more is apparently about to fall. The wooden houses on both sides of the alleys shake so much as one walks about them, and their floors are so far from level, that it is surprising that they have not collapsed, in spite of the support given them by the adjoining buildings." [1] These buildings were ordered demolished by the Board of Health. The owner of the property obeyed the order, and upon the area thus cleared has erected one large five-story brick house with accommodation for forty families. This house is not what a building for so large a number of people ought to be. Its halls are narrow and much too dark, and there are but two main entrances for all who live in the building. But in point of physical healthfulness there is undoubtedly a change for the better. A similar illustration of this type of improvement is the wiping out of Kenna Place, leading off Grove Street between Phillips and Revere streets in the West End. At the present time a block of apartment houses

Estabrook, *Some Slums in Boston,* p. 16.

covers the area where formerly were wretched rookeries.

The third type of permanent improvement is the remodeling of an unsanitary block so radically as to make it habitable. This is well illustrated in the notorious Keith's Alley, leading from North Street towards Hanover. In 1898 a block of three three-story brick houses on the left had no rear ventilation other than that gained by two small air shafts covered in at the top. Towering above the block in the rear were brick buildings four and a half and six stories high. Across the alley, about eleven feet distant, was a block of two three-story wooden buildings, whose only rear windows opened on a narrow crack between them and a five-story brick warehouse. The only water-closets for these blocks were in the open space at the upper end of the alley. The Board of Health ordered the houses vacated. The owners of the property then proceeded to make radical changes. A large section was cut out of the centre of the brick block, giving light and ventilation to the rear rooms of the inner houses. The closets were taken out of the yard. New closets, with suitable plumbing, were put into each house and opened on the air shafts, which were themselves opened at the top to the outer air. Similar changes were made in the wooden block on the right of the alley. Both blocks may now be considered as at least out of the worst class.

Cheap lodging-houses, which are more numerous in the North and West Ends than in other parts of the city, have of late years engaged the attention of the Board of Health, and some extremely salutary changes have been effected. Many of the most objectionable have been closed. By stringent regulations and constant supervision, the remainder are now fairly clean and well ventilated, and supplied with cleanly furnishings. Overcrowding has been to a large extent prevented by nocturnal visits on the part of the health authorities.

The " lanes," " alleys," and " courts " of the city are, according to a recent report of the Health Department, " in a bad sanitary condition and subject to a great deal of complaint." The difficulty lies in the proper adjustment of responsibility for their cleanliness, since they are private property. Uncleanly habits of their owners keep many of these open spaces in a most undesirable condition. Not until the street-cleaning department of the city shall have the entire authority to clean them at the abutters' expense will the difficulty be satisfactorily overcome.

Some of the facts concerning disease and death in the city will indicate the present need of in-

creased sanitary effort.   During 1900 Boston's
population was 560,892, and 11,670 deaths were
reported.   This would make the city death-rate for
the year 20.81 per thousand inhabitants, or one
in each 48.06.   This death-rate has been lowered
in only four of the last fifty years, two of these
four years being 1898 and 1899.   Ward 6, in the
North End, shows the largest number of deaths
under one year of age, 184, or 8.74 per cent. of the
whole number of deaths under one year; and the
largest number of deaths between one and five
years, 177, or 13.7 per cent. of the whole number
of deaths between one and five years.   The death-
rate in Ward 6 was one in each 41 ; in the whole
city one in each 48.   In Ward 8, of the West End,
where the adult lodging-house population lowers
the rate, it was one in each 58.   In Ward 25, a
suburban district, the rate was one in each 81.
Wards 7 and 13 show a total death-rate slightly
higher than Ward 6, though in the mortality of
children under five years, the North End is far in
excess of any other section.

In the matter of specific diseases Ward 6 is not-
able again in having the largest total number of
deaths from pneumonia, meningitis, typhoid fever,
and diphtheria; and the second largest number
of deaths from cholera infantum and bronchitis.

This ward also leads in homicides. In Ward 8 the mortality figures are not so striking, although its percentage for deaths of children between one and five years of age is exceeded in only two other wards. This ward leads in the total number of deaths from diseases of the heart, and is second only to Ward 6 in the total number of deaths from pneumonia. These wards do not have so large a number of deaths from consumption as do several other wards of the city. Consumption specially afflicts the Irish in the severe New England climate, and makes its greatest ravages where they are most numerous.

Wards 6 and 8 lead with 1386 and 1033 births, respectively, out of a total of 16,351. Ward 11, in the Back Bay, reported only 238. That is to say, in Ward 6, of the North End, there was one birth to every 22 of the population; in Ward 8, of the West End, one in every 28; and in Ward 11, of the Back Bay, one in every 81.

It has been thought by some students of the housing problem that the tenement-house congestion in the North and West Ends would be relieved by the building of small houses in the suburbs and the cheapening of transit facilities. Dorchester and West Roxbury have shown great gains in population since 1895, and a large number of small houses have been built in these sections. But it remains true that Ward 8, of the West End, increased in population during the same period faster than any other section of the city, except the two suburbs named. It now has the distinction of containing the largest number of persons to the acre, 173.6. Ward 9, in the South End, ranks second, with 132.2, and Ward 6 third, with 104.3. The relative growth of these two wards may be shown as follows : —

	1895.	1900.
Ward 6....................	27,860	30,546
Ward 8....................	23,130	28,817
	50,990	59,363

The same figures for Dorchester and West Roxbury are as follows : —

	1895.	1900.
Wards 20 and 24 (Dorchester)	39,768	59,682
Ward 23 (West Roxbury)	18,283	23,637
	58,051	83,319

Let it be noted, however, that the acreage of Dorchester is 5590 and of West Roxbury 7660. There were in 1900 only 10.6 persons to the acre in Dorchester, as compared with 104.3 in the North End, and 3.1 persons to the acre in West Roxbury, in contrast with the 173.6 of the West End. Evidently the time is far in the future when the cheaper rates in food and the pleasures of association with one's kind can be overcome by the attractions of healthier surroundings and suburban houses. The tenement-house problem of the North and West Ends is destined to be a vital one for many years to come.

In this connection a few figures from the United States census of 1900 will be instructive. The percentage of Boston dwellings containing three or more families is 19.9. In 1890 it was 17.2. Ward 6 is reported as having an average of 3.3 families to a dwelling; Ward 8, 2.8. These are the largest averages among the wards, the average for the whole city being 1.8. Of the whole number of families in the city, 41.3 per cent. live in dwellings containing three or more families, as against 37.5 per cent. in 1890. In Ward 6, out of 5843 families, 4754 live in dwellings containing three or more families; in Ward 8, 3818 out of 5065 families live under similar conditions.

The present condition of the tenement houses in the North and West Ends is not satisfactory from any point of view. The Health Department of the city has not succeeded in preventing overcrowding, or in compelling owners to provide the necessary ventilation and sanitary arrangements. Although a considerable number of the very worst houses have been removed, a very large number of wretched dwellings are left. They are not quite bad enough to be condemned without payment of damages, but they are entirely unfit for human habitation, according to the standards set by modern sanitary science and modern ideals of home life. In March, 1899, the consulting architect of the city reported to the mayor the result of his investigation of these unfit houses. He described dirty and battered walls and ceilings, dark cellars with water standing in them, alleys littered with garbage and filth, broken and leaking drain-pipes, interior rooms or closets and damp basements used as bedrooms and even then overcrowded, dark and narrow stairways, dark and filthy water-closets, closets long frozen or otherwise out of order, tenements inadequately lighted and unventilated because of high buildings closely surrounding them, and houses so dilapidated and so much settled that they are dangerous.

In the fall of 1901 the Health Department ordered a comprehensive examination of all tenement houses in the city. Each inspector reported the details in regard to the sanitary condition of every house in his district. These reports have been filed with the department, though they have not been tabulated by streets and wards, as they should be if they are to be of the greatest value. A compilation of the reports of twenty-six tenement houses in South Margin Street, in the West End, reveals the following situation : —

The number of tenements reported upon was 118, containing 350 rooms. In these rooms 540 persons are living, though the number allowed by law is only 446. Of the 197 bedrooms, 97 contain less than 600 cubic feet of air space. Thirty-eight of the bedrooms are dark rooms, and 33 of the tenements are reported as overcrowded. Six houses are said to have defective drainage. Sixteen have cellars that are damp or filthy or both. Eleven yards are in bad condition. Nineteen out of 20 garbage receptacles are reported as defective or insufficient or both. Seventeen out of 67 water-closets are in bad condition. The name of the owner is posted in only 9 of the 26 houses.

It is to be said, of course, that the personal habits of the tenants are largely responsible for such conditions, and that these habits are not under municipal control. Undoubtedly many a suitable tenement house is turned into a place of misery by the ignorance and vice of its occupants. Beyond a certain point in sanitary regulation the health authorities of a city cannot go. Nevertheless the housing problem is one that cannot be dismissed as

merely one of many incidentals under the care
of the city. It must receive the attention it demands. Not only does the health of the city
depend largely on the condition of its tenement
houses, but the morals as well. Such a problem
has become serious enough to require the most
thoughtful attention of able men and women who
have devoted their best energies to its solution.
It cannot be properly handled by those who are
compelled to make it subordinate to other duties.
New York City has found it necessary to establish
a separate Tenement-house Department. There
are many good reasons why Boston, though a much
smaller city, should do the same.

Complaints against the present building laws of
Boston have arisen from several quarters. Those
who have been inclined to invest money in improved
tenement houses are now deterred on the ground
that first-class buildings, erected under present
requirements and rented to families who cannot
pay as much as sixteen dollars a month, would
yield practically no return on the investment.
Others complain that under the head of repairs
the present laws allow old buildings to be recon-
structed without conforming to restrictions applied
to new buildings. This leads to the perpetuation
in an increased degree of the evils of the old

houses. Finally the Health Department, in its report for 1901, complains that the present building laws over-emphasize the matter of fireproof construction and pay too little attention to light and ventilation, thereby permitting air shafts that are utterly inadequate and halls and stairways which are almost totally dark.

Such complaints make it clear that there is need of a careful revision of these laws from the various points of view of fireproof construction, economical arrangement, adequate ventilation and light, artistic architecture, and inexpensive accommodation. Such a revision should be made by a commission made up of architects, builders, physicians, and sanitary and philanthropic experts. A petition has been presented to the mayor of Boston by the Tenement-house Committee of the Twentieth Century Club asking for the appointment of just such a commission. Public-spirited citizens, whose opinions would carry great weight, have indicated their willingness to serve on a commission of this kind without other compensation than the opportunity to aid in improving housing conditions. Changes in legislation proposed by such a body would certainly receive the most careful consideration on the part of the members of the Massachusetts legislature.

Meanwhile there are various lines of improvement which can and undoubtedly will be undertaken. The investigation of the tenement houses made by the Health Department in 1901 furnishes the data for much effective sanitary progress. The demolition of single unfit buildings continues, although the lack of funds retards activity in this direction. Having no money in hand for the payment of possible damages, it is inevitable that the authorities should avoid condemning any building for which a claim for damages could be successfully established. This results, as has already been said, in the demolition of only the very worst buildings. That more than this needs to be done is recognized by the Health Department, and the sum of $10,000 has been requested from the City Council as a sinking fund to provide against damage suits. It is essential that some such appropriation be made in the near future.

The department has also recommended the widening and extending of certain narrow streets and alleys. " There are a number of congested districts in this city where improvements of this kind could be made to great advantage; such, for instance, as Webster Avenue from Hanover Street to Unity Street, which could be widened and made a street, thus doing away with a lot of unsanitary dwellings and improving all the others. Another great improvement could be made by the extension of Hale Street, formerly Crescent Place, to South Margin Street." [1]

Nor has the need of more open spaces been overlooked. In the report for 1900,[2] the department recommended that " as Cross Street is to be widened in the near future, the territory bounded by Salem, Stillman, Endicott, and Cross streets be taken possession of by the city and made a breathing spot, thus doing away with a number of old, unsanitary, and dilapidated tenement houses, and also abolishing Morton Street, which is one of the narrowest, dirtiest, and most unsanitary streets in the city of Boston."

Such recommendations cannot long go unheeded. The housing problem has come to be recognized in England as the most vital of all municipal problems, and heroic efforts are being made to solve it. It is receiving in Boston the attention of an increasing number of those who are most intelligent concerning the needs of the city. The situation must be handled in a comprehensive manner, with adequate recognition of the future, and in a full sense of its bearing upon the city's welfare and progress.

---

[1] *Annual Report of the Health Department for 1901*, p. 42.
[2] Ibid., p. 42.

CHAPTER V

LIVELIHOOD

In ways of earning their bread, as in other
things, North and West End people stand out quite
distinct from the remainder of the city's population. Something of their industrial civilization
they brought with them. The city, from the nature
of its growth, had made these districts the likely
lodgment of struggling immigrants as they arrived.
To a considerable extent it had also ordained the
currents in which the local industry should run.
This is particularly true with respect to the North
End. The sharp limit of the water-front, with its
docks, warehouses, and great traffic; the North
Union Station and its approaches; the markets
reaching out toward the railroad terminal in one
direction, and toward the harbor in another —
effectually stamp their impress upon the district.
The boundaries of the West End do not take a form
so definitely commercial, but the section is much
more affected by railroad activity than the North
End, while it has easier access to the great centres

of trade in the heart of the city. Beacon Hill prevents the growth of trade to the south of the district, while the bank of the river is not available for commercial use on account of the drawbridge tolls, added to the high cost of land. Between the hill and the river is a narrow strip of territory which the West End population is gradually invading. Here there are numerous stables, and the workshops of many jobbing mechanics and artisans. The northern slope of the hill, rejected by the prosperous as being exposed to all that is worst in the Boston winter, furnishes convenient location for two strongly contrasted grades of attaché to downtown establishments, clerks and Negroes.

There is not much large-scale manufacture in or near the North and West Ends. The only considerable plants are, one for the generation of illuminating gas, —which is soon to be removed, — the other for the generation of electric power for the transit system. These are both on the North End water-front. The North End has some tin factories and furniture factories, and in both districts there are large establishments for the manufacture of confectionery and cigars. In general, land is too expensive in these parts for any industrial enterprise requiring space.

The great stores of the city, all of which can easily be reached from any point in these districts by walking, are related to them not merely as centres of employment and bases for household supply, but as markets for clothing made at home or in small workshops, and as headquarters for laying in the materials for peddling.

The direction taken by shopkeeping within these districts, even more than other aspects of their economic life, is largely a matter of nationality. The Italian and Jewish colonies are to a considerable extent self-sufficient, with the full variety of trade in the hands of men of their own race. But in the Italian quarter the clothing trade is controlled by Jews, and the Jewish quarter is being invaded by Italian greengrocers. Here and there, ever more rarely, is a weather-beaten signboard with the name of some belated New Englander, struggling to maintain his foothold against intruders on his market by offering to speak several sorts of foreign tongue.

There are a few Jewish and Italian liquor sellers, but the Irish still hold their regrettable monopoly of that noxious trade. The saloons are the last commercial relic of Irish occupation. They are exceptionally numerous because to these two districts are apportioned the full number of saloons supposed to be appropriate to the great crowds that are found near or within their boundaries during business hours. The business has been a very lucrative one in times past, and many well-to-do Irish families throughout the city owe their rise in life to it ; but this condition of things has changed. Not a few saloon-keepers, in fact, find it difficult to make their living out of the trade. In all parts of the city, even where the Irish strongly predominate, the cause of temperance is making headway, because it is the general testimony that the saloon business is noticeably falling off. There is additional reason for such falling off where Jews and Italians are displacing a population of Irish origin, both being more temperate races, taking milder liquors, and using them at home. The Jew seldom enters a saloon. Italians in considerable numbers patronize the saloons kept by their own countrymen at the North End. Here they learn to drink beer instead of the Italian wines to which they have been accustomed.

There is a special and permanent fitness in the Italians' choice of abode just next to the great fruit and vegetable markets. The citizens of Boston owe a great debt to the Italians for organizing and developing the retail fruit trade throughout the city. The Italians have, in fact, created a

wholesome appetite for fruit among the mass of
the people. Believing in their goods, they have
special skill in selecting, arranging and caring for
it. Even the newest immigrant, with his push-
cart, makes his wares attractive, and unwittingly
acts as the dietetic missionary of the back streets
throughout the city. In their stores at the North
End the Italians have striking displays of vegetables in their season, red and green peppers having
all seasons for their own.

As has been suggested, the Jews seem to prize
the Italians' taste and cleanliness as a purveyor of
food. The contrast between the Italian and Jewish
grocery would seem to be appreciable in every case
to more senses than one. As to meat, however,
the faithful Israelite still prefers the ceremonially
even to the aseptically clean. The tendency of the
Jew toward wearing apparel as his stock in trade
is strongly shown by his ready recourse to the peddler's pack, and even by his falling back as a last
resort upon "rags." The Jew's surprising power
of making headway is seen in his very first essays.
The Jewish immigrant has moral capital to begin
with. He is seldom or never illiterate. He always
has a friend who can loan him a shelter if not
money. And he is not by any means always im-
poverished when he reaches our shores. Borne

forward by his indomitable pertinacity, armed with a few words of English, he shoulders his junk bag or his peddler's pack. Jewish peddlers in some cases start out on long circuits through New England, and are gone for months. They are not much seen in the immediate vicinity of the city. That route of caravan trade has been recently taken up by some Semitic cousins of theirs, the women of the new Syrian colony at the South End.

The Jew's capacity for trade in cast-off utilities appears frequently, of course, in the pawnshops, " misfit parlors " and junk shops. These lines of trade are, however, not so successful as formerly. The charges of pawnbrokers are restricted by law to one and a half per cent. per month, and they are likely to suffer severely if they accept stolen goods. New ready-made clothing has become so cheap at the downtown stores that the demand for second-hand garments, except those of " Harvard students," has quite fallen away. Trade in junk has also suffered by the lessened cost of manufacture in various lines. It would appear, however, that every effort is made to exhaust the remaining possibilities of the rag and bottle business, judging from the number and persistency of raucous-voiced Hebrews who file through the back alleys of various parts of the city.

The junk collector or peddler in a surprisingly short time is found as the proprietor of a small basement store, or the owner of a wagon in which he hawks vegetables or ice in summer, wood and coal in winter. The owner of a clothing or dry-goods store is in a more secure position, not dealing in goods that are so perishable or so limited to their season ; but these small merchants are constantly feeling the competition of the great department stores among their more thrifty customers, and of the installment stores among the less thrifty. There is, in fact, a new type of peddler, a man who, by a special understanding with a department store, sells its goods to customers on the installment plan. This is an alliance on the part of the small Jewish trader and the department store in order to meet the installment store with its own weapons.

The more prosperous shopkeepers are German Jews on Hanover Street. Their trade is on a considerable scale, and they own their places of business. On Salem Street the property is still held by old Boston families. Clothing stores are the most conspicuous, and the dealers do not wait passively within for their customers. Food supplies and household furnishings of the cheapest grades are all dealt in. An exception must be made in the case of the butcher shops. These have the trade of Jews from all sections of the city. They sell the better qualities of meat, and are especially careful about their supply of fish. There are three bankers on Salem Street, whose business seems to be chiefly concerned with foreign exchange. In the West End, Jewish trade is increasing rapidly, but this growth, up to the present, takes the shape of innumerable small enterprises. Many of them must go to the wall before there can be any possibility of well-conducted and prosperous establishments in the streets of which the Jews have taken possession.

The sale of jewelry is a staple form of business among the more prosperous Jews of these parts of the city. For this, as for other sorts of trade, they prefer to be a little removed from the Jewish quarter, where they can have the trade of their congeners and of the world as well. There is some personal and incidental trade in gold and gems, as was characteristic of the Jews in the Middle Ages. A case in point was that of a kosher butcher who was also in a quiet way a dealer in diamonds. This survival is the more interesting because the Jew has come to realize intensely that he is at last in a country where he will not be compelled to flee at night; that his treasure need no longer be such as can be tied in a napkin. The old land hunger has returned upon him in a passion for "real estate." With a keen sense for earning his living by profit rather than by wages, and with the necessary capacity for strict attention to detail, this easiest and surest form of profit-making is to him an economic vision of hope and happiness. The increase of Jewish ownership in real estate during the past ten years has been amazing. The number of Jewish landlords is so large that the pioneers among them complain bitterly that there are "too many in the business." A considerable number of Jews now give their occupation as "real estate;" but even petty traders are property owners by the way. One man who has been a peddler for fifteen years owns two houses. A certain small shopkeeper in the North End is the owner of three houses, which accommodate ten families besides his own.

Jewish real-estate holdings are more numerous in proportion in the parts of the city under review in this volume than elsewhere in the city, but in the South End and Roxbury such holdings are rapidly growing. In the North and West Ends in 1900, estates with a total assessed valuation of $6,344,700 were charged to persons of names unmistakably

Jewish.[1] Practically every parcel of this property represents but a very slender cash investment, but it is managed so painstakingly and shrewdly that mortgages are rapidly reduced. The method of the new landlord is in nearly every case the same. He purchases an old building, tears out the plaster partitions, rearranging them so as to give a larger number of rooms, builds an ell so as to cover as much of the ground as possible, tears down the old front wall and erects a new one of showy yellow brick, which seems to be particularly attractive to tenants' eyes, and almost universally makes the front cellar do duty as a basement store. The old material is used as far as possible. New material is of the cheapest grade. The labor is provided by ill-paid recent immigrants. Such a development implies a large amount of money-lending on the part of brethren who have been particularly successful.

The two most characteristic forms of small capitalist that have developed among the Continental immigrants are the Jewish sweater and the Italian padrone. Originally the sweating system was a method on the part of small manufacturers to escape the cost of rent, heat and light by having the em-

---

[1] The property of well-known downtown merchants is not included in this total.

ployee do the work in his own home. The sweater also sets out to secure the advantage of the principle that a man's home is his castle, in order to avoid legislative regulation and official inspection. He seeks as his employees the most ignorant and helpless of the immigrants; enlists all the members of a family, including little children; pays them by the piece at cruelly low rates, so that very long hours of work are necessary, amid congestion that conduces surely to ill health and low morality. The scale of wages for other work-people is seriously endangered. These evils, in their worst aspects, may fortunately be spoken of as things of the past in Boston. Ten years ago, as the result of public agitation, a law was passed by which work at home is under very careful inspection as to the sanitary surroundings in which the work is done. Licenses are given only in case of strict cleanliness in the tenement of the applicant, in the hallways leading to it, and in the yard at the back. A fine of fifty dollars is provided for the offense of giving out work to an unlicensed person. At present, licenses for home work in the North and West Ends are comparatively limited in number. They are held principally by Italian and Portuguese women, who eke out a little in time spared from their domestic duties.

The sweating system has thus, to all intents and purposes, disappeared from districts where it once flourished, and where all the local conditions for its growth still exist. The effect of the anti-sweating legislation was at first in some ways disastrous. The orders which had formerly been fulfilled in Boston sweat shops were immediately transferred to sweaters in New York. The local garment industry in its cheaper grades was for a time prostrated. Many garment-workers went to New York, some to Canada.

In due time, however, a considerable share of the old industry was reorganized in separate workshops, which are subject to factory inspection. There are certain attractive sides to this work. The Jew dislikes the military regulations which necessarily govern a factory. He enjoys the friendly intimacy of the shop. The master provides, as far as possible, for his Sabbath rest and worship. The smaller shops are attached to a little tailor store — it is usually a " ladies' tailor " — and are scattered through various parts of the city. When they work for private customers they are not subject to inspection. The larger shops are found in the North and West Ends, for the most part in warehouse buildings. The force in each shop includes from five to thirty men and women. The men are chiefly Jews; the women, Italians and Portuguese. Some of the evils of the sweating system still persist, — low wages, long, uncertain hours, evasion of sanitary regulations, very irregular employment according to dull or busy season, the competition of recent unskilled immigrants. It is from these shops that the unfinished clothing is given out to the licensed home-workers.

The rise of the Jewish master tailor presents an instructive instance of the evolution of the capitalist. He works endlessly, living with his family on an impossibly small expenditure. He lays by a small amount. He gets his landlord or his butcher as his security. He purchases a sewing machine and a pressing table on the installment plan. At first he makes less than his employees; but by perseverance, by quick perception as to organizing and subdividing the industry into specialties, often by keeping up a human feeling between himself and his employees, he gradually develops his business until he can command the services of certain specially skilled workmen to act as leaders in his shop, and can present inducements to foremen in the large clothing stores for the sake of winning their patronage.

Within the past three or four years, a considerable business in the raw material of the garment industry has sprung up at the North End. There are now eight small firms dealing in woolen goods. It is possible for them to compete with downtown wholesalers by keen attention to small considerations in buying, by paying low rents, and by handling poor grades of goods. Their business is not confined to the local garment trade; they supply small Jewish tailors in different parts of New England.

The Jew is narrow in the range of his occupations. The growth of a class of mechanics and artisans has awaited the development of a class of small capitalists. Jewish real-estate ownership is already bringing an increase of Jewish workmen in the building trades. The Jews have the ingenuity and mechanical ability which would fit them for industrial crafts, and many of them have followed such vocations in Russia.

The Italian represents a varied list of occupations. In the North End colony there are artisans, bakers, barbers, confectioners, musicians, tailors, scissors grinders, shoemakers, marble cutters, and workers in plaster. The Italians have discovered how much the average young clerk or mechanic, on occasion, enjoys having some one else polish his shoes. At a number of points throughout the city they have opened good-sized rooms wholly given over to bootblacking, and these rooms seem to furnish rather profitable occupation. Many Italian boys are bootblacks at large in the old-time way, making Boston Common their headquarters.

An increasing number of Italian women, with a few men, engage in agricultural work in the market gardens of Arlington, Belmont, Lexington and other adjoining towns. The women bring some intelligence and endless assiduity to such work, and the market gardeners are much pleased with this new source of labor supply. A cluster of bright headdresses among the growing crops in a New England field is a distinctly novel sight. It is a thing, however, which brings a sigh for all in American tradition which goes against overburdened womanhood. Often, in addition to their field labor, these women walk the entire distance from the North End and back each day.

Fully fifty per cent. of the men of the Boston Italian colony are engaged more or less regularly at heavy labor with pick and shovel, in railroad building or in the construction of gas and water works. Such toil always nowadays calls to mind the Italian. This is quite as true in various parts of Europe as in this country. The one-time conqueror of the world is now its slave.

When the Italian laborer appeared among us, he was indeed in bondage, under a cruel taskmaster. The Italian padrone, in the days of his ascendency, took a disastrously large commission for the purchase of the immigrant's steamer ticket, upon his wages after he arrived, upon the rent of his miserable overcrowded abode; and finally, in many cases, with the assistance of an Italian banker, appropriated his savings wholesale. The padrone's methods have been much limited as the years have passed. The Italian government, which formerly looked upon all emigrants in the light of deserters, now takes a more liberal attitude, and has regulations in force to protect its citizens as they leave the country. The stranger arriving upon our shores now has friends, acquainted to some extent with the English language and with the ways of the country, who inform him as to wages and conditions of labor, and perhaps receive him as a lodger in their own little tenement. The absconding banker is becoming rare, especially as the Italians are learning to put their savings in the old, well-established savings banks of the city. One of the Italian banks at the North End does business under a name recognizably Irish, — this in the hope of convincing Little Italy that it is an American institution. The American Express

Company has recently established a branch near North Square, offering in Italian terms to send money safely to Europe. The Italian banks still appear to drive a thriving trade, if the lavish display of gold and greenbacks in their windows may be taken as proof. Their close relations with the padrones is shown by their acting as headquarters for information about employment for groups of unskilled laborers at various points throughout the surrounding country.

A few Italians have taken up the business of hotel-keeping, but the standards of these men have been so lax as to make them very objectionable in that capacity, — so much so that their progress in that direction has to some extent been blocked by the police. It must not be thought, however, that all Italian business enterprise is of the nature of preying upon the community. There are several successful Italian firms in the wholesale fruit trade. The manufacture of macaroni is a natural and growing avenue for Italian business talent. The making and selling of plaster casts of statuary, for which so large a demand has within a few years been created, is thus far an Italian monopoly. The number of Italian real-estate owners is very considerable. In the North End, in 1900, $2,325,-800 worth of property was ascribed in the city records to persons having Italian names. A few artists, musicians and handicraftsmen of distinct ability have begun to appear among them, and there is prospect of many more in the rising generation ; but such persons are likely to move to other parts of the city.

A very large majority of the Irish in the North and West Ends are unskilled laborers. On the whole, they do not suffer as much as would be supposed under the competition of recent immigrants. To a considerable degree the Irish and the Jews represent non-competing groups, their industrial capacities being so divergent. Then the large amount of work carried on by the municipality, for which the Italians might be candidates, is restricted to American citizens. This, as well as labor under the great corporations, whose franchises come from the city government, is dispensed almost entirely as political patronage. As the politics of these two districts is still in the control of the Irish, men of that nationality practically monopolize these forms of labor so far as the North and West End population is concerned. It is probable that not less than one third of the families of Irish extraction in these districts have breadwinners that are employed through political influence.

There is among them a large number of dock laborers, freight handlers, and teamsters. The skilled trades have some representation. Members of the younger generation are very likely to seek mercantile employment. The Irish huckster is giving way to the Italian with his push-cart. The prosperous Irish citizens of these parts, omitting saloon-keepers and politicians, are a few substantial shopkeepers who still remain, and a few contractors, who for the most part might be classed as politicians.

The Portuguese are sufficiently numerous to have some small supply stores of their own. Like the Scandinavians in the North End, they are primarily sailors and fishermen or longshoremen. They are found to some extent in skilled mechanical work, as pattern-makers or cabinet-makers. Some of the young men become barbers. The young women go out as domestic servants, though a few are shopgirls.

The Greeks are in active and, so far as their numbers go, successful competition with the Italians as sellers of fruit and sweets. Indeed, they are leaving their ancient rivals far behind. They are becoming noticeable for their achievements in developing the confectionery trade in the neighborhood of the great downtown stores which attract women purchasers. The Greeks know that the mother on returning home must always come bearing gifts.

There are several small but enterprising Negro shopkeepers at the foot of the hill in the West End. A branch of Booker Washington's Business Men's League exists in that quarter. The vast majority of them, however, follow the menial occupations to which they are fated, — waiters, servants, sleeping-car porters, bootblacks. Some occupy the more independent positions of janitor or elevator man. Occasionally a colored man employed in a store combines the functions of porter and clerk. There are but few colored members of skilled trades, and even the barber's trade seems to be closing to them. A considerable number of burly Southern Negroes work in the markets, carrying quarters and halves of meat on their backs. There are also a few colored teamsters. Persons of leisure are by no means lacking, supported by their wives, who go forth as laundresses or scrubwomen.

Men of American and British American antecedents, found in the West End lodging-houses, are chiefly clerks in stores and counting-houses, though there are among them not a few mechanics and artisans, who, having only themselves to provide for, manage to live in a somewhat more

ambitious way than most of their fellow workmen.
Here and there through the lodging-house streets
are a few members of the learned professions, for
the most part in rather doubtful standing. Each
nationality among the tenement houses of both districts, including the Negroes, is gradually developing
its quota of professional men. There is a noticeable tendency on the part of the brighter young
men, especially among the Jews, to become lawyers
and enter the lists for a general city clientele. Too
often they seem to have an instinct for methods
which do not lend credit to their calling.

The lot of most immigrant women, so far as
actual labor goes, is not so severe as it was before they left their old homes. Factory development takes from them spinning, weaving, knitting,
and to some extent even sewing. There are distinct signs of leisure among the Italian housewives
at the North End. It is this state of things which
makes it possible for some of them to undertake
agricultural labor, and for others to scour the city
for wood, which they carry on their heads by the
cart load, skillfully navigating through the most
crowded streets. Italian girls and young women
quite commonly work in the confectionery factories.
Some of them, and some Jewish girls as well,
are now found behind the counters of the depart-

ment stores. But Jewish women seldom leave their homes to work. Marriage comes early, and unmarried women are as scarce as beggars in the Jewish community. Where there is a store, the family lives adjoining it, and the wife and daughters assist actively in conducting the business. A considerable number of Jewish and Italian women work with the men in the garment shops. Irish women have almost disappeared from the sewing trade in this part of the city, as a result of the disastrous competition of the newcomers. For many of them the change was a tragedy. Others have found more secure employment in the downtown factories and department stores. In the lodging-house district in the West End, there are of course many young women from the country and some from the British provinces, who have positions as saleswomen, stenographers and writing clerks in large mercantile establishments.

The pressure upon children to become wage earners as soon as the compulsory period of school attendance is passed, so as to supplement the family income, is, except in the case of Jewish girls, well-nigh universal and very insistent. Office boys, cash boys and messenger boys in the city are largely Irish. Jewish boys monopolize the downtown newspaper trade. Italian boys are bootblacks. Colored boys are fortunate in beginning with the occupations which they will follow as men. Boys of other nationalities follow juvenile occupations, which in a few years leave them on the employment market almost as helpless, as far as experience and training is concerned, as they were when they left school. The evil effect of the streets is very apparent upon all children of these districts, but they are all having better opportunities of education than their parents. Few will fall below the level of the immigrant generation, and an appreciable proportion of them, through special training and opportunities, are rising to a wholly new level of capability and resource.

There is a much greater uniformity of industrial status in these districts than in any other part of the city. The North End is so particularly characterized by this sameness that it proved difficult to register on a map the slight shades of difference from block to block in that district. It is a great community of the unskilled — of those, on the one hand, who have not yet had time enough to rise, and those, on the other, who are the stragglers left behind by the more enterprising of their kind.

As there are in these districts several large establishments supplying temporary quarters for homeless men, it will be understood that the tramp finds ample winter quarters here. The typical guests at these places subsist by street begging and petty thieving, with occasional jobs. The daily goal of their hopes is a night's lodging and strong drink as much as possible, with or without food. Their " change of air " takes the form of a few months down the harbor at the House of Correction or the Almshouse. In the cheap lodging-houses, besides tramps, there are undoubtedly a few genuine " journeymen," traveling in search of work. Some sailors and fishermen also stop here during the interim of their voyages, — such as do not go to the special boarding-houses for men of sea-faring occupations. Among this floating population, and closely allied to it, is a considerable class of casual workmen. Their way of life is partly created by the uncertainties of employment that go with all dock and water-side industries, though as important a cause is the general degenerating tendencies that spring out of tenement-house life. Specimens of this grade may be seen at any time lounging about or staggering away from the saloons on Commercial Street. It must not be thought, of course, that these degraded specimens constitute more than the residuum of the men engaged in the industries of the harbor. The mass of the men regularly attached to the dock and shipping interests find their employment more or less irregular, and there is danger always that this irresponsible class beneath, with its crude, ravenous desires, will offer to do their work at a lower wage than they in their more human way can live upon.

During recent years there has not appeared any serious problem of the unemployed in these districts. There are, of course, occasional difficulties, as when the anti-sweating law went into effect, throwing many Jews out of work, or when by a change of city administration many Irish employees find themselves " on the bricks," or when within a few weeks there are several thousand newly arrived Italians thrown upon the labor market. But ordinarily the permanently unemployed are a very small remnant. Many Italians may be seen loafing about North Square, but as a rule they are simply waiting between jobs on large construction works. The Jews are not inclined even to wait between jobs, though they cannot turn so easily as formerly to garment-making or even to junk collecting, since those occupations have been placed under license, with special restrictions and regulations. On the whole, however, the only Jews who are not working are the white-bearded elders who sit on the synagogue steps.

How people subsist when out of work is a question which is exceedingly difficult for the outsider to understand. Ordinarily families have some bit of savings to fall back upon. Then there are the small basement stores giving credit. There are occasional small jobs. Perhaps the wife can go out to work, or the children are pressed into employment. Relatives and friends often go to surprising lengths in supplying food and loaning money. There are successive journeys to the pawnshop. All the time subsidies of charitable relief are unfortunately more available than recourses in the way of self-support.

The lowest grade of regularly paid employment in these districts is garment work. It is done by the day or by the piece. In the shops, women earn from $3 to $5 a week, men from $9 to $12 and upward. The comparatively unskilled nature of the work, and the almost unlimited supply of operatives, make competition for employment very intense. Women sewing at home cannot earn more than thirty or forty cents in a long day.

Italian gang laborers formerly received only $1.25 per day, but they are now freely offered $1.50 or $1.75. This is for work at a distance. They have to pay their carfare, and there are always possibilities that their wages will be heavily drawn upon for their victualling and shanty accom-

modations. Considering how much time they lose
during the year, they are probably no better off
than the fruit hawkers, who make on the average
$5 or $6 per week. Italian women on farms earn
$1 per day. The Italian hurdy-gurdy grinder,
with the tambourine girl in peasant costume, who
as a rule hires his instrument by the day, has a
somewhat larger income than this, and considers
himself much superior to his horny-handed countryman — a leisured aristocrat, so to speak.

Among the Irish part of the population, the
standard wage is $2 per diem, the rate paid to
the laborers in the city departments. For similar employment on corporation works and in connection with building operations the wage is $1.75.
There is also a choice between the two sorts of
employment in the number of months in the year
during which men must lie off — the time being
shortest in city work — and the amount of stren-
uousness exacted, the city here being also the
most indulgent employer. Teaming, cab driving,
freight handling and dock work are paid for at
rates a little lower. Longshoremen work by the
hour at from twenty-five to sixty cents, the latter
amount being for evening and Sunday labor. Sailors receive $30 per month. Fishermen still have
the old-time coöperative system of payment, — the

ship having one fourth of the value of the catch, and the remainder, after expenses have been deducted, going to the master and the men.

The North and West Ends are both singularly deficient in artisans and mechanics. Men of that grade of skill in the Irish population have to a large extent moved elsewhere, and the type has developed but little among the Jewish and, as yet, among the Italian population. The specially capable and enterprising ones rise quickly out of the ranks of the unskilled, leap over the skilled-labor stage, and become clerks or shopkeepers. Most of the skilled labor class is found in the better streets of the West End, some of them being young men in the lodging-houses on the hill slope. Their wages run from $2.25 to $3.25 per day, with more or less loss of time during the year, according to season. Some of the Jews have a profitable type of skilled labor in cigar-making. The wages are from $15 to $25 per week, with little loss of time during the year. Jewish and Italian bakers receive about $10 per week. In all trades which they enter, the Italians are still somewhat below the usual standard of wages. This is true of the barbers, for instance, who receive from $6 to $10 per week. " Italian labor " is a standing bugaboo among the working classes of the city, and only time can remove its

meaning.   Negroes engaged in personal service
have comfortable incomes.   The wages of waiters
are of course often but the smaller part of their
receipts.   Sleeping-car porters are the magnates of
the colored servant class.   They often take in $100
a month.

Shopgirls receive $5 or $6 per week.   Women
stenographers and clerks in business offices have
from $6 to $10 per week, and more in cases of
special ability.   The ordinary weekly wage of men
clerks ranges from $10 to $15.

The mass of small Jewish shopkeepers do not
make more than a bare living out of their trade.
Many of the little basement stores are only auxiliary sources of income.   In some instances, even the
basement store is a source of substantial gains.
Under such circumstances the rent is very low
and the prices correspondingly less.   In one case
of a basement store, this method of competition is
so successful that, with the whole family employed,
an annual business of $10,000 is transacted, with
a net profit of twenty-five per cent.   This is the
rate of profit on which all Jewish dealers calculate.
Some of the woolen firms do a gross business of
$40,000 or $50,000 a year.

The question of times and seasons in the North
and West End industry is a complicated and serious

one. This is particularly true in the garment trade. There is a slack time of sometimes two months, from August to October, and another of equal length after Christmas. The Jews are embarrassed with regard to the Sabbath. Recently arrived immigrants lose both Saturday and Sunday, but after a time conscientious scruples begin to give way. The loss of both days is too heavily felt, and the employer, who is naturally under special pressure to have work finished at the end of the week, can ill afford to retain help which drops out at the moment of special need. So far as Jewish stores go, conditions vary between being closed during the whole of both days and being stealthily open during the whole of both days. The police, however, follow up with some degree of vigor the matter of Sunday closing.

Garment work done at the homes cannot be regulated either as to days or hours; and to some extent work is carried from the shops by employees to be finished at home, against the chance of discovery by the factory inspectors. The workshops, besides coming under strict sanitary restrictions, are of course subject to the State regulation of fifty-eight hours as the maximum weekly working time in all manufacturing establishments. The limit of sixty hours for the week's work in mercantile establishments, which was set a year ago by the State, will, when its enforcement is fully organized, bring much relief to many employees in the small stores in this part of the city.   For those who work in the large downtown stores, the working day is universally not so long as the maximum limit allowed by the law.   Italian laborers have their busy season during the spring and summer.   As a rule they have no protection as to the hours of work, and their day ordinarily is one of ten hours.   The dock and water-side laborers work by the hour at somewhat irregular intervals.   Expressmen and truckmen have long and elastic hours.   The city laborer, as part of model conditions, has the eight-hour day.

The effort to classify the different industrial grades of these districts, and to make out the relative numerical strength of each, is beset by special difficulties, and the result can only be broadly suggestive of the situation.   The entire mass of the garment-workers, with the exception of a few men obviously attached to downtown tailoring establishments, must be included among the unskilled. Some of this large number already belong to the higher grade, and many will no doubt within a few years stand either among the skilled or among the clerks and shopkeepers.

On the other hand, all of the trading class, with the exception of peddlers and organ grinders, may be included among the clerks. Many of these, so far as income is concerned, are no higher than the unskilled, but they represent in their personal history a step up from the level of unskilled labor and a step nearer the social condition of the shop-keeper class.

The proportion of the dependent classes may be broadly estimated from the reports of public and private charities in these districts. Such reports indicate that about twelve per cent. of the population in the North End, and about nine per cent. in the West End, have received some form of charitable relief within the past two years. These proportions would include practically all of those who belong distinctly to the grades of casual and intermittent workers, together with tramps, loafers and semi-criminals. These three lowest types, judging from returns made by proprietors of cheap lodging-houses for the police records, may be esti-mated at three per cent. for the North End and two per cent. for the West End.

The industrial character of the bulk of the population may be analyzed satisfactorily by means of the Assessors' List, which for purposes of iden-tification gives the occupation of each man over twenty years of age in the city. The list for 1901 for these districts contains 7853 names for the North End, 13,170 for the West End. A classification and count of the occupations represented show that for the North End unskilled laborers, including garment-workers and a few other inferior trades, number 5068; skilled workmen, receiving standard wages, 1317; clerks, superior workmen and shopkeepers, 1239. Those entered without occupation, chiefly old men, foot up to 121, while to professional men and downtown merchants not more than 108 can be credited. For the West End the corresponding figures are: unskilled, 5603; skilled, 2431; clerks, 4699; without occupation, 197; professional and commercial, 240.

These numbers for men in different parts of the districts represent slightly different totals for the entire population. The total is slightly larger in proportion in the lodging-houses than in the tenement houses, reflecting the large proportion of women lodgers. Taking out the percentages already allowed to the loafer, casual and intermittent classes, and charging a majority of these to the unskilled laborers and a majority of the remainder to the unskilled workmen, we may distribute those without occupation, the veterans, proportionally among the three chief classes.

A large part of the population is huddled into old houses originally built for the use of single families. Many of the smaller tenement houses are built in rear yards and courts. There are many large newly built tenement blocks, in which the evil devices involved in making over old houses are perpetuated in the new. This process is still going on at a rapid rate, particularly in the West End. The most recent new or remodeled structures generally take the form of apartment houses with some appearance of privacy at the entrance, some modern conveniences and often but one family to a floor. The outer appearance is extremely deceptive, and a few years will work havoc with the flimsy materials out of which these buildings are constructed; yet for the present they represent an advance for the tenants. A somewhat poorer yet very worthy class is found in the large blocks of model tenement houses representing " philanthropy and five per cent."

The Jews, inured through long centuries to overcrowding and uncleanliness, adjust themselves to such surroundings with unfortunate ease. The Italians, while not models in the matter of cleanliness and the reserves of life, seek to make their windows and narrow courts suggestive of the green world from which most of them have come, and in

which a better order of living was not so overwhelmingly difficult. The Portuguese and the
Negroes, not standing so high as neighboring types
in the matter of the more serious sanctions of life,
are both strongly inclined to cleanliness in their
homes. There are actually streets in the West
End where, while Jews are moving in, Negro housewives are gathering up their skirts and seeking a
more spotless environment.

Much attention has been given by public authorities to the cheap lodging-houses in this part of
the city, and some slight leveling up in their
standard is apparent. There are a number of
second-rate hotels in both districts, — some of them
resorts of a degrading type, some better grade
lodging-houses, some simply saloons with liberty
to sell liquor on Sunday. The boarding-house
does not seem to have passed away quite so completely in the West End as in the South End,
and there are not so many separate basement
dining-rooms; but the background of life on the
slope of Beacon Hill beyond the State House is
essentially the same as that of the respectable-
appearing decadent streets of the South End.

In spite of the fact that these districts are so
near the city's best base of supply for meat and
vegetables, the people trade at very small shops,

and of course are compelled to follow the extravagant method of buying in small quantities. The Jewish meat supply is in the hands of a local Jewish monopolist, and the savage riots of the New York Ghetto were reproduced in the North End when the price of meat recently rose so high. The evidence was quite clear that the local wholesaler had undertaken to increase the momentum of rising prices in order to secure special personal advantage.

The Jews' faithfulness to the dietetic code of the Mosaic law makes them no more strange and individual in their notions about food than are the Italians. They use but little meat. Crabs and razor fish are a staple. Occasionally they have chicken or pork. Beef is a rare luxury. The Italians like their food greasy, highly spiced and flavored with garlic or onions. A dish so dressed will have for a body nothing more substantial than macaroni. With this they will have French bread, beer and some partly spoiled fruit or dried olives. Such a diet is inexpensive so far as first cost is concerned, but a sturdy growth cannot be made upon it. The frequency of rickets among Italian children, and the general high average of sickness among adults, is owing very largely to their choice of food. Their liking for this strong-tasting but innutritious food is so deep seated that if they go to a hospital they consider themselves wronged when they are placed upon a diet of milk and beefsteak.

As in the South End, there has been of late years a marked increase in the number of restaurants, which are common along nearly all the chief streets. Hardly one of them is in the least clean or attractive. The little Italian eating-places in the North End have about them some of the atmosphere of the Continental café ; but in the West End restaurants, the hapless lodger finds not even that solace to counteract the poor quality of his food. Nearly all the Negroes continue to have some sort of home attachment, and they have good food when they can possibly afford it. Their comparatively high standard as to the conditions of home life probably reflects their hereditary associations as servants in homes of the well-to-do. It is needless to say that a Negro does not neglect his clothes. Many young colored people from the West End, — as seen, for instance, at a band concert on Boston Common, — while showing an undue expenditure in clothes, are yet dressed becomingly.

The Jews are also very fond of fine clothes, or at least of the appearance of such. The women, as family incomes increase, appear in cotton velvet or brocaded satinet, with colored feathers in their hats, mock sealskin coats and dubious jewelry. The Italians are more frugal, and do not cultivate an appearance of elegance. The women are satisfied with simple fabrics in bright colors. The men do not affect broadcloth, as Jewish men do, but are contented on Sunday — if the day be marked by nothing more — with a gay necktie, curled and unctuous hair and a brilliant polish to their shoes.

The desire for clothing of American cut is one that rises strong in the breast of the immigrant immediately upon his arrival, and the imported styles become less and less in evidence every year. Long beards among the Jewish men, and wigs among the women, are seen but little as compared with a few years ago. The inclination of the Jews to move away from the antiquated tenement houses of the North End into the new flats of the West End, where they have figured plush furniture, flowered carpets, and even pianos, is very marked. In such ways there is sometimes among the Jews, particularly on the part of the women, a distinct tendency toward extravagance. The secret of such an unexpected phenomenon is undue social ambition. Probably no nationality is so keenly alert as the Jews to the various marks that register gradual advancement to higher and higher social levels.

All the nationalities at the North and West Ends make considerable contributions to the support of religion, an outlay which, even from the most superficial point of view, is an exceedingly useful public investment. Parents are more and more putting themselves at pains and cost to secure the benefits of education beyond the grammar school for their boys, and, to some extent, for their girls. This is of course especially the case among the Jews, whose intellectuality is a distinguishing trait. All classes spend some money upon the theatre — on the whole, beneficially. The Italians give much attention to public recreation. Considerable expense is incurred by them on feast days and Italian national holidays.

Even microscopic incomes do not forbid to the Italians, much less to the Jews, the practice of thrift. Italians save to go back to Italy, or to bring friends over. Some save and become landholders and small business men. Many of those who are diggers in the ditch put by one hundred dollars in the course of a year. Italians do not easily fall back upon charitable agencies; but, for those who slip, determined spurring is needed in order to get them well under way again. Jews are not likely to need charity, but when they do they seem not to have much self-respect in the

matter, looking upon such relief as another resource to be availed of to the utmost limit.

Among Jews there are two types of providence.
One sort of person places his family upon the lowest possible line as to home conditions, food and
clothing, in order to make the utmost margin between his expenditures and his income. He intends
some day to have things different, but he wishes to
become a capitalist and make his living by profits
rather than by wages, at the earliest possible moment. His family is under degrading conditions;
he himself is ill nourished, and his children are
dwarfed physically and morally. The other type
is also eager to become a capitalist, but he wishes,
from the beginning, to have his family under
healthful and encouraging conditions. Instead of
taking up his abode in some swarming, reeking
court at the North End, he lives in a comfortable
little flat at the West End. He does not save so
rapidly, but he is in condition to earn more,
to enjoy more, and to be an increasingly more successful man in the future; his children, meanwhile,
are laying the foundation of a fair education and a
reasonably healthy physical and moral adult life.

The inhabitants of the North and West Ends
have their obvious economic sins. The shame of
a variety of underhanded methods in trade, not

easily punishable by law, must be laid at the door
of a certain type of Jew.   More serious than any
of these things, however, is the danger that lurks
in the low standard of wages and expenditure
which all Jews and Italians bring in with them,
and in which great numbers persist.   So long and
so far as this state of things continues, the newcomer remains an enemy to all that is best in
American life, and cannot expect to be received
into the friendly fellowship of American citizens.
The American " standard of living and of life " is
being intrenched in various ways, — by the commonwealth and the municipality, by working-class
regulations and sentiments.   It has suffered seriously, and still is threatened.   The issue will
depend on the effect of the total civilization of
the city in amplifying the range of wants among
these new peoples.   In this way the energy, productive capacity and ambition of the mass of
them will be brought to a higher point.   At the
same time, that base, passionate enterprise will be
tempered which would ruthlessly sacrifice kindred
and neighbor for the dream of ultimate prosperity.

CHAPTER VI

TRAFFIC IN CITIZENSHIP

" AFTER all, the predominating issue is — work."
The congressional candidate had made a few flour-
ishes about matters of concern to the nation, such
as militarism and trusts. This was his way of arriving at reality in the North End. He then proceeded to explain that by securing from the national
government an appropriation of millions of dollars
to deepen the harbor at Boston, he would open up
to the men whose humble abodes are near the harbor docks an almost endless vista of jobs. The
deeper harbor will lead to the erection of new
docks, which men must needs be employed upon to
build. Docks mean dockers. New ships will come
and must be manned. This growth will imply new
factories and new warehouses, which men must
build, and which once opened will remain as well-
springs of employment forever.

The tendency to localize and domesticate the
universal is one of the master motives of ward politics. There is in the mind of the voter a marked

absence of such faculty of abstraction as will en-
able him to feel himself receiving advantage from
the general action of the community in its large,
ordinary functions. These are to him like the
atmosphere. He wishes to see some new, divisible
fruitage produced toward the enlargement of his
meagre life. This feeling is so pervasive that the
fulfillment of the individual voter's insistent need
becomes the decisive test of political and public
service.

Honesty and special capacity in public officials
is a virtue which has some value in campaigns, but
even then it is usually so indiscriminately ascribed
to all candidates as to make it the mere material
of compliment and persiflage. A hundred times
more worth while than general honesty in the eyes
of the local electorate is fair play. The serious
charge against an office-holder is not " he was dis-
honest," but " he was greedy ; " he did not impart to his constituency enough of the results of his
influence and power. The remedy does not seem
to the people to be that of the business man, nor
yet that of the scholar in politics. Civil service
reform means to them administration in the hands
of a class that may be honest in an arid sort of
way, but not serviceable or responsible, so far as
they are concerned. The " greedy " politician can

be and is soon displaced by one who will be
" fair." There is an ingrained and powerful feeling that the hope of the poorer and alien classes
is in holding blindly together. The reformer is,
in fact, looked upon with some of the distrust and
fear in which in the Middle Ages the equally truth-
loving heretic was viewed, — as one who would turn
distraught humanity aside from the only way of
salvation.

Ordinary public standards of intellectual fitness
count for little or nothing in these parts of the city.
It is, in fact, a distinct hindrance in a candidate to
have the air of training. Occasionally some young
politician is charged with being a graduate of Harvard ; and the charge is denied resentfully. One
of the foremost political magnates, a man of un-
doubted native ability, who has held high elective
office as a lawmaker, is yet unable, after several
attempts, to secure admission to the practice of the
law. Such a fact hardly creates a ripple of interest among the rank and file of his following.

There are political virtues of different degrees,
but the greatest of these is loyalty. Ward politics
is built up out of racial, religious, industrial affiliations ; out of blood kinship ; out of childhood associations, youthful camaraderie, general neighborhood sociability. Party regularity is simply the

coalescence of all these. It is the brightest star in the crown of a political veteran to have been "always regular." The frequent petty insurrections only show the power of this loyalty. They are family quarrels. The offending member is still more loved and even more trusted, so far as family interests are concerned, than any outsider. The very disinterestedness of the outsider makes the family recoil from him. The sudden way in which the most acrimonious political breaches are healed over shows the underlying fraternal bond. Ward politics is an amplified scheme of family communism — a modernized clan. Some day it may perhaps become apparent to the historian, looking back, that this clan life in the midst of civilization went with the industrial and social confusion of the time. The poor in our cities have as fierce a contest with industrial conditions as the barbarians had against wild nature. The similarity of social formation, of ethical standard, goes with the similarity of the facts of the two kinds of life. The present-day barbaric outlook must be altered if we would impart truly civilized conceptions of politics or of life in general.

In these northern wards, as in the inner wards at the South End, one of the parties is so strong that there is never any contest, and the minority party is of consequence only in general city elections. The strain and conflict which go with politics occur only when there are faction fights. These are not uncommon, and while they last are more intense than any contest across party lines. Where the party nomination is equivalent to an election, it is natural that there should be keen competition within party lines. In the fierce glare of a faction fight, the true perspectives of ward politics come out. The charges brought against leaders by their opponents, and the claims of service rendered which are made in reply, show the actual motive and trend of politics in the ward.

Sectarian feeling is appealed to by asserting that a certain leading politician used the church as a tool, and that he was dismissed from the altar by the reverend pastor. He is accused of having invited a non-Christian to officiate as bearer at a funeral. Racial feeling is goaded by the charge that a Jewish office-holder had expressed profane contempt for the Irish; and an Irish alderman is denounced for not having rushed to the defense of his Italian constituents when they were classed with Negroes at a meeting of the board. That a certain leader is making use of politics for his own enrichment is sustained by the charge that he is treasurer of a corporation receiving numerous

contracts ; that he is one of a real-estate syndi-
cate whose land is assessed at one third of its
value ; that he and his brothers own seven saloons
among them ; that one of his lieutenants in the
State Senate wronged and duped the voters of
the constituency by taking money rather than
patronage for his vote on a street railway bill.   It
is asserted that a prominent local political figure is
not a resident of the ward, and packs the voting list
with other non-residents.   A poster calling attention to these facts says : " Home Rule is the fundamental principle of free government, which principle men died to establish.   Why, therefore,
should the people of this ward allow residents of
Concord, Acton, Winchendon, Lawrence, Winthrop, Beachmont, East Boston, the South End, to
govern them ? "   This same tyrant and usurper
has, it is said, secured the dismissal of many men
from their work, and made " saddened and broken
homes because heads of families voted as they
thought was right."   Not content with a relentless
policy toward foes, he is, it is said, traitorous to
friends ; and it is even hurled through the dense
pipe-smoke into the teeth of the populace that one
such victim of treachery actually died of a broken
heart.

The scene changes.   Look on that picture and

on this ; trace here the lineaments of the man whom King Demos delighteth to honor. He went on the hottest days to contractors and corporations seeking jobs for men in the ward. He was noted for the " conspicuousness of his presence when wanted." The people did not have to " play hide and seek " with him ; when they desired his services he could always be found. He represented his constituency " so earnestly, so successfully, so untiringly " in the search for employment for them. He voted for the abolition of civil service regulations that he might have more jobs to dispense. He voted to control corporations having contracts with municipalities in such way as to make corporation patronage as valuable a political asset as that of the municipality itself. He opposed a measure to punish housewives who undertook to use milk cans or jars for any other purpose than that for which they were intended. He promoted a measure compelling ice companies to sell five-cent cakes of ice, and a measure requiring gas companies to sell their product for seventy-five cents per thousand feet. He urged the boarding out of neglected children in families of the same faith as that to which their parents belonged. He sought the relaxation of some of the restrictions on the use of the Sabbath ; and, though his constituents might not acknowledge this as a special service to themselves, worked for the abolition of dark cells and of the death penalty. Lastly, he supported an increase in the tax-rate, but only in order to give more employment to laborers — not for the sake of providing " high salaries for Back Bay dudes."

The machine politician especially opposes reform measures like that of civil service restrictions and the secret ballot. These make it more difficult to organize and control the vote, to secure the appointment of particular men, and, what is more exasperating, to hold the allegiance of men after they have been installed in city jobs. It is not uncommon for political appointees whose positions have been placed under the protection of civil service regulations to throw over all obligations to the political machine, and even to move away to a remote suburban district.

Such facts make it all the more important that the work of party organization should be painstakingly done. In bringing out the votes of these wards, the ward committees may be said to exhaust the possibilities, to use everything and neglect nothing, in order to produce results.

Here, as in the South End,[1] the street-corner gangs and a variety of loosely organized clubs form

[1] *The City Wilderness*, p. 114, sq.

political groups, ready made to the hand of the ward heeler. In the North End certain political clubs leap into activity during campaign time. In the West End there is a remarkable political organization having rooms on the most prominent square in the ward. This club keeps up an active existence all the year round, and is the headquarters for the entire business of machine politics of the ward.

Apart from all formal organizations, each ward is divided into several sections, and local lieutenants are appointed to hold together, and bring to the front at the proper time, the vote of their neighborhoods. The local lieutenant devotes himself unremittingly to the people of his section of the ward. He keeps himself acquainted with their whole round of life, and constitutes himself the adviser and helper of them all. By unresting vigilance, together with a careful and comprehensive system of political account keeping and statistics, he knows within a few votes just how much strength his section holds for the party ticket. As campaign time approaches committees are appointed, who divide among themselves the responsibility of seeing and making sure of all the voters in these sub-districts. The ardor of propagandism exhibited by these local committees quite surpasses the proselyting zeal of any type

of churchman. Indeed, the most aggressive soli-
citors of trade could hardly equal them; because if
inducements fail, they have an organized power
of constraint behind them which amounts almost
to that of the tax collector or police magistrate.
The care and shrewdness with which this work is
done is illustrated by the fact that in the West
End it is sometimes the custom to appoint one man
to get out eight voters, and soon after to appoint
two other men each to get out four of the same
eight. In the North End every imaginable sup-
porter of the party has his name enrolled in a card
catalogue. Every such person is visited in advance
of the caucus, and to the utmost limit of the resources of the machine — with its knowledge of
each man's ties, obligations, ambitions, necessities
— satisfactorily "fixed." At the caucus, and
again at election, voters, as they appear, are checked
off by party representatives. When proceedings
are half over, trusty men are dispatched in every
direction throughout the ward to chase in the
tardy ones. "So run I not as uncertainly; so
fight I not as one that beateth the air" might be
taken as the watchword of the ward politician. It is
because he sends the arrow so straight to the mark,
the axe so sure to the root of the tree, that the far
less determined reformer fails to overthrow him.

Very special efforts have to be made to adapt political methods to the particular spirit and necessity of the different nationalities in these cosmopolitan wards. There is a constant tendency on the part of the Irish to move away to better favored parts of the city, where they will not be subjected to so crowded conditions and to unpleasant association with recent Continental immigrants. As the local political leaders are nearly all of Irish origin, and as the Irish are their surest and best reliance, they make determined efforts to retain in the ward the remnant of the Irish population. The Roman Catholic churches of these districts, which with enormous establishments are in danger of being left stranded, are working toward the same end. It is a fixed rule in Ward 8 that no man can receive a job without pledging himself to remain a voter in the ward as long as he holds the job.

The Jews and Italians are gradually becoming voters under pressure of leaders of their own, who show them the advantages of so doing. Nowadays, the Jew junk collector must have taken out citizenship papers before he can get a license, and the Italian laborer has no prospect of being engaged on city work unless he be an American citizen. Peddlers, junk dealers, fruit sellers, organ grinders, sewing-women, clothing manufacturers, — all must have dealings with public officials. Everybody knows, too, that by mistake or otherwise the laws of a strange country are easily broken. Under such circumstances the value of an accommodating expert in public administration is soon realized. The newcomer, in establishing his home, finds that some credit is necessary. The gas company requires security. The politician — not unknown to corporations — gives it. The politician expects votes in return. He has ways of enforcing his displeasure if the votes are not forthcoming. In each identical bearing of the social mechanism where oil is needed, it is possible to put sand.

Finer considerations are by no means lacking. It is coming to be a matter of racial pride and loyalty among Italians and Jews to place themselves on an equality with those who assume superiority over newcomers. They wish to escape the contempt with which the ignorant treat foreigners; they crave the full round of American experience. Soon they realize that their children are to be Americans, and this makes American citizenship more clearly their own destiny.

As to party affiliations, both of these nationalities, when first arrived in Boston, were inclined to be Republicans. They seemed to recognize in

the Republican party a distinctly American organization. The word *republican* is one that the
Italian is familiar with, and it has inspiring associations for him. The Republicans have not had
the sagacity to take advantage of this situation.
They have allowed these wards to be under a type
of leadership which is certainly as corrupt as that
of the opposite party, without any of the redeeming
qualities that go with its strength. This state of
things has conduced to the change in political
alignment which has taken place. It was not a
spontaneous movement. Neither the Jew nor the
Italian, be it said, is instinctively drawn to the
Irishman, nor he to them.

The Irish have made great efforts to win the
Italians to the Democratic party. They are co-
religionists, and they can love each other for their
common enmity to the Jew. At least half the
Italian voters in the North End are now Democrats. They make good political workers. They
organize effectively, and are quite disinterested.
The chief difficulty about them from the political
organizer's point of view is that they are split into
many rival camps, according to the city or province
in Italy from which they came. The leaders of
these different cliques, in their claims to recognition, are very prone to exaggerate the number of

their naturalized followers. The Democratic leaders have managed also to secure a considerable following among the Jews. Were these districts not so overwhelmingly Democratic, the Jews could be kept more closely within the Republican fold. As it is, the poorer ones are very likely to be Democrats. They are made to see, in the machine's tangible, lucrative ways, the advantage of supporting the local political powers that be. They are very difficult material for the politician. They are individualists, quarreling constantly among themselves, each demanding to have as good a share as the most favored one. They do not act in a mass under impulses of loyalty. They are of that very uncomfortable sort who "have to be seen often." They demand stated and regular returns for political allegiance, or else their allegiance is gone.

The Negro vote is for the most part gerrymandered into a Republican ward. There is some competition between the parties for their suffrage. There are three classes of Negro voters, each class including a considerable number: those who are purchased at so much a head; those who act under leaders for a consideration of some sort; honest voters whose support is held by their being "recognized" in various ways.

The inducements brought to the minds of the

voters in these wards, it will be seen, are of a concrete, unmistakable sort. Of outright bribery it must be said that there is very little. Every political step, however, involves some sort of indirect bribery. The whole course of local political procedure is beset with trickery and fraud. There are specialists in naturalization, each of whom stands as sponsor to large numbers of newcomers, swearing falsely as to the length of time they have been in this country. They retain certain interpreters to serve their purposes. The reading test is managed with considerable ease. Under a friendly registration officer, any rude attempt at pronouncing the words of the Constitution is considered satisfactory. Immigrants, provided they are familiar with the Roman alphabet letters, after a little coaching, summon intelligence and courage to pronounce a series of English words, syllable by syllable, in an incoherent way; and a North End wardroom is not the place for stiff academical requirements.

It is perfectly true that there are often, if not always, some hundreds of voters in these districts who do not pretend to live in this part of the city. Many of the " boys " who have moved away from the North End still retain a " residence " there. They spend a night or two at a certain address at the first of May, rarely even complying with the letter of the law, and then have themselves registered as voters from that address. It is quite possible, in case of local faction fights, to decide the issue at a caucus, or in city elections to affect the general result, by this " carpet-bagger " vote.

The choice of men to stand as candidates for party nomination at the caucus is subject to a variety of considerations. The foremost politicians have probably climbed the ladder of elective fame so far as ward politicians can. The West End boss, who has been to the top, deigns, like " the old man eloquent," to return to lower posts of statesmanship ; but he is exceptional. The usual plan is for the leader to put forward some specially trusted intimate, often a brother or a cousin, for the important nominations. Specially bright " talkers " are likely to be advanced for honors in the City or State legislative chambers. Faithful party workers are " rewarded " by a term in the Common Council. It is the policy, also, in both districts, to " recognize " the Continental elements by giving some of their number small elective offices. Some of these are beginning to rise above the Common Council. One Jew and one Italian from the North End have served in the lower branch of the legislature. Every man selected to go before the caucus is required to agree, in the presence of witnesses, that if he is elected to office he will act entirely as the ward organization directs.

The filing of caucus nomination papers is every year the occasion of some absurd, disgraceful exhibition. A heeler gets into the party office by a window, or down through a skylight, in order to have his faction's list of nominees placed first on the caucus ticket. Or the announcement of the time for filing nominations, of which public advertisement is required, is placed in an obscure part of the first edition of the afternoon papers, and those in possession of the secret have their nominations filed while their opponents are still waiting for the news.

As a rule, local contests in the North and West Ends never extend beyond the caucus, except in a merely perfunctory way. The West End is so boss ridden that there is rarely any public campaign at all. The democracy does not meet and reason together for the common good. Important elections take place in this district without a single meeting for a discussion of the issues involved. This seems to represent the extreme step in setting aside our American precedents. The West End doctrine is that platform discussion is " hot air ; " that the newspapers are all " fixed " by corporations'; and that the welfare of city and nation is neither here nor there to Ward 8. This does not mean that there is nothing to an election but the leader's fiat. On the contrary, the campaign in the shape of "personal work" is carried to the bench and counter, the threshold and fireside, the saloon bar and the street corner, — wherever the voter is found. Exhaustive organization, not talk, is the West End style of canvass. In either district freedom of speech is sometimes subject to actual abridgment in the case of bolters. In the West End a dissenting faction had made all arrangements to hold a meeting in the wardroom, but arrived to find the lights out and the door securely locked. In the North End there was to be, under insurgent leadership, a special Jewish rally in a new synagogue which was practically completed. Influence was brought to bear upon the contractor to post a notice that the building was unsafe.

At rallies, when there is a local contest, much time and attention is given to specific instructions as to the proper candidates to be voted for under each heading on the ballot, and careful warnings are given as to the proper sources of light, provided light is necessary. Indeed, a ward rally at the North End toward the close of the evening assumes the character of a district school, in which the pupils of different grades are given their different appropriate lessons by the chief political pedagogue, to be learned by caucus day.

It is said that a peculiar sort of "crib" has been devised by which some of these pupils occasionally escape the mental burden of their lesson. For a certain office there are a number of independent candidates, whose fitness for the nomination consists in the fact that their names are confusingly like those of the "regulars." A tooth comb is taken and the teeth removed, except those which are spaced so as to point to the names of the "regular" candidates on the caucus ballot, when the end of the comb is pointed at the name of the office to be filled; or better still, a piece of cardboard has oblong holes cut in it, which, when fitted over the list of nominees, leaves only the approved names in sight. Thus equipped the recent Italian immigrant may be enabled to vote "right" with an accuracy of which enlightened voters — whose eyes might wander — would be quite incapable. At this point political ingenuity comes within a hair's breadth of making the machine automatic.

At the caucus itself instruction is still liberally and insistently dispensed; though then, of course, false doctrine is likely to be even more loudly proclaimed. In this case there is everything in the voter's knowing the particular source from which the instruction comes. The officers of the caucus are on the alert for opportunities. There is a provision by which a voter who has any physical defect of hand or eye may seek help of the officers of the caucus. Sometimes a halting intellect is symbolically bodied forth in a bandaged eye or an arm in a sling. Then it is important to have the right man ready to "assist." Sometimes caucus officers exercise terrorism over certain voters by assisting them against their will, particularly those who are under the influence of liquor. These actions, however, are very closely watched by the opposing forces at the rail, who loudly protest to the captain or lieutenant of the police. Such an official is always present at this up-to-date folkmote, clothed with summary authority, and supported by from twenty to fifty roundsmen and two or three plain-clothes detectives.

The faction leaders outside the rail give close vigilance to watching the line of voters as they pass in to the polling booths. When the "fight" is a warm one, a large number of votes are challenged. The ground of most of the challenges is false registration, — covering the case of "carpet-baggers," whom every one knows to be non-residents, but whose failure to comply with the letter of the law may be difficult to prove. Quite often Republicans are found voting in Democratic caucuses. Occasionally a man is challenged as a repeater; that is, as voting on the name of another man, who may be late, absent, ill, in jail, or dead.

It is perhaps needless to say that the object of these challenges is not a disinterested desire to stop such corrupt practices. If the vote proves to be a close one, the challenges are followed up. As the caucus has now practically the same legal sanctions as an election, there are severe penalties involved. Usually, however, nothing is heard of them afterwards, and many people in the district come to look upon false registration, and even repeating, as part of the safe and profitable risk of the game of politics. After one caucus, in which the opposition made specially strenuous protests and entered many challenges, one of the local heelers was heard to remark, " Well, we ran in a couple hundred of them, anyway." A voter is sometimes challenged simply in order that the faction leaders may know exactly what the nature of his vote is. It was the intention, under the secret-ballot system, to make it impossible for the politician to keep account of stock and know about the actual delivery of goods. This worthy intention is easily defeated. A voter is challenged just as he is about to deposit his ballot. It is then necessary for him to identify his ballot by writing his name on the back of it. Confederates of the faction leaders, when the count comes, can discover whether the challenged voter has voted "right." This method is operated so effectually, and the machine so severely punishes irregularity thus discovered, that the security of the secret ballot is to a considerable degree lost.

It is only when a defeated faction refuses to abide by the result of the caucus that the full excitement of the campaign is carried beyond the primary and into the final election. Aside from such fraternal strife, there remains in general city elections the stimulus of supplying a large local vote for the party candidates; and as both wards carry an enormous list of city appointees, this incitement is always sufficient to keep the machine actively at work up to election time.

The power of such political organization is in that it is incessantly at work. It hardly has a season in which it is more busy than at other times. It has no vacations. Election won or lost, the organization comes at once to the steady, all the year round task of keeping the forces together and, as far as possible, satisfied. After a victory each ward tries to secure the greatest share of the spoils, and Wards 6 and 8 are noted for getting more than their share. In case of defeat various shifts are made to keep as many men as possible in office. There is at least a slight hold on power in the Board of Aldermen, or there are members of the legislature who can secure jobs from corporations. Many go back to their old trades. Loosely attached ones move away, remaining available for "residence" purposes when needed. In general, the same interlacing of relationship and association which lifts the fortunate into city positions serves to break their fall in the event of party failure. In any case, everything is done to stimulate the voters to watch and work for the future. It is a strange fact that party loyalty seems to rise higher during the lean years than during the fat years. Bolters choose the times when the party is in power as the favorable time for their insurrections; because, while many are provided for, more are not, and there are infinite possibilities for jealousies and bickering. As a City Hall official expressed it, " Every time I give a job I make one friend and ten enemies."

The brother and lieutenant of the Ward 8 boss, when in the legislature, dismissed some very important measure limiting the power of a certain corporation by saying that he was too busy attend-

ing to securing work for the unemployed to pay
attention to such matters.   The task of placing a
large number of men in city work is indeed a very
engrossing and exasperating one.   There lies in
waiting the disappointment of seeing them all discharged.   In Ward 6, at a recent political over-
turn, 212 men were removed.   No wonder that the
boss in the ward campaign that followed the mayoralty election, with a lenient and fostering air, stated
that if there were any men still in the city employ
who feared that they might lose their jobs by coming to the caucus, such men would be excused from
coming.   This announcement was the accompaniment of whispered rumors that a child had starved
to death, and a man had committed suicide.   It can
easily be understood, therefore, that there is a certain solemn hush about the last campaign meeting
before a city election, when the turn of events
affects so deeply the well-being of so many of the
families of the ward.

Civil service regulations offer obstacles in the
way of patronage, but the law is to some extent
evaded.   A boss secures the discharge of a large
number of men " for the good of the service " or
" for lack of work."   After a little time he begins
to draw liberally upon the civil service list, which
he has been careful to have filled up in the mean

time by his own men. Sometimes it is possible to make a new classification of labor, to have men enter their names under this new head, and then to have a call sent from the city departments for workmen of the new description. It has been asserted that on one occasion certain politicians in the West End surreptitiously secured the civil service examination papers in order to make sure of landing their men. The story goes that one half of the questions were changed, with the result that all the West End candidates made a mark of exactly fifty per cent. There is immunity from these embarrassments in the placing of laborers with corporations that have close relations with the municipal government. This is more and more an integral part of the machine scheme. Contractors and tradesmen who deal with the city departments are also confidently looked to by political leaders as sources of employment.

As matters of personal interest, of course only the larger stakes in the game concern the political chief and his aides-de-camp. Aside from securing a few well-paid appointive posts at City Hall, each ward expects that the teaming, street construction and other large city work carried on within its limits shall be done by some of its citizen contractors. These contracting firms are usually of

an improvised sort, and are often only a name
to cover up the operations of two or three politicians. Large profits are made in these ways.
Matters are so arranged that when the administration changes, the good-will and fixtures are transferred to a firm ostensibly connected with the
party newly in power, but the ownership probably
remains the same.

It is in connection with land transactions that
the professional politician finds his special financial
opportunity. Some of these schemes come near to
the line of legitimate business. For instance, at
the time when the new bridge to Charlestown was
to be erected, there was intense rivalry between two
groups of local politicians as to which should determine the precise location of the bridge. One
group had options on one row of buildings, the
other on a different row. The successful group
first secured a large amount of money for damages
to their buildings, and then profited by the rise
in value of their property after the improvements
were completed. Such money-making exploits on
the basis of inside knowledge of facts, and even
on the basis of facts actually created for the purpose, are, of course, the commonplace of much of
the large business enterprise of the present day.

Without that degree of excuse is the practice

of managing the purchase of real estate by the city at a price greatly in excess of its real value, the amount in excess going as booty to the chief political agents in bringing about the purchase. At least two local politicians have frequently been engaged in undertakings of this kind. "Land deals" are, in fact, so common that among old hands at City Hall it is taken for granted that no purchase of land by the city can be made without some official receiving his "dot."

The relation between politics and local trade of every sort is close. Shopkeepers find that it is very necessary to be on friendly terms with the machine. Their trade may diminish otherwise. A provision dealer in the West End was placed under a boycott not long ago because he had a political bolter engaged in cutting meat for him, but the provision dealer pluckily endured the temporary stress. The liquor trade is everywhere just on the edge of politics. But as the licenses are given by a State board, over which ward politicians can have but little influence, the relation of the politician to the saloon-keeper is simply that of two men who can give each other aid in forwarding their different projects. In several forms of Jewish trade and enterprise, the politician finds financial opportunities. The junk dealer seeks a license. Theoretically it costs five dollars; in practice it costs fifty. The jerry-builder seeks a license to make over an old building and crowd new additions upon the land. The politician can help him, for a consideration. After crowding the building over every possible inch of land, he wishes to gain more space by adding bay windows that jut out over the public street. In many cases the narrow streets in the West End, newly built up by Jewish landlords, have bay windows three feet deep reaching out on both sides, and almost continuous along the whole length of the street. A certain former Republican alderman, now holding a more important position, is said to have pocketed twenty-five dollars for each of these obstructions. As a result, among some of his companions he is called " Bay Window," by way of jolly nickname.

It must not be thought, however, that the politician never serves his constituency for naught. He has an endless number of thankless tasks laid upon him. He must see that this poor family's rent is paid; he must secure legal assistance for that oppressed immigrant; he has to arbitrate local disputes; he must secure for the sick admission to the hospital; he is pressed to use his best endeavors to get ambitious but incapable girls into the high or normal school; he must find places for them as stenographers or teachers when they have finished their education; he must put the poor, worthy and unworthy alike, in the way of receiving help from church or municipal charities; he is besieged for opportunities of work by widows and helpless people. He makes it his business to befriend the culprit before the law, advancing bail, securing witnesses, getting the complaint smoothed down, the penalty eased. As a philanthropist, under enlightened standards he could hardly be allowed to pass; still, he is inclined to believe himself one, and many of his constituents share the opinion with him. He is certainly human in the variety, the universality, of his interests and service. Up to a certain point, also, the boss must necessarily be a man of character. As seen in these districts, the political chiefs, whatever may be said about their public morality, answer to the severest tests that private domestic rectitude may place upon them.

Ward politics is largely an affair of young men. It brings them into some sort of equal association with persons of influence and power. Ambitious youths, with no one to help them to a professional or commercial career, and having prejudices to meet in those lines against their race and religion, find an open, inviting opportunity in politics.

Middle-aged men do not care for its excitements, and cannot so well afford its risks. It is a difficult task to get the older men to come to the caucus and wait for hours in line. Still, the family claim is so strong that cases are not uncommon in which a successful young politician, holding an important position at City Hall, will find a place for his father as laborer in one of the city departments.

The intricacies of family relationship have so much to do with holding the party together that the sentiments of women have telling force. Two minor politicians in the North End have recently found themselves discredited because they were saloon-keepers and non-churchgoers. The influence which led to their undoing came chiefly from what was said here and there over the table at home. Either fault by itself might have been condoned, but the double delinquency could not be endured. No man need hope for votes from these constituencies who is known to be discourteous to women or inconsiderate of children.

Politics, far more than any other interest, gives dignity to the larger social life in these wards. The man who succeeds in business moves away into pleasanter surroundings; the man who succeeds in politics must, in effect at least, remain. Politics lifts and localizes at the same time. It is, therefore, on the political, not on the economic or educational scale, that social dignities are registered. Politics forms a titled aristocracy. No considerable social occasion is complete which is not illustrated by some of these men of rank.

The political affairs of a ward are nominally in the hands of a ward committee for each party, but aside from the difficulty of finding among the voters of the ward twelve or fifteen men of sufficient special capacity and experience to serve on such a committee, the situation is so complicated, requires such varied, flexible and instant action, both for the regulation of internal affairs and for playing the local forces in the large outer field of a mayoralty campaign, that the single powerful leader is a natural and inevitable development. Even the reformer, if he reaches his conclusions on the basis of the facts as they are, is compelled to admit that the conditions require some sort of boss. The boss, too, must be near his people, and, in essential respects, like them. "He's our kind" is the keynote of loyalty to political leadership; and this, indeed, is usually as true, though the sentiment may be more subtly expressed, among the educated classes as among the working classes.

The two leaders in Ward 6 and Ward 8 have, until about a year ago, been engaged in a relentless duel with each other. The trouble began in a nominating convention. Charging that the Ward 6 man did not trade votes as he agreed to do, the Ward 8 man swore that he would let his right arm wither before he would ever take the hand of his professional brother. The two wards, being close neighbors, are in the same aldermanic and senatorial districts. Each boss strove to organize support in his rival's ward for alderman and senator, and every weapon in the arsenal of political chicanery was put in commission. Each proceeded to organize a band of insurgents in the territory of the other. Each played defensive tactics against the other by bringing hordes of " carpet-baggers " into his ward. After such strokes had been dealt back and forth during successive campaigns, the Ward 8 leader was able to institute a deadly attack from the rear. This was done by means of an organized, persistent policy of treachery to his party, through which he continued to retain a large share of his power after the opposition party had come into control of the city government. By placing at work men belonging to his opponent's ward at a time when all of his opponent's most loyal followers were being discharged, he effectually checkmated the enemy. The two bosses have now established a *modus vivendi*, to the peace and quiet of the city as a whole. The capitulating Ward 6 man, however, is now looked at somewhat askance by his "regular" colleagues in other parts of the city.

These two men, strongly contrasted in personal traits and in some of their methods, yet are alike in representing the ward boss as no other political leaders in the city now do. There are other leaders as powerful or more so, but this is because they have gained large influence in the public councils of the party or the municipality. There are no others who give such unremitting personal attention to the perplexing maze of petty affairs which makes up the internal life of their wards. In this respect the Ward 8 leader clearly outstrips the Ward 6 leader — so as to be known throughout the city as the man who, against ever-increasing obstacles, holds the vote of his ward absolutely in hand. His galvanic mastery of his followers is, in fact, so absolute that he can juggle with the votes of fifteen hundred men, throwing them, at the same time, for the regular candidate for mayor and for an unknown insurgent candidate for street commissioner.

Both bosses exercise that combination of autocracy and benignity, frankness and mystery, which goes with paternal sway. Both know how to bring out and give scope for capacity in the young before it knows itself. Both know how to check and mar a career that is leading toward ends alien to their own. Both have their power balanced with an overwhelming load of responsibility. The anxieties brought about by the general pressure for place, the constant unrest and outright treachery of their following, the personal clashing of rival suppliants, — all these, while outside foes may be clamoring, constitute a body of corroding care such as only the strongest men could endure. The Ward 6 leader, a man of nervous, impetuous type, some years ago found that the strain of living in the thick of all this became too great, and removed with his family twenty miles out into the country. Here, then, in the land of popular representative government, is the curious anomaly of a political leader of a large constituency, elected to every sort of office by them, who has for years made his home a score of miles away, under conditions in every respect different from their own. Every one knows the fact, but it is spoken of under the breath, except when an insurgent movement breaks out. It would be impossible for him to retain his hold but for the large family connection which the boss enjoys. One of the humors of a recent revolutionary uprising in the ward was a burlesque programme of a play, in which the characters were

King John and a long list of princes of the blood royal.

This leader comes of the well-to-do Irish, most of whom have given up all connection with the North End. His family for many years kept an old-country grocery, including " bottled goods." He has had a fair education in the Boston schools. His executive force became apparent in connection with schoolboy interests during his course in the English High School. He was in politics as soon as he became a voter. His ascent was exceedingly rapid. He leaped from the Common Council to the State Senate, and thence leaped again to Congress, being almost the youngest member during his first session. He was elected to Congress by the odd rallying cry, " The people believe in rotation," displacing a man who had represented the district with special ability and distinction. The time came, however, when his rallying cry was due to be used against him. Since being, in turn, rotated out, he has become the editor of a weekly paper combining religion with its politics, which was formerly the possession of the only general municipal boss the city of Boston has yet known.

" The young Napoleon of the North End " is not inaptly named. He is short, dark, sharp featured, with set lips. He has quick movements and an anxious look. His home life is said to be very attractive, and he is very hospitable to his city friends at his country establishment. His opponents accuse him of obviously making use of the church to further his ends; his friends say that he has rendered the church very important aid. Certain it is that he is a loyal church-man, and that there is nothing in his private life to belie his profession. For keeping up his influ-ence in the ward, he is noted among the politicians of the city for vast and intense activity, for the acute and subtle manipulation of personal and social interests, and for successful dickering with other political leaders of his own party. He has apparently had a comfortable income, in and out of office; but there are no signs of his having any considerable property. Though there is always more or less unrest under his leadership, the people of the ward are proud of his personal success, even when not held to him by the bond of benefits received. He has shown an aggressive interest in several very important movements at the North End for the bettering of the way of life among the people. The North End Park, a playground and swimming beach, is his "monument." He does not fail to make frequent public reference to his connection with these enterprises. In general, he follows the type in making the central figure at public meetings, at charitable bazaars and in the columns of the papers. His grand ambition is to attain the dignity of " His Honor, the Mayor."

The king of Ward 8 utterly scorns all such vanities. Caring nothing for glory, living after the homeliest fashion among his own people, having no family, and only the semblance of other business, he rivets his attention upon his craft of ward boss. He is of the poor Irish, and there are touches of the cabin life of his ancestors in his plain, homely ways ; on the other hand, his name, a very unusual one, is that of an ancient Irish chieftain. He began life as a newsboy, but even then he used to take his recreation by going to the State House to listen to the legislative debates. He came to the front just as some of the last of the well-to-do Irish leaders were passing from the West End to pleasanter quarters.

He has no tendencies toward any sort of dissipation, abstaining from liquor, and even from tobacco. He is said to have given as a reason for his abstinent life a promise long ago made to his mother. He is fondly attached to his brother, who wanders somewhat from his own chosen ways. He is punctiliously devout ; and though availing **himself** fully of church *esprit de corps* for his

purposes, yet as a worshiper he seeks an obscure corner, not the foremost seats.   He always distrusts
the stranger, meaning by the stranger any one not
of his own tried and intimate followers.   It is this
narrow, intense form of allegiance which he seeks
and creates that makes him a sort of clan chief,
hated and feared almost as much by the regular
forces of his allies as by the enemy, but supported
by the unquestioning loyalty of clansmen to their
chief.   The North End is split up into many gangs,
and there a revolt is always imminent.   The West
End boss sees to it that there is but one gang, the
membership of his ward political club.   The annual
incomes of municipal employees in the membership
of this organization aggregate not less than $80,-
000 or $90,000.   Under the peculiar West End
system for being on both sides of the fence politically, none of its members walk the streets all
night in agonized suspense before an election, as
city employees in the North End sometimes do.
These facts suggest the indissoluble nature of the
tie which holds the club together.   The boss has
his " real-estate " office in the club, and the members always know how to find him.

In contrast with the North End leader, this man
is stolid and unrefined.   He looks darkly out of
eyeglasses set against beetling brows.   His chief

feature is his lower jaw, which is broad, square and protruding to the point of caricature. He walks with a dapper step, and has a rapid, choppy utterance, which gibe oddly with his large head and heavy features. He speaks but seldom, however. He will walk for blocks or drive for miles with one of his associates beside him and not utter a syllable. He is without magnetism ; on the other hand, he is not arbitrary or domineering, though very severe and sudden with anything savoring of disloyalty. His personal mastery comes of his sheer executive force and strength of character. He is always in command and on the field in person. His easy self-possession reaches its height at the caucus : the wonderful knowledge which he has of his ward is every moment apparent ; even jaw-breaking Russian names he calls out before the clerks have time to consult the lists ; his manipulation of affairs suggests the compositor setting type with the linotype invention, and the result of it all is as surely his act. He is connected with no social organizations, though he provides in his scheme for the social ambitions of others, making use of such motives for his own ends. At bottom he is the financier. Thrift is the keynote of his life, and the real ambition of his life is that of the money-getter. He saved money when he was a city laborer at $1.75 per day. He has numerous real-estate holdings, and is said to be worth at least $100,000. It is said that he desires to be a general city boss. If so, he seeks not the honors but the emoluments.

He constantly inculcates thrift upon his followers. He is also a stern advocate of a temperate, self-controlled life. He gives the advantage always, in distributing patronage, to men of sobriety and steady character. Unmarried and accused of being a woman-hater, he constantly urges marriage upon the young men of the ward. He very often gives his followers substantial aid in setting up a new household, and it is part of his code of laws for the ward political club that the club shall give each member who marries a generous present. Such a policy of social upbuilding in the ward does not displace the usual charities of the boss, but supplements them by something truly sagacious and far-reaching. This policy reaches its height in his special efforts to discover promising young men, encourage them with their training, launch them upon their careers, give them positions of confidence and power in the politics of the ward, and place them in high-salaried positions in the city government, or establish them as contractors, to win still larger sums from the public.

The fanatical fixedness of purpose with which this man insists on keeping up his patronage list and his representation on the appropriation and finance committees of the City Council, along with his peculiar narrowness of range and inability to trust the outsider, constitute him probably the most serious menace to good government that now exists in the city of Boston. There could hardly be a more curious and tragic instance of a man holding absolutely to a programme of right living in his personal life and standing with unwavering loyalty by his friends and neighbors, yet commonly suspected of exercising every ingenuity of unscrupulousness in public affairs, and even treating his own political party with barefaced treachery. He controls a sufficient vote, so that his party is compelled to bargain for his support. He is constantly creating deadlocks in party conventions, in order that the vote of his ward may count for several times more than that of any other. The opposing party may nearly always win him for the proper price. There are times when this adept of ethical legerdemain sells out to both parties, and by the help of disaffected elements in other wards actually delivers the goods.

The length to which he will go when kept back from any part of his booty was shown when Josiah

Quincy was elected mayor a few years ago. Mr. Quincy considered his demands in the way of jobs, contracts and committee appointments altogether exorbitant, and refused to grant them. With his ablest lieutenant, he entered the State legislature. Here they combined with the opposite party to hinder Mr. Quincy's projects for improving the city charter. A youthful member of his staff, five-and-twenty, a miracle of brazenness, was placed, by means of a similarly treacherous alliance, in the chair of the Common Council. Here some of Mr. Quincy's most interesting plans for enhancing the health and happiness of the masses of the people were hopelessly blocked. Leading citizens, regardless of dividing lines, sent in formal petitions. The whole organized force of the working people of the city, chiefly of his race, sternly demanded favorable action in matters so vital to them. Far-seeing leaders of his party saw here a signal political point of vantage. But with his ward in solid files behind him, and holding the balance of power between the two parties in the Council, he stood immovable. And all to satisfy the desire of vengeance in the heart of this strange political Shylock, with his flinty exaction of human life as forfeit for his lost ducats.

He has in his ward what might stand as " monuments," — the Charlesbank Gymnasium and the West End Branch Library. He takes little interest in these enterprises; in fact, he hardly more than acquiesced in their establishment. They are now falling almost entirely into the hands of the Jews; and he, though contriving to hold a following among that race, is secretly a bitter anti-Semite. In part, this may be because in their worst traits he resembles them; " it is not the colors, but the shades, that hate each other." The chief reason is not a subtle one. The cement of clan has held together the foundations of his power. Those foundations are being sapped. His own people are being displaced and scattered. The Jew is becoming omnipresent about him — as a spectre warning the Irish boss of his coming downfall.

His supremacy will not pass away, however, before he has drilled leaders of the Continental immigrants in ways that are subversive of the American party system, not to speak of every holy tradition of our free Republic. The evil methods will remain; yet not because of him or any of his like. They exist because, to immigrant as to native humanity, liberty is an empty thing without the means of life. Machine politics provides for the purchase of opportunity by the payment of freedom.

CHAPTER VII

LAW AND ORDER

THE North End, with the addition of the North Union Station and one half of the great market region near Dock Square, go to make up Police Division 1. From the first of December, 1900, to the first of December, 1901, the total number of arrests in this division for all offenses was 4300 males and 575 females, or 4875 altogether. Of these, 3124 were for drunkenness, 306 for assault of one kind or another, 232 for simple larceny, 37 for breaking and entering dwellings and buildings, 77 for offences against chastity, including night-walking and the keeping of a noisy and disorderly house, 75 for gaming on the Lord's Day and at other times and being present where gaming was going on, 3 for murder and being accessory to murder, and 6 for manslaughter. There were taken into custody, also, 203 suspicious persons, and 37 vagrants and tramps of both sexes; 87 disturbances were suppressed; 368 sick and injured persons were assisted, and 32 dead bodies were cared for.

But the North End is bordered and crossed by great highways of travel and traffic from one part of the city to another. Therefore the figures given represent a much greater population than that which makes its home in the North End. A separation of almost any one of these groups of figures into residents and non-residents would give some surprising results. As a matter of fact, of the entire number of persons arrested in this division, fully two thirds live outside the limits of Boston. Naturally, the majority of these non-residents are arrested for drunkenness or immorality of some kind, since a great number of men, and some women, from neighboring cities and towns, especially from those to the north of the city, resort to the North End for purposes of wrong doing.

If the remaining third of the total number of arrests is separated into residents of the North End and those of other parts of the city, there is another surprising result. On the basis of a careful estimate, no less than one half belong outside the North End. For what offenses these non-residents are arrested it is not easy to say; but probably for drunkenness and immorality in general, as in the case of those living away from the city.

Thus it appears that out of the 4875 persons

arrested in the division during the twelve months ending December 1, 1901, fully 3250 did not belong in Boston at all, and only about 825 resided at the North End. In view of the fact that this last-mentioned number comprises all who were arrested for any offense whatever, including drunkenness, in a population of nearly 30,000, it seems astonishingly small. According to the police showing, therefore, the North End, so far from being exceptionally lawless, is, on the contrary, law-abiding to a degree that is not generally supposed.

Certain measures recently taken by the police in the North End have had an important bearing on the moral welfare of this section of the city. One of these was the closing of the last of the dance halls in the spring of 1900. These dance halls for a number of years before they were shut up had been the sole survivals characteristic of that period in the history of the district when the moral tide was at its very lowest ebb. This period, which covered fifteen or twenty years from about the middle of the century which has just closed, presents a picture of vicious and criminal activity that seems incredible to one familiar with the North End of the present day. " Jilt shops " — those resorts under the name of brothels into which the sailor was enticed merely for robbery — were strewn thickly along Ann Street, now North Street. There was a rat-pit where sporting men from all parts of the city gathered, and where fights among the spectators were of the most frequent occurrence. In the saloon above this rat-pit the drinks were served by girls with painted cheeks and in low-necked dresses. Entertainments of the lewdest character were given in a resort off North Margin Street and elsewhere. The " North End Block " sheltered a swarming population of thieves, murderers, prostitutes and gamblers. In and around Richmond Street was gathered a mass of depraved Negroes and white people who constituted what was known as the " Black Sea." A stranger venturing too near this " Black Sea " was very likely to be engulfed by it, only to be tossed back later, robbed and stripped, if not lifeless.

The dance halls had come into existence early in the century ; but during this period they reached their greatest number and sank to their lowest level. Those that survived the period, while less and less open, and having a constantly diminishing patronage, remained essentially unchanged to the very end. Indeed the charge on which they were closed, that of being houses of ill-fame, might have been brought with equal propriety against them during the eighty or more years of their existence.

Licenses were not required, since admission was free and no liquor sold. The women were paid a small fee by the proprietors in addition to what they received from their victims. The proprietors, who bore all the running expenses, including the cost of the music, ostensibly derived their profits from the sale of the so-called " soft " or non-alcoholic drinks. No private rooms were connected directly with the halls, but such rooms were to be found on the floors above or elsewhere in the immediate neighborhood. That the proprietors controlled some of these rooms there is no doubt.

The closing of the dance halls really registered the moral change that had taken place at the North End within the last quarter of a century. The conditions out of which such resorts had sprung, and upon which their continuance really depended, had ceased to exist. During their later years the dance halls had been more and more of an anachronism. A rapidly decreasing number of their women *habituées*, and a smaller and smaller percentage of their patronage, came from the neighborhood. At the same time, local public sentiment was growing constantly stronger against them, as being a disgrace and a menace.

Thus the shutting up of these dance halls may be said to mark the end of a long and interesting chapter in the history of the North End, — a chapter of moral decline to an almost inconceivably low point, and of at least partial moral recovery. But after all, it is the narrative of what has taken place on the soil of the North End rather than in the hearts and minds of the people; for the changed moral situation has been due, for the most part, to the change of the population. The moral decadence began with the incoming of the vicious and criminal of all races to take the places left vacant by the departure of the people of the better grades; with the coming of the self-respecting and industrious foreign immigrant began the moral revival. In other words, the history of morals at the North End is at bottom little more than the history of the social changes that have taken place here.

This should not be construed as meaning that religious, educational and coercive agencies have not been at work all along, or have been ineffective. On the contrary, they have done much to keep the North End from sinking to any lower point of moral degradation, and to aid it in its moral recuperation. The work of the churches and schools is described in other chapters of this book; that of the police only is in point here.

Even in the most turbulent days of the North

End, police activity was by no means lacking.
Haunts of vice and crime were broken up, lawbreakers of every sort were driven away or taken
into custody, and life and property were safeguarded.
In 1851 a single descent of the police on the notorious Ann Street resulted in the apprehension of
165 persons guilty of every sort of vice and crime.
In another raid on the same street a few years
later, 51 street-walkers and inmates of houses of
ill-fame were taken into custody. The police
annals of this whole period are full of tales of
sensational encounters with burglars, murderers
and other desperate characters. As late as 1870
or later, it was not considered safe for a police
officer to go alone through certain quarters. Two
officers went together and also took care to walk
in the middle of the street. Nevertheless, the
police force in this part of the city was far too
small for the situation that it tried to meet. In
1854, when the Police Department of the City
of Boston superseded the Boston Watch and Police, there were in the North End division one
captain, two lieutenants and thirty-three patrolmen. To-day the force in practically the same
division numbers ninety.

A recent event that has had an important bearing on the moral welfare of the North End was the

loss by one of the hotels of its innholder's license. An innholder's license, it will be remembered, carries with it the privilege of serving liquors with food at any and all times excepting between the hours of eleven at night and six in the morning. Unlike the dance halls, this hotel, as it was conducted, had never been rooted in local conditions. With others of the same general class here and there in the city, it owed much of its business to the breaking up, by the police, of the organized houses of prostitution throughout Boston. Women frequented its spacious café on the second floor, where they were known to be present and could easily be found. Men and women also came in company. Some of the women lived in the house, hiring their rooms by the week, month, or for a longer time; a few drifted in from the near-by dance halls before these were closed. The waiters had each a favorite among the *habituées*, for whom they solicited custom, and shared in her illicit earnings. Practically none of the women belonged in the North End, and nearly all of the male patrons were non-residents.

The loss of its innholder's license involved, of course, the loss of those privileges of selling liquor on Sundays and holidays, upon which the prosperity of such an hotel depends. As a result, the character of the house was completely changed. The café was made into a general dining-room, which, together with a similar room on an upper floor, was visited by a constituency of a distinctly better grade than that of former days. The hotel held merely an ordinary bar-room license. But this change proved fatal to its financial interests; within a few months it has been obliged to assign.

Prostitution was not wholly banished from the North End by these two events. Finding the doors of their former haunts shut against them, some of the women established themselves in near-by tenements or took to the street. Yet they did not long escape police vigilance, and were taken into custody or compelled to leave the district. At the present time there are no disorderly houses at this end of the city and but little street-walking. That prostitution no longer exists here cannot, of course, be affirmed. There is an unwritten law of the local hotels which points unmistakably to its continued presence. This law is that a woman who comes with a man, presumably her husband, and remains over night, shall not be allowed to depart alone until her companion has been seen and gives assurance that his valuables are intact. Thus the unpleasant consequences of a reported robbery in the house are avoided. But prostitution no longer flaunts itself openly. On the contrary, whatever of it still remains here is well under cover and avoids rather than seeks attention.

The immigrants, who form the characteristic resident population of the North End, have brought certain evil ways of their own; they are also inevitably affected by the moral contagion in their surroundings. The Italian men, especially those of the so-called lower classes, are as a rule very lax morally, and the younger Jewish men are becoming so more and more. Dispensary doctors are able to give evidence of the serious inroads of sexual immorality among their Italian male patients, and to a less extent among their Jewish ones. Several Italians who are unmarried or without their wives may live with a common mistress, ostensibly the housekeeper of the group. This woman may be American or Irish, but is never an Italian.

The women of both races, on the other hand, are chaste with comparatively few exceptions. In the café of the hotel described, a Jewish girl rarely appeared, and an Italian girl almost never. No girl of either race frequented the dance halls. In the case of the Jewish women, chastity is due to religious and home influences; in that of the

Italian, there is, in addition, the special protecting and avenging arm of the male members of the family. Any man attempting to lead an Italian woman astray is liable to be visited with a severe penalty from her father, brother or other male relative. Within a few years an Italian was murdered in the North End to prevent his returning to Italy, where he was likely to take up again an illicit relationship in which he had involved a kinswoman of the murderer. The custom still obtains among the Italians that a girl, especially if she is of marriageable age, shall never appear upon the street without a chaperon. The loyalty that goes with race seems to afford the Jewish girl, in a negative way, something of the same protection, for when she does lose her virtue it is seldom or never through a man of her own race. Although many of the Jewish men are bigamists, or at least are supporting more than one woman — one in Boston and one in New York or elsewhere — there is probably no instance in the North End where a Jewish woman is living with a man to whom, in her opinion, she is not properly married.

The number of liquor licenses held in Police Division 1 is 128. Of these, 10 are innholders' licenses, and the remainder, with the exception of 21, are ordinary saloon licenses. The

21 excepted are distributed among the drug-
gists, grocers and wholesale classes. Thus there
are in this division 97 bar-rooms, including those
in the hotels. Apportioned equally among the
inhabitants of the division, these would give one
saloon for about every 309 men, women and children. But with the exception of the Italian
saloons, few of them derive any considerable part
of their trade from people living in the North
End. Indeed, should all but the Italian saloons
suddenly become dependent upon strictly local
patronage, the larger number would go out of existence at once. The Jews, who with the Italians
constitute the great mass of the population, are
not frequenters of the saloon. Moderate drinking
is very general among them, but it is carried on
for the most part in their houses and places of
social meeting. Up to a few years ago, no Jew
engaged in the liquor business, at least directly.
At the present time, however, two or three large
saloons are carried on by Jewish proprietors.
Irish and Scandinavian bartenders are employed
in them to draw in the trade of the Irish and
Scandinavians. The Italians, though they are beginning to drift into the American saloons, patronize chiefly the saloons of their own people. These
saloons, which are distinctly Italian in character,

are situated on North street and one or two adjoining streets, and are resorted to for social as well as drinking purposes. Indeed, gaming rather than drinking seems to be their chief attraction. A man buys a glass of light wine or beer, and sitting down at one of the little tables, with which these saloons are well supplied, passes two or three hours in some game of chance with his companions, or in watching the play that may be going on.

The great bulk of saloon patronage at the North End, as has been said, is by non-residents. The prohibition enactment in places on the north side of Boston sends into the North End by the ferries and the railroads entering the North Union Station a great crowd of people after liquor. These furnish the great majority of the men and women arrested for drunkenness. According to the average ratio between resident and non-resident offenders who fall into the hands of the police here, all but about 450 of the 3124 persons taken into custody for drunkenness during the twelve months ending December 1, 1901, had their places of abode outside this section of the city.

Here, as well as throughout the city, the number of arrests for drunkenness is falling off appreciably year by year, the result, to some extent, of a more lenient policy on the part of the police in dealing with " drunks." Whenever circumstances permit, a man under the influence of liquor is put in the care of friends or quietly sent home, instead of being taken to the station house, whence he can be discharged only by the courts. Yet there seems to be an actual diminution in the amount of excessive drinking. This is due, in some measure at least, to the increased consumption of beer in place of harder liquors.

Observation tends rather to confirm than to disprove the correctness of this estimate, low as it appears. Excessive drinking is not a characteristic either of the Jews or of the Italians. Indeed, instances of it among the former are extremely rare, and by no means common among the latter. The 3124 arrests for drunkenness referred to included no arrests of Jews and only five or six of Italians.

This moderation in the use of alcoholic drink is easily explained as part of the general frugality that characterizes both races. In the case of the Jews it has a further explanation in the habitual self-control of this people. Perhaps, also, the enlightenment of the race in the matter of health, resulting from the inculcation and observance of their dietary and other hygienic laws, serves as an additional restraint from immoderate drinking.

Among the Jews and Italians alike, beer has displaced to a very large extent the home-made wines and the light wines of Europe; but among the Italians especially, stronger liquors are beginning to displace both. In the Italian home the bottle of " rock and rye " is seen with increasing frequency by the side of the bottle of Chianti. While this change in the direction of more intoxicating drink is due more or less to mere imitation of American ways, it is also a result of the demand for stronger stimulants created by the severer strain of life in this country. With the increase in the use of ardent spirits, the amount of drunkenness will of course increase, and in time sobriety may cease to be a characteristic of the Italian citizen.

There are no gaming-places, strictly speaking, in the North End. Men play for drinks or even for small sums of money in the pool-rooms and in some of the saloons; but gaming-places with roulette wheel or other implement of chance, or where large sums are staked at cards, are not to be found at this end of the city. Consequently, whatever gaming is carried on here is of a comparatively harmless character, and is confined for the most part to the resident population.

Groups of boys, especially newsboys and boot-blacks, may be seen at almost any time in side

streets, doorways and elsewhere, shooting craps or
engaged in some other game of skill or chance.
The public playground adjoining the Paul Revere
school is a favorite gathering-place of these youthful gamesters. Here they congregate in considerable numbers, especially on Sunday mornings, sta-
tioning sentinels on the street at either side to
guard against surprise by the police. But this
and other similar precautions do not always avail,
for occasionally the police make a descent upon
the boys and take one or more into custody as a
warning to the rest. Of the seventy-five persons
arrested in this section of the city for gaming during the year 1901, the majority were juveniles.

The gaming spirit which shows itself in the boys
is conspicuous on all sides in the men. Generally
speaking, the Jews and Italians are habitual
gamesters. Necessarily, the stakes are small, but
the play seems to lose none of its zest on this
account. Unlike the Jews, who shun publicity in
this as in most of their other diversions, the
Italians frequent the Italian saloons, where they
will play hour after hour, perhaps merely "for the
drinks." Every evening during the week, and
many an afternoon, especially in winter, any one
of these saloons is crowded with men sitting at
the tables over their wine or beer, intent upon a

game of chance played with the fingers. Cards
are not allowed in the saloons, but are very generally played elsewhere. Those who play at home
take their table out of doors if a suitable place is
at hand and the weather permits. A group of
these open-air players may not infrequently be
seen on a pleasant summer afternoon in the courts
leading off Hanover and North streets. Here the
bits of bright drapery flung over the galleries of
the surrounding houses, the plants in the windows,
and the gayly colored head-coverings of the women
moving about give a foreign air to the scene.

While the Italians engage in " finger play " in
their saloons, and gather about the card-tables
in the open air, the Jews carry on their play in
the privacy of their homes, shops and clubrooms.
" Pinnacle," the favorite of their card games,
seems never to lose its fascination for old or young.
One passing along Salem Street may see in the
rear of one shop after another a group of men,
some of them quite venerable in appearance, engaged in this game. Now and then, especially
among the Italians, a quarrel results from some
turn in the play, which brings what is going on to
the attention of the police; but the gaming itself
by either race is seldom of a character to warrant
police interference.

Strangely enough, crime at the North End, while comparatively small in amount, is to a considerable extent of the most serious character. Between such minor offenses as drunkenness, simple larceny or gaming, and the greatest of all crimes in the eye of the law, there are few gradations. During the last eight years twenty murders, whose perpetrators were found out and convicted, have been committed in this section of the city. Of these murderers fourteen had their homes here. During the twelve months so often referred to, three men were arrested for murder and four for assault with intent to murder — all residents of the North End. Thus a population that on the whole is orderly and law abiding almost to an exceptional degree includes an element of a strikingly different character.

But these murderers and would-be murderers are of a single race, — the Italian, and of the Sicilian or Calabrian branch of that race; and they by no means are representative of the population, or even of the Italian people. Moreover, while some of them premeditated their crimes, the majority acted on the impulse of the moment; hence are homicides rather than murderers. Of the twenty convicted of murder within the last eight years, only one was convicted of murder in the first degree.　Some of the murders were to satisfy a blood feud perhaps of long standing, or to avenge an insult or injury to a kinswoman of the murderer.　Indications of the Mafia are to be found at the North End, but none of the murders here have been traced directly or indirectly to that organization.

Although the Italians often exert themselves in behalf of a guilty countryman, they do so in order to save the Italian name from the disgrace that his punishment would cast upon it.　Their action does not mean that they condone the offense or even have any special regard for the individual.　Unfortunately, such efforts are having a most pernicious effect upon the more ignorant of their countrymen in lessening respect for law and in creating among them at the same time an erroneous impression as to the protective power of money. Not infrequently an Italian undergoing search in the police station is found to have a roll of bills on his person, which he keeps, as he says, to use when he gets into trouble.

To remove one cause of so many murderous acts by their countrymen, a number of Italians several years ago petitioned the governor to revive and enforce the law against carrying concealed weapons.　With the revolver and stiletto out of reach, they believed whatever fierce passions might be aroused would in most instances subside before a crime was committed. But on the general ground of individual freedom, the governor refused the request; and nearly every Italian, as soon as he arrives in this country, procures a revolver, which, together with his stiletto, is always at hand to resent an affront or to avenge an injury.

Other than murder, and assault with intent to murder, there is but little serious crime at the North End. Of course, where so many saloons stand open to the passing throngs, there are more or less assaults — 289 in the year of which the police statistics have been given. Burglary is of infrequent occurrence, a district of this description offering but few inducements to the professional thief. Italian boys, and to a less extent Jewish boys, steal junk whenever an opportunity presents itself, and commit other minor offenses. In the Italian rising generation especially, an increasing spirit of lawlessness is very noticeable. Gangs of these boys are beginning to present a serious problem, the so-called " American spirit " appearing to have peculiar possession of them.

The Jews seldom fall into the hands of the police, but they cannot be called a race " void of offense against the public order and welfare."

They are especially prone to contentions with one another, as well as with their Gentile neighbors. No other people come to the police station so often to make complaints and demand redress. The ground of their grievances is usually that of abusive or threatening language or some form of personal violence. In nearly all cases their feelings have been hurt more than their bodies. Either side will produce witnesses to almost any number in support of its affirmations or denials. The readiness of the Jews to commit the crime of perjury has passed into a proverb in this part of the city. But the characteristic thrift of the race does not desert the complainants even in the heated recital of their wrongs, real or fancied; for unless they see in the satisfaction which they demand some pecuniary gain to themselves, they usually drop their accusations. Isolated and aggravated cases of arson and swindling and other serious crimes with a similar motive have occurred among the Jews in both the North and West Ends. There are occasional instances of such crimes which suspicion ascribes to them, but where evidence has been skillfully covered up. In general, the law of the land is feared rather than respected by Jewish immigrants; and a considerable proportion of them show a tendency, in many petty ways, to violate its spirit while formally observing the letter. On the whole, however, the Jewish community is law abiding to a marked degree.

That portion of the West End under review lies wholly within the bounds and comprises about four fifths of the territory of Police Division 3. Inasmuch as it includes nearly all of the characteristic part of the division, the police statistics for the division as a whole may be taken as a trustworthy guide to the criminal tendencies here. During the year ending December 1, 1901, there were 4192 arrests in the division, including 2804 for drunkenness, 261 for assault, 8 for murder and being accessory to murder, 6 for manslaughter, 12 for robbery and assault to rob, 50 for breaking and entering dwellings and buildings, 165 for simple larceny, 124 for offenses against chastity, including night-walking, 13 for keeping a noisy and disorderly house, and 47 for gaming, being present where gaming implements were found or keeping a gaming-house. In addition, 248 suspicious persons and 11 vagrants and tramps were taken in charge, 514 sick and injured persons were assisted, 135 disturbances were suppressed and 28 dead bodies cared for.

The West End, as well as the North End, is traversed by great thoroughfares to the North

Union Station and to adjacent cities and towns. Moreover, the variety theatres and dime museums on Bowdoin Square and Court and Howard streets bring throngs of people into the district. Hence, as at the North End, much of the wrong doing here is by strangers and sojourners. Of the 4192 persons arrested in this division in 1901, 2338 were residents and 1854 were non-residents. On an average, between two fifths and one half of all offenders have their homes elsewhere in the city or altogether outside Boston. This ratio falls below that in the case of " drunks," since the saloons clustered about the West Boston and Craigie bridges and the North Union Station derive no little amount of their patronage from the suburban places, especially those in which prohibition is in force. It is rumored that the proprietors of some of these saloons contribute annually to the no-license campaign funds in the city directly across the Charles.

Like the North End, the West End to-day is in a state of moral recovery, although it never reached such a point of degradation as the North End forty or fifty years ago. Its moral regeneration likewise, so far as this has come about, has been due to similar causes, — the breaking up of centres of vice and crime and, in those sections where morality was at its lowest ebb, the displacement of the vicious and semi-criminal population by Jewish and Italian immigrants. Within the last three years seven hotels of the same general type as the North End hotel described have been closed by the police, with excellent results. But this movement in the direction of moral betterment has had less local support than at the North End, chiefly because of the large lodging-house population here. Proverbially, lodgers concern themselves but little about neighborhood conditions. Hence the West End presents a better field than the North End for the observation of what may be done by police measures in making " vice difficult and virtue easy."

That section of the West End between Green and Allen streets and the North Union Station differs but little in the general character of its population from the North End, and may be regarded as an extension of that part of the city. With a few rather unimportant qualifications, what has been said of the criminal tendencies at the North End applies equally well to this particular region. Occasionally a crime is committed here unlike any that is apt to occur at the North End, as, for instance, burglary. Prostitution is to be found under particularly hideous forms in the West

End. Certain of the Italians marry abandoned women of other nationalities for the sake of sharing the proceeds of their shame. In the vicinity of Green Street a dozen or more of these men with prostitute wives have established themselves, each couple occupying a separate lodging or tenement and carrying on usually a "speak-easy," or kitchen bar-room. The extreme difficulty of getting convicting evidence against these places serves as a sort of protection to them. Whether the husbands have other occupations or not, they spend much of their time in soliciting for their evil resorts. This sort of traffic, however, is not confined to the Italians, but is the branding mark of "lovers" of whatever race.

The "lovers," both white and black, constitute a numerous class in the West End. They are generally well dressed and not unattractive in appearance and manner. In fact, their success depends very largely upon the maintenance of a pleasing address. The majority have no employment but subsist wholly upon the money provided by their mistresses. When this is not enough for their wants, they do not hesitate to resort to abusive treatment in order to get more. "A bit of the strap" is not an uncommon method for inciting a girl to renewed efforts in her calling of shame. Indeed, the terrorism which the "lovers" often exercise over these women, and the heartlessness with which they will desert one favorite for another, deepen beyond measure their infamy. Nevertheless, however brutal he may be, a man of this sort seems to have no difficulty in finding a woman to support him. Formerly the police were wont to belabor with their clubs such a character wherever found; this irregular though not uncommendable treatment is no longer permitted. Groups of this class, well dressed, well fed, and smoking cigars, stand about on the streets or loiter over the pool-table or bar; while the girls who support them are urged on by fear lest their earnings fall short of the sum demanded, and violence or, what they fear even worse, desertion, be the penalty.

A few well-known houses of ill fame, and certain other houses of a suspicious character, still exist in the West End. Real-estate interests, and sometimes even public sentiment itself, stand in the way of closing them. At one time the police were about to succeed in breaking up the oldest and best known of these houses through keeping a persistent watch upon it; but the neighbors objected so strongly to a continuance of the surveillance, because of the annoyance to themselves, that the attempt had to be abandoned. However, the number of such places is far less than formerly. Access to those that do survive is closely guarded. Strangers cannot gain admission unless satisfactorily vouched for. Solicitation from windows or doorways is practically unknown except in the lowest haunts of the Negroes. Street-walkers may still be seen, but their every movement is watched by the police. The moment one of these women is seen attempting to ply her evil trade, she is warned, if not at once placed under arrest. Some of these street-walkers are " badgers," or women whose business it is to entice men to rooms where they may be robbed by accomplices. While prostitution is still carried on here, its methods have changed within recent years. Instead of the parlor house there is the variety theatre, the low-priced café, and especially the hotel. With one or two exceptions, West End hotels are houses of assignation. " Lovers," or " runners," are also taking the place more and more of women seeking their own victims.

The places of amusement which centre about Court Street between Hanover Street and Bowdoin Square have already been spoken of as bringing into the West End throngs of people living elsewhere in the city or in the suburbs. They serve also, of course, to bring into this part of the city great numbers of men and women of the theatrical profession who furnish their entertainment. Now while such people are as a rule orderly and well behaved, they call around themselves, in the hotels and boarding-houses, and in the theatres, an objectionable class of both sexes. These hangers-on — young men about town, prostitutes, gamblers and crooks of various descriptions — give much of that character to the professional quarter and surrounding region popularly attributed to it. However well deserved this character may have been, it no longer holds to the same extent; for within the last few years the Howard Street neighborhood has undergone a distinct change in the upward direction. Fights are much less frequent than formerly; and in the number of vicious and criminal acts there has been a marked falling off. One cause of this improvement has been the closing on Howard Street of three hotels through the withholding of their liquor licenses.

The Negro quarter at the West End includes among its population a class of the vicious and semi-criminals, both black and white. This element is larger relatively than once it was, through the removal of so many of the respectable and well-to-do colored people to Cambridgeport, the South End and elsewhere. Yet poverty and social degradation are no oftener synonymous in the case of the Negro than in that of the white man. Close by some of the worst haunts on the back slope of Beacon Hill are blocks and sections occupied by decent and law abiding, though extremely poor families.

Sexual immorality, the characteristic shortcoming of the race, is made by many of the Negroes directly or indirectly a means of gain. There are numerous women who seek white men as well as those of their own color on the street; and instances are not uncommon of colored men, often with white wives, following the inhuman ways of the Italian husbands who have been referred to. Even among apparently respectable families, prostitution is indirectly made an additional source of revenue through the rental of rooms by the evening or night. Robbery often accompanies prostitution, and not infrequently is the chief motive in it.

In the section given over to the Negroes, alley leads off alley, with perhaps a narrow passage to a different street from that by which the first alley was entered. Sometimes these unsuspected exits wind between high buildings, or, in one instance at least, go directly under a building. From this particular underground passage open the doors of a number of tenements, apparently the only means by which the tenements can be reached. A curious group of wooden houses at the corner of Phillips and Anderson streets has recently been torn down. Between the buildings ran wooden walks — now on one elevation, now on another, the different elevations reached by flights of steps — and bridges extended from the upper story of one house to the corresponding story of another, and from roof to roof. It suggested to the visitor the scene of the flight of Bill Sykes from the police, and his subsequent suicide, as described by Dickens in " Oliver Twist."

Now the very opportunities for vice and crime that this general section affords must draw thither the vicious and criminal. Wherever wrong doing can be carried on comparatively free from observation or with small danger of apprehension if detected, there the wrong doers will congregate. The stage of real life seldom waits long for actors to carry on the play for which the scene is set. Dens for infamy will sooner or later become dens of infamy. Moreover, the dark and unsanitary dwellings, of which there are many, and the overcrowding, which is to be found here and there, combine to foster, if not to call into existence, tendencies to immorality. Moral ills as well as physical ills spring from unwholesome surroundings. Therefore the first remedial agencies here should be light, air and sanitation. Not until the housing conditions have been radically improved can the community be reclaimed. If Garden Street Arch, Grove Street Terrace or Strong Place is to be brought up to a uniformly decent standard, the initiative must be taken by the Board of Health. When the conditions of a moral life have been provided, then will come the time for the churches and other moral and religious agencies.

As at the North End, gaming has been nearly stamped out. What survives is carried on behind closed and carefully guarded doors. The game is invariably poker, since the implements for roulette or faro could not be concealed quickly and effectually in case of a visit from the police, or easily removed to another place when flight becomes necessary. Forty-seven arrests for all offenses involving gaming is the record for the year ending December 1, 1901.

Policy, likewise, while not suppressed completely, is kept well "on the run." Chances are sold in and around the hotels and saloons and on the street, but with every precaution against attracting the attention of the police. While this evil has peculiar attractions for the Negroes, it is by no means confined to them.

The saloons at the West End, of which there are eighty-eight, differ but little from those at the North End, excepting the Italian saloons among the latter. Like the North End saloons also, they have a very large non-resident patronage. For this the numerous places of amusement described, as well as the thoroughfares to Cambridge and the North Union Station, divide the responsibility. Here, as elsewhere in the city, a drunken man is seen with surprising infrequency when the enormous number of saloon patrons is taken into account.

There is comparatively little serious crime, as at the North End. Of the nine persons arrested for murder achieved, attempted or alleged, a number were fugitives from outside the city. Members of the under world gravitate in this direction rather than to the North End, because of the places of amusement here. Certain bar-rooms and hotels, especially in the vicinity of Howard Street, are more or less gathering-places of this class. Here and around the theatres and on the streets the police would look for a "suspect," rather than in any particular lodging-house block or section. Indeed, no particular lodging-house street is especially given over to crooks of any kind.

As to life and property, both districts are safe to a degree. In nearly every case the victim of an assault or robbery is partially to blame for what befalls him. The well-behaved can come and go at any and all times in either of these districts with little or no fear of molestation. Of course the man looking for adventure is very apt to find what he seeks. As regards gaming, both sections are practically closed; and, in respect to prostitution, are far from being "wide open." The old dance halls have gone, and though a few new ones have appeared, they are not of so low a type. Saloons are numerous in each, but excessive drinking is rather on the decrease than on the increase. With the exception of an occasional murder or murderous assault among the Sicilians, crime of a serious nature is of comparatively infrequent occurrence. Although the number of arrests year by year, with the exception of those for drunkenness, has not fallen off very noticeably during the last few years, the offenses for which the arrests were made are increasingly of a minor character.

Whatever may be true of individual patrolmen, there is no evidence that the police in general are protecting prostitution or any other form of vice or crime. Indeed, most of the signs point in quite the contrary direction. Connivance with wrong doing there may be on the part of a man on the beat here and there, but it does not extend far up in the force. A prominent member of the under world has declared emphatically that he could do no " business " with the captain at the West End. Nevertheless, there are men who sometimes succeed in collecting considerable sums of money from wrong doers by representing themselves as influential in police circles, if not the direct agents of police authorities. These " middlemen," as they are styled, merely trade on some chance acquaintance with a member of the police department, and as a rule work solely in their own interests. There are instances where they have been so bold as to actually assume the name of some prominent official. In most cases they soon come to grief through the failure of their victims to receive the exemption from police interference guaranteed.

At the North and West Ends alike, an upward moral tendency is more and more apparent, hastened in the case of the former by a constantly growing public sentiment. Whatever other causes this tendency may have had, it is due in no small measure, especially at the North End, to the supplanting of the low and vicious element by people of cleaner lives and higher ideals.

CHAPTER VIII

LIFE'S AMENITIES

THE outer aspect of great cities, even of contrasted American and European cities, grows less dissimilar year by year. Nevertheless, enough of the Old World can yet be found in some sections of the North and West Ends so that the stranger coming into these parts almost forgets that he is in America. The language heard on every side is in a foreign tongue, and the palpitating interest and variety of the street life give one a feeling that he is having a glimpse into some far-off town or village. A wealth of song and story is brought to mind by some word or gesture, a Neapolitan lilt or two belligerents biting thumbs even as did the ill-fated Montague and Capulet.

The light-heartedness of the Italians, and their keen love of pleasure, make an atmosphere so full of gayety that a spectator for the time is led to overlook the many discomforts which must naturally fall to the share of a people so closely crowded together. But perhaps these discomforts affect the

Italians less than any other race, for they love the
open air and the general fellowship of their kind,
and every possible moment is spent beyond the
confines of the house walls. The first glimpse of
spring brings with it thronging streets, crowded
doorways and well-filled open windows. With
uncovered heads, the women and girls saunter up
and down the sidewalks, or with their bits of cro-
cheted lace, intended for home decoration, sit in
some doorway or at an open window, where they
may gossip with a neighbor or join in a gay street
song. Here too may be seen the curved knitting
needle used by the older Italian woman as she
rounds out the stocking for the coming winter.
The men crowd the curbstone or open street, discussing the politics of their country, their personal
injuries or the possibilities for assisting some less
fortunate brother. Groups of men and boys, numbering fifteen or twenty, congregate in some street
or square, and immediately there is such emphatic
utterance, fiery denunciation, violent gesture and
all-pervading excitement as would convince the
unaccustomed that a mass meeting was discussing
the wrongs of a nation, rather than that a casual
group of neighbors was exchanging gossip.

The street offers much to vary what is otherwise
often a life of mere monotony and toil. The street

piano, which is an ever-present, ever-welcome entertainer, starts the children dancing. Their feet have already forsaken the steps of Italy. It is not any peasant dance through which they flit, with the native lightness and aptness of their rhythmic land; it is the prancing, burlesqued grace of the Afro-American cake walk. The hurdy-gurdy is played by Italians of the south, and each instrument is usually accompanied by a man and a woman, the latter's deft handling of her tambourine often calling forth enthusiasm from the onlookers. These women retain the full peasant costume as a dramatic property. The short, full skirts are usually made of some cotton stuff. The kerchiefs worn about the shoulders, of the brightest yellows, the richest browns and purples and the most brilliant reds and greens, bordered with bands of colored flowers, are not in the least dimmed by the bright blues, magentas and Roman stripes of the aprons, which are always a part of the street dress. Even the folded kerchief thrown over the back of the head, as a protection from the rays of the sun, is more or less gay. The arrangement, however, of these bits of color is often of the very crudest. The kerchiefs, the quaint jewelry, the long ear pendants and the talisman worn about the neck are much coveted bits of decoration, highly prized by the possessors and passed down from generation to generation.

Nowhere out of Naples can a truer picture of southern Italian life be found than in the home of the street piano and its grinder. While on the street these people are really working, caught in the whirl of American life ; but when they have turned in for the night, and all the hurdy-gurdies have been housed, the performers are free to relapse into their native temper. The court in which a large number live is transformed as if by magic, and the Bella Napoli, with all its gayety, its lights and shadows, suddenly stands out upon the scene of the North End of Boston. Everything is there, — the song, the tambourine, the accordion, and lastly the dance and the glass of Chianti. There, indeed, the tarantella, the favorite and famous dance of southern Italy, is performed exactly as it is among the crags of Capri, or at sundown beside the inhauled fishing nets of Sta. Lucia. Nothing is wanting — the dark, rich coloring of the skin, the heavy hair, the bright touches of color in the dress, and the sturdy peasants whirling, balancing, treading the many figures, while the accordion plays on in rapid time until one after another drops out exhausted and fresh dancers take the floor. These bits of home country life are enacted in the streets and courts unfrequented generally by the outside world. It is to the familiar visitor of the byways that one must turn for guidance if he would really know the people in their most care-free moments.

The loyalty of the Italian to the land of his birth, and his love of the dramatic, make him seek every opportunity for a folk festival. The anniversaries of the various benevolent and secret societies are often celebrated by processions of men and children carrying gay banners. These, together with the bright sashes of the little ones and the insignia worn by the men, cause one to feel that the Italians are truly a nation of children, born to turn their world into a stage, with every-day life as the sufficient material of the play. Although they cannot be said to be a people of deep religious feeling, the historic associations of their church, and its unequaled pageantry, appeal to their emotional natures. Easter is the greatest festival of the entire Christian year. The long gloom of Lent quickly recedes, and Easter Sunday is truly a gala day alike to the rich and the poor. Mass is attended on that day by all who are able to leave their homes and who are within the pale of the church. For church decorations, potted plants are coming into favor, taking the place of the paper flowers and tinsel ornaments which have given such a tawdry air to altar dressings. Images of the Virgin and Risen Christ are often carried in processional with " music and banner." These processions are frequently seen in the streets, as they pass from the school buildings to the churches. The various classes in the Sunday-schools, and the different church socie- ties, are conspicuous by reason of their particular ornamentations, and with the banners and various religious symbols the whole makes an impressive sight. Easter is also a favorite time for the cele- brating of weddings, as the Catholic Church pro- hibits the solemnizing of any marriages during the Lenten season. The dinner on Easter Day is one of the great events of the year. The entire family is collected, and certain dishes, peculiar to the sea- son, are prepared with great care ; ravioli, a kind of pastry, together with macaroni in some form, are usually among the dinner delicacies. The de- coration of the table is perhaps of as much interest as the food itself. This is peculiarly true so far as the children are concerned, for their places are indicated by confetti and sugar toys, the latter of the gayest colors. This Easter dinner is usually followed by a dance. Indeed a succession of many large dancing parties is given at this time of the year.

The more elaborate of the candy toys used at

the holiday seasons are the work of the Neapolitan confectioner of North Square, whose reputation as an artist in sugar has made it possible for him to secure for his work prices that are not dreamed of by other shopkeepers. Many tales could be told of these gay bits of sugar: how they are used first to decorate the festal board, how they are afterwards carried by the children like a favorite doll, until the bright color has been replaced by dust and grime, and how they are finally broken into fragments to sweeten the breakfast cup of coffee, — thereby combining thrift and æsthetics in a characteristic if not felicitous way. A visit to this rare workshop and salesroom, all in one apartment, is well worth while, particularly at the Christmas and Easter seasons. For weeks in advance the confectioner has been at work, and the variety and gayety of his wares are unequaled. He has grown very proud of his skill, and though deeply grateful for the admiration shown by sight-seers, he scorns to betray this weakness. With the simplicity of this childlike race neither the candy-maker nor his neighborhood customers find any incongruity in rendering, alike with the flowers and fruits, the doves and lambs of Eastertide, — loftier symbols of the holy and happy season. Barley sugar to them is a material not more or less profane than wax or ebony or gold. A sugar saint excites no astonishment, nor does a deftly moulded figure of the Christ upon the cross, done in translucent pink and amber sugar, suggest to these people any unseemliness.

It is one of the great resources of the Italians that they can extract pleasure from the humblest and most commonplace events. The simpler enjoyments are entered into with quite as much zest as the greater. The hot summer evenings are made delightful by their readiness to avail themselves of the ferry-boats, whole families getting cool, fresh air in this way. The roof parties are perhaps the most popular summer gatherings. The weeding of the tiny herb gardens that are to be seen upon the roof of almost every Italian tenement house, and the making of the brilliant tomato conserve, when accompanied by friendly chat, cease to be labor. This is also true of the many excursions into the country in search of dandelions, mushrooms and other table dainties. The family picnic in one of the breathing spaces of the city again shows their quickness to get pleasure wherever pleasure may be found. Such a group enjoying supper on the Common on a hot afternoon is a sight familiar to all.

On a fête day the houses from cellar to roof are

decked with the red, green and white of Italy, as well as the Stars and Stripes. Everywhere some effort is made toward holiday dress. Chinese lanterns, too, often play a large part in the decorations. During a recent visit from a distinguished guest, North Square was brilliantly lighted with colored electric lights, showing the readiness of the Italian people to adapt themselves to modern methods.

In winter the streets are comparatively quiet. Doorstep and window chats are transferred to the living-room. Small quarters do not limit sociability. It is rare that a family is permitted to spend the evening alone. Some lodger or boarder friend from the neighborhood drops in, and over the glass of wine or mug of beer tales of the home country are told. The men of the family enjoy the life of the neighboring saloon, where, aside from the social drink, various games can be played. It is at one of these saloons that the favorite game of peasant Italy, "bocce," is played almost every evening, and as this is the one place in Boston where it may be found, there are many spectators. The older people rarely mingle with people of another nationality, except the better educated ones, who sometimes go to enjoy a good play at one of the uptown theatres. The operas, too, and many of the best concerts are attended by those who can afford such luxuries. Those who saw the hearty and appreciative welcome which her countrymen in the upper gallery gave to Signora Duse will never forget it.

The Italians have no theatre of their own. Occasionally traveling showmen with marionettes have stayed for a season in the North End and then gone their way. Amateur theatrical performances are not infrequent. These busy people find time after the long hours of the barber or tailor or candy shop to learn their parts, attend rehearsals, and finally to give their play in some hall of the city ; and a very creditable performance it is, though the play may be the most stilted and old-fashioned of dramas. An air of domesticity pervades the audience. Mothers bring their babies, and the performers converse with friends before the raising of the curtain. The members of the orchestra are invited by name to dispense their music with more liberality. " Pipe up, Tony," says one friend to another, and they scrape and pound and blow till flesh rebels and they turn upon their too appreciative and too urgent following. The desire for amusement and excitement among the younger men and boys is not always satisfied with these more wholesome pleasures, and some of them, though in no large numbers, find their way to the cheaper theatres and museums. The Italian girl, however, unless she has stepped beyond the confines of morality, is rarely seen in any public place of amusement save in the company of an older person. No daughter is more carefully looked after than the child of Italian parents. In a ballroom the wall seats are occupied by the many matrons in attendance, whose beaming faces show the delight they take in the good times enjoyed by their charges. Many of these older people show their newness to this country by the style and arrangement of their dress. The three-cornered kerchief tied over the head, and the gay shoulder shawl, are not an infrequent sight in the dancing hall, while the daughters of these same mothers appear in gowns made in the latest fashion. Sometimes these young people regret the lack of hat or bonnet in the street costume of their parents, for they are desirous of having them dressed like the " American lady." As yet the Americanizing of these young Italian girls has not taken from them their refreshing naturalness. Their cards are filled before they have had time to remove their outer wraps, and at the first strain of the music the floor is filled, and they fairly dance into the arms of their partners, and this with no touch of immodesty. The guarding of the unaffianced is, however, lax as compared with the restraint exercised after her betrothal, and indeed often after her marriage. By nature the Italian is most jealous and demands of his mate, not only absolute devotion, but often abstinence from almost the commonest civilities from other men. These punctilious demands are not confined to the better classes; they are quite as carefully obeyed in the humblest families. A certain fruit vender, who cannot aspire to a push-cart, but must conduct his business from a basket carried on his shoulder, can tell, with as much pride as the owner of a fruit market in the Back Bay, how for two whole years, during his daughter's engagement, she was never seen on the street, except in company with her mother on the way to and from church, until the day of her wedding. Her fiancé, he will explain, was not in Boston, and they were anxious to give him no cause for suspicion. Nor does the bestowal of the dowry and the family jewels belong to any one grade of society. The poor fruit peddler's daughter received from her father a dowry of two hundred dollars. Her mother's gift to her on her wedding day was six pairs of ear-rings and six finger rings, all of quaint design and of the purest gold.

No one has really made the acquaintance of the Italian people of our city, or indeed of any city, until he has seen them in the art galleries. A

Sunday afternoon in the Museum of Fine Arts shows them at their best. Whole families, many of them unable to speak English, find their way here. They walk through the rooms as if treading upon sacred ground. Undoubtedly they recognize in some of the statuary copies of familiar objects in art-loving Italy. The Italian standard of beauty is not always high or even correct, but love of beauty as they perceive it is a vital part of their lives. If they often rejoice unwisely in what is gaudy, it is nevertheless true that none more than they, and few as much, draw deep and genuine delight from the best that our public galleries have to offer.

Jew and Italian are near neighbors in the North End. The two neighborhoods touch, but the line between them is sharp, the atmosphere of each absolutely alien to the other. The genial, care-free expression of the men in the Italian district is suddenly missed when the border-line into the Jewish quarter is crossed. There we find the shrewd yet ingratiating look which so often means financial gain at any cost, even at the cost of self-respect. This, in the long-bearded Jew of the older generation, is clothed with a cover of conscious martyrdom. Then, too, from the Italian woman, always hard worked, yet thoroughly alive to varying interests, we turn to the forlorn, almost degraded woman of the Jewish household, whose every action reveals the narrow, oppressive atmosphere which she has breathed for so many generations. The great intellectual gifts of this race have been far from equally shared between the sexes. Book learning for the Jewish woman has in the past been thought unnecessary, and the lack of education is keenly written in the faces of the older women.

Resemblance between these two localities lies merely in the crowding of the streets and the incessant trading thereon. While there is much that is of peculiar interest in Jewish life, there can be, where there is so much squalor, but little real beauty. On the streets the commercial instinct is everywhere evident. The dangling old clothes, the pawnshop windows filled with everything that could possibly be turned into money, the baskets, barrels and carts of foul-smelling fish, do not add to the charm of the scene, and are hardly offset by the boxes of green vegetables and ripe fruits which border the sidewalk ; but the human element, the owners of the shops and wagons, with their forlorn expressions of anxiety to sell, the patriarchal old men, the intent, purchasing housekeepers and the energetic young salesmen who do not hesitate to drag customers into the shops, are of never-failing interest. The general dinginess of the locality is perhaps centred in the unattractive Jewish restaurants and meat shops. The windows of the former are filled with indifferent eatables, and from the grimy ceilings often hang festoons of long sausages, while the meat shops display a great variety of fresh meats, some of the most loathsome parts of the fowls and carcasses being placed on the counters in such quantities as to lead one to suppose that they are in great demand, if not looked upon as delicacies. These eating saloons and meat shops contrast strangely with the occasional corner or basement where second-hand Hebrew books are sold, and where the beautiful parchment and leather bindings tempt one to dream of their scholarly past. Fine old brass candlesticks are often for sale in these places. It is to such bits of brightness that this region owes much of its small aspect of cheer.

During the warm weather the streets teem with life. Every doorway is crowded with the older people, while the sidewalks and highways are populous with children, some in an almost undressed condition. They are all great lovers of music, and the advent of any musical instrument sets the youthful feet at once to dancing. The Jewish children dance as if by instinct, and their correct ear for music makes them apt pupils in the side-walk branch of the art.

There can be no greater contrast drawn between Jews and Italians than in their several ways of celebrating holidays and feasts, — the Italian seeking the air and sun on every occasion, the Jew finding sanctuary in his home for festival and rite; yet it is during the various holidays that the Jewish quarters appear to best advantage. These seasons first make themselves apparent to the Christian world by the festal gowns of the women and children. Among the older Jewish women, especially among those belonging to the Orthodox church, the married ones are easily distinguished by the coarse brown wig often made of some material other than human hair, the absence of which after marriage was formerly looked upon as a mark of immodesty. At times a kerchief or a piece of black cotton lace is used to take the place of the wig; but like many other customs, this of covering the head is disappearing before the general Americanizing tendency.

While the Jews are a people having large families, their inborn love of money-making leads them to crowd into the smallest quarters. Families having very respectable bank accounts have been known to occupy cellar rooms where damp and cold streaked the walls. Yet it is in their homes that the Jews rise to their best level. The family life is usually worthy of admiration. The parents are devoted guardians. The father feels strongly the responsibility of instructing his sons and daughters in the laws and customs of the faith. The mother is the affectionate and interested companion of her children, big or little. Even in the homes of the poorest, candles are always lighted for the Friday evening service, and the family assemble for the beginning of the Sabbath. On Saturday, after returning from the synagogue, the day is spent in visiting or receiving calls. The neighbor, with the ever-convenient shawl thrown over her head, comes to have a chat and a glass of tea from the steaming samovar. Many of the living-rooms of the Jewish people are furnished with beautiful specimens of hand-made copper dishes and brass candlesticks, all of which are brought from the old home country. The great need of increasing the family income often makes it difficult for the immigrants to keep these fine pieces of copper and brass. Strange as it may seem, one of their own countrymen usually stands near, ready to offer to these financially stranded ones a sum not one quarter of the market value of their treasures.

As a result, these interesting objects are gradually finding their way into the houses of well-to-do Americans, while the Jewish kitchens are becoming more and more filled with iron ware such as is sold in all of our house-furnishing stores.

The Jews have some social life in their various benevolent organizations, culminating in an occasional dance; but their intensest interests of this sort centre about their many religious ceremonies. In every home the circumcising of the newly born male child, the betrothal and the wedding of a son or daughter, are occasions of great moment, and are looked forward to as times of feasting and merrymaking. The wedding is perhaps the most interesting of these three functions. The ceremony is rarely performed in the bride's home, the lavish hospitality of the occasion necessitating the hiring of some hall for the reception, even when the pair are married in the synagogue. The oriental love for splendor and display is everywhere seen. Since it is possible to hire all things, even the wedding gown and veil, these are often, by the desire of the bride, mere temporary finery, in order that the money saved thereby may be used to increase the general gorgeousness of the occasion. The hospitality is unbounded. Not only are parents and brothers and sisters constantly on

the alert to see that the guests are cared for, but
the bride herself omits no effort for their comfort
and enjoyment. Entire families are among the
guests, from mothers with nursing babies to grand-
fathers and grandmothers, and all share the common joyousness.

At the ceremony, the father or mother of the
bride accompanies her to the canopy under which
she stands, facing the east. She is followed by
an attendant, who is the wife of the best man.
The lights carried by the friends of the bride
recall to memory the wise and foolish virgins of
Holy Writ. The rabbi tells the pair that they
take their vows as descendants of Abraham, Isaac
and Jacob; gives them a dissertation on married
life, and his blessing. After they have tasted the
consecrated wine, the groom crushes the goblet
under his heel to show to the world his determination to overcome all evil in the new life upon
which they are entering. Dancing follows the
ceremony, and lasts long into the night. Everybody tries to make everybody else happy. Young
men and young women dance with small children
as well as with each other, and pay an exquisite
deference to their elders. The wedding supper is
served at many tables, so that all can sit down
to the feast. The men often take their seats

before the women, and always eat with their hats on.

At the ceremony of the circumcision, great honor is conferred upon the man chosen to hold the child, such a one usually being high in authority in the church. He has no further duties toward the child. Such ceremonies are followed by feasting and dancing, — home-made wine, cake and conserves being provided in abundance. This free-handed hospitality is never accompanied or followed by intemperance.

The Jewish year has many holidays, from the New Year, which comes in the early autumn, to the single national holiday, which is celebrated as a day of thanksgiving in the early summer. At the Feast of Booths, green bowers are erected on roofs or in back yards. The Feast of Lights brings into use whatever wealth of candlesticks a family may possess. A feast is often preceded by a fast. Purim follows closely upon the Fast of Esther, and its coming is characterized by masquerade balls, the exchanging of gifts, and festivities generally. The holiday which entails the greatest preparation is the season of the Passover. It is then that children are everywhere seen munching the unleavened bread, while huge packages of it are piled in every grocery shop.

The amusements and merrymakings of the Jewish people cannot be described without further mention of their great love for music. The operas are largely attended by Hebrews, many being willing to undergo some sacrifice to hear a great artist. They are also devoted to the theatre, and as the best are too expensive for the poorer people, they go in great numbers to the cheap places of amusement. This is peculiarly true of the boys and girls; and an evening spent in the Dime Museum, the Nickelodeon or the music hall will confirm the observation. There is no regular Jewish theatre in Boston, but several times during the year Yiddish plays are given in one of the up-town houses by a company imported from New York. These plays are pictures of family life, usually Russian in character, and are exquisite in their simplicity. The acting is of an artistic quality rarely seen in our playhouses. The audience at such plays is most interesting. The familiar scenes, the old joys, the old wrongs and restraints touch deeply; progress is measured by departure from old customs. The vigor with which the Americanized Jewess applauds revolutionary sentiments with regard to the overbearing husband in the play is very significant.

No class of people in Boston has perhaps less opportunity for recreation than the Portuguese immigrants from the " Western Islands," as the Azores are popularly called. They come to us from their island homes, hoping to taste of riches, the supposed reward of all who go to America, only to find themselves swallowed up in the heart of a large tenement district, their homes the closest and darkest, and their outdoor life gained only at the expense of long hours of toil. The pride of the former landholder will not allow them to go out of their homes to work, and as a consequence the usual occupation of the women is the finishing of men's clothing. They easily obtain licenses for the work, as they are the neatest of housekeepers; but it is, of course, one of the poorest paid industries. Even when the clatter of the sewing machine has ceased and the living-room is deserted for the better air of the street, the work of sewing on buttons and picking out bastings does not cease. Indeed, the latter is often assigned to children of five years or so, while the older people, as all who have reached the age of thirteen years are considered, undertake the more difficult work.

With the early autumn comes the yearly exodus to the cranberry bogs of Cape Cod. This is a season of work and pleasure, looked forward to with the greatest delight. It is like a great family reunion, for here they meet their kinsfolk who have settled on the Cape, as well as many relatives and friends from the city whom they rarely see in their cruelly over-worked lives. And after the busy day of picking, screening and measuring the cranberries is over,—which begins with the drying off of the dew on the vines and ends with the setting of the sun,—they are ready for an evening of genuine relaxation. The great frame shanties, where many workers are housed, afford opportunities for the exchange of many a bit of gossip and for many a game and dance. A cranberry-picking in our sparkling September weather is a sight never to be forgotten. It has sometimes been compared to the hop-picking in Kent, which affords many a Londoner the only country outing he ever gets; but just as the Londoner can offer no such richness of color in skin or hair or costume as can these children of the sun, no more can the mild moistness of the English autumn be compared to a brilliant September day on Cape Cod.

The great poverty of the Portuguese prohibits many gayeties; indeed, it almost prevents the simplest hospitality. The glass of wine and the home-made cake so familiar in the home of the well-to-do are rarely seen in the homes of these islanders, yet their cordiality and sweetness of spirit are manifest. Constant privations have led to some evils, their conjugal irregularities being attributed to poverty. A woman abandoned by her husband sees no necessity for the expense and trouble of any legal steps before accepting a second spouse. She marries again, regardless of the existence or whereabouts of the deserter.

Church festivals vary the monotony of their lives to a small degree, and the occasional dance or picnic gives to these temperate and unusually industrious people a little of deserved good cheer. They have their benevolent societies, whose treasuries must be replenished from time to time, and this can best be accomplished by means of an entertainment.

The West End has ever been the great habitat of the colored race in Boston, and in spite of the exodus of the past few years to the South End, to Cambridgeport and to the suburbs at the north, many yet remain, while the churches and the social gatherings bring back others who no longer have an abiding-place there. The chief recreation of the colored people of the West End centres about their benefit or secret societies. The average city Negro belongs to many "orders," "circles" or societies, which hold frequent meetings. They are usually carried on in the homes of members, and at these meetings business and festivity blend. Then there are balls and receptions, which are often most elaborate. A marked feature of these events is the large number of visitors from distant cities. There is a characteristic note about every such affair. Whether it be due to the high degree of skill gained from years of training in domestic service, their inborn love of the ornate or simple ebullition of animal spirits, there is certainly an air of effulgence and exuberance about a social gathering of colored people to which no other race can attain. Yet here as everywhere, by one of the paradoxes of fate, the Negro, who is the tragic figure in our national life, is called to play a comedy part. Barred out from the society he most admires, his mimicry only excites mirth, and when he touches the white race on grounds of social equality it is the meeting of outcast with outcast. Back of some of the haunting scenes of vice in the West End stalks the spectre of race prejudice which has shut off from their kind once respectable persons who have married members of the black race. On the other side of the shield we see in the faces of refined and cultured colored men and women the triumph of nature over the degrading relations which slavery enforced. It is surely as unjust to judge the colored race by its worst as it would be so to judge the whites; while on the other hand, the story of the ascent of the black man is unparalleled in rapidity by that of the more favored race. Among the educated class the remarkable evolution of the woman's club of recent years has played its part, and in the State Federation of Working Women's Clubs there are no more earnest and intelligent members than a group of young colored women. The Negro has dwelt with us long; but so fixed are our notions of his character and limitations that it is with a shock of surprise and wonder that we come upon a gathering of the best of the colored race, differing not one whit in manners, in taste or in appearance, save for the richer color of the skin, from any similar group of white people. The traditional traits of the Negro, dearly loved by story-tellers and playwriters, the florid manner, the brilliant garb, the antics and the inconsequence are not far to seek; but what has been achieved by the few may be achieved by the many, and the life of the community may yet be made greater by the awakening of this youthful, untried race.

The Irish are, of course, the most numerous of our foreign-born population; but they have been with us so long and so intimately that they have become more closely identified with the native life than

have other races. The more ambitious have, as
a rule, moved away from their first homes in the
North and West Ends, pushed out by the invading
Jew and Italian. A very great number of people
are still attached to the Irish Catholic churches. A
degree of social life centres in the churches. They
furnish only a single bit of pageantry to the streets.
The processions of children crowned with wreaths
and wearing colored sashes, which are to be seen in
the Whitsuntide season, with the banners, mottoes
and little images which are carried, suggest the
spectacles dearly loved by the peasants over-seas.
Aside from church relations, there are dances for
some unfortunate brother, or the annual balls and
picnics of labor organizations and of the innumerable social clubs. The Hibernian is first, last and
always a social being, and this instinct does not
fail him even in his times of distress and bereave-
ment. For this reason, genuine grief and sympathy are not incompatible with keen appreciation
of a convivial touch in the wake and of the pomp
and drama of the funeral. The near-by summer
resorts draw crowds from the Irish-Americans
every Sunday or holiday or evening off. In the
winter the theatres attract large numbers of them.
In some cases they become regular subscribers to
the less expensive playhouses of good repute. The

distinguishing characteristic of Irish-American social gatherings is, of course, their political significance.

The theatre and things theatrical fill a large place
in the life of the people of the North and West Ends.
Not only is there a very numerous theatre-going
population, but in the district between Scollay
Square and Bowdoin Square there exists a world
almost untouched by any outside life. The hundreds of performers in the cheap theatres and
museums thereabout come and go, taking no part
in our common life. The crowding of the " profession " is so great, and competition is consequently
so fierce, that to keep pace they must rehearse and
retouch and embellish their " acts " during their
spare moments. Their stock in trade is some physical peculiarity — a flexible spine, an iron jaw, a
brazen voice — or some gift in the way of dancing,
dreary repartee or mimicry. They form partner-
ships — conjugal ones, too — for business ends, and
sever them when it seems desirable so to do, with
no thought of their relation to the community.
They have few acquaintances beyond the walls of
the theatres, and as their specialties pall or rivals
crowd them out, they one by one drop from the
ranks and are submerged in the crowd. In spite
of the irregularity and irresponsibility of their

lives, much that is innocent may be found in them. There is no glamour about the stage for these people. Their daily round is just so much work to be done, with the hope, often unfulfilled, of another job in the future. As to the character of their performance, there is much that is harmless, a part that has actual merit, and a part that is positively bad. The audiences are drawn not only from various parts of the city, but, in the more notorious places, from all parts of New England. The rural visitor who wishes to plunge into dissipation in Boston hies to these hunting-grounds of the thief, the prostitute and the gambler.

The several places of amusement attract different kinds of audiences. One of them — the Bowdoin Square Theatre — is the home of sensational melodrama free from indecency. Another appeals to a morbid love of the abnormal, and "freaks" of all kinds may be found there. At the others the performance consists of a medley of innocent accomplishments, inane chaff and the grossest vulgarity. Too many of the younger people of foreign extraction are finding their way to these places; but it is doubtful if as yet they form an appreciable proportion of the audiences.

There is one note always discernible in the daily life of the foreign peoples of the North and

West Ends, and nowhere is it clearer than in their moments of leisure. In spite of the survival of types, in spite of the inevitable longing for the home country, in spite of all the differences of race and tradition, the strongest and most impelling of motives, the most cherished of ideals, is that of becoming American. Color, melody, comfort and content — indeed some of the sterner virtues themselves — are sacrificed before this Goddess of Democracy whose protecting arms, these people from foreign lands have been led to believe, will afford them and theirs a share in the joys of life. Not so ugly as it seems at first glance, then, is the ready adaptability with which the newcomers take on the least commendable of our customs. The Italian girl who forgets her cadenza and sings the most nasal of street songs, her mother who prefers the scrubbing of offices to the handicraft of her ancestors, her father who forsakes his native wines for beer, are unconscious idealists ; and beneath one and all of these humble acts lies a meaning which we who are born to our inheritance would do well to prize. " 'T is not the custom of the country " is a phrase that is changing the manners of the centuries and shaking the beliefs of ages past.

CHAPTER IX

TWO ANCIENT FAITHS

BETWEEN the early religious situation at the North End and that of to-day, Christ Church, whose house of worship stands on Salem Street, is the single connecting link. When it was organized in 1723, it was the second church of the Episcopal faith and order in Boston. At the Old North, Increase Mather was ending his long pastorate, and Cotton Mather, his son and colleague, was in the height of his power. Peter Thatcher was occupying the pulpit at the New North, his call a few years before having been the cause of a remarkable dissension in the church. The New Brick Church had been recently organized by one of the factions in this quarrel. Conveniently located by the side of the Mill Pond was a little wooden structure in which the frowned-upon Baptists were worshiping.

An especial interest attaches to Christ Church because of the stately and now historic building which it has occupied from the first. In the steeple of this edifice, according to tradition, were displayed the signal lanterns of Paul Revere which warned the country of the march of the British to Lexington and Concord ; from its tower General Gage witnessed the Battle of Bunker Hill; and in one of the burial vaults beneath its nave the remains of Major Pitcairn reposed until transferred to Westminster Abbey.

Indeed, the historic associations connected with its house of worship have served to keep the church where it is, notwithstanding the decreasing number and wider and wider scattering of its adherents. Of the hundred or more communicants on its rolls to-day, less than twenty reside within the limits of the North End, and a good part of the fifty or sixty members of its Sunday-school come from East Boston and Charlestown. The Sunday morning service — the only service of the week which is regularly maintained — brings together a small congregation made up chiefly of sight-seers.

Other Protestant survivals are three agencies of different denominations for religious and social work among the sailors. Sea-faring men have been a class more or less numerous at the North End ever since the days when the town dock was where Faneuil Hall now stands and wharves reached out into the water from the present North Square.

All three agencies hold religious meetings, give aid to seamen in distress, provide lectures, entertainments and suppers, maintain a reading-room and visit among the sailors in their homes and boarding-places and on shipboard. The Mariners' House, under Methodist management, provides a home where seamen can obtain board at moderate rates. If in circumstances of need, they are received and cared for free of charge. The Baptist Bethel restricts its efforts less than the others to the sea-faring class, carrying on a Sunday-school and several educational and industrial classes made up of children and young people from the neighborhood. It spreads its net wide by calling itself "a church for seamen and landmen," and now employs an Italian missionary to look after people of his own race living round about.

Not all the Protestant religious agencies in the North End to-day are survivals of the past. In 1894 a Methodist Episcopal minister of Italian birth began work among his countrymen. The following year a church of seventy members was organized, which five years later had a total enrollment of over five hundred, of whom one hundred and seventy-five constituted its actual resident membership. One reason of this growth, which came exclusively from the Roman Catholics, was to be found in the social and educational privileges provided by the church. Unfortunately, however, the logic of the come-outer has appeared in a division of the church itself. Part of the people, with the pastor, have taken up the Congregational form of organization.

Certain specially degraded conditions of life, formerly more characteristic of the North End than now, brought the "slum corps" of the Salvation Army to their relief. A small mission for Scandinavian seamen, and one more survival of other times in a single personal representative of the "Society for the Employment of Bible Readers in Boston," fill out the number of Protestant religious agencies. With the exception of the two Italian churches, all nine minister chiefly to sojourners or to social outcasts and the extremely poverty stricken, leaving the more stable and normal classes, who make up the bulk of the population, practically untouched. Even in the case of the Italian Protestant fragments, they include unattached and shifting individuals rather more than family groups. The serious truth is that if any or all of these Protestant agencies should drop out completely, the general religious situation in the North End would be affected almost not at all.

At the West End there has not been, of course, so long a religious history as in the North End, and there are no survivals of old-time church life. Several of the old buildings, including that of the West Church, associated with great names in its pastorate, are still standing, but have been turned to other uses. There is in the West End a larger constituency available for Protestant ministrations than in the North End. This is true chiefly on account of the colored population.

A Negro church, the Zion Methodist, is the oldest existing religious organization in the West End. It dates from 1836. Through the removal of so many Negroes from this part of the city, barely a third of the moderate number of its attendants live in the vicinity of its house of worship, on North Russell Street. The rest have their homes in the South End, Cambridgeport, Charlestown, and even farther away.

There are three other congregations of colored people in the part of the West End covered by these studies, — the Revere Street Methodist, the Twelfth Baptist and St. Augustine's. Not far away is the Charles Street Methodist. With the exception of the last, they are small — the Revere Street Church comprising scarcely a handful — and draw but a minor part of their audi-

ences from the immediate vicinity. Among them
there is no coöperation and but little common acquaintance. Indeed, an association of the colored
churches of the district would be very distasteful
to the Negro. In his religion, as in other things,
he would forget, and have all others forget, that he
is colored. He will never of his own accord draw
the line between himself and the white man.

St. Augustine's is a missionary outpost for colored people, sustained by the Church of St. John
the Evangelist. It possesses an advantage over the
other Negro churches in that it has a white rector
and a corps of white assistants, for white religious
workers are more acceptable to the colored people than religious workers of black skin. This is
due partly to the higher moral character that as a
rule white preachers and missionary visitors possess, and partly, also, to the aggressive feeling
of equality between one Negro and another that
is characteristic of the colored race. The women
helpers of St. Augustine's are members of the
Sisterhood of St. Margaret, a religious order of
the Episcopal Church, whose headquarters in Boston are in Louisburg Square, a short distance away.
The rector is one of the group of Cowley Fathers
who constitute the ministry of the Church of St.
John the Evangelist.

Alone of the five churches mentioned, St. Augustine's is establishing vital points of contact with its neighborhood. Indeed, it is the only one of the five whose removal would involve serious loss to the Negroes of this section of the West End. Even those who have no connection with the church often turn to it when they need the offices of a minister or desire personal counsel. But this local activity is only a part of the work of St. Augustine's. The majority of its one hundred and fifty communicants, with a proportion nearly as large of the attendants upon its services, are scattered throughout the city and suburbs, especially in Cambridgeport. Among those recently removed to the South End, a branch Sunday-school, with occasional religious services, has been established. St. Augustine's, with all the authority it can command, endeavors to hold its followers to a reasonably high standard of morality. Although it is not always successful, moral lapses are perhaps no more frequent among its adherents than among those of many a white church. Aside from the hold it has on its own members, it exerts a marked restraining influence from wrong doing upon the entire colored population.

Of course the Negroes of the West End do not confine their church-going to organizations of their

own race or to the district in which they live. In
fact, within half a mile or more of Beacon Hill,
there are few churches, not excepting the Roman
Catholic, into which they fail to find their way.
The considerations which guide them in the selec-
tion of a place of worship are by no means peculiarly their own. Too often, as with men and
women of another complexion, their motives may
be resolved into the desire for social distinction.
The woman who can claim membership in Trinity
parish is apt to feel socially superior to her female
neighbor attending the Zion Methodist or Twelfth
Baptist. St. Augustine's itself wins and holds
many of its followers less by its ritual than by the
social prestige it is thought to confer. Those who
go into the Roman Catholic Church do so because
here, as they believe, black and white will be treated
as equals.

A considerable part of the colored people have
no church affiliation whatever. Nor, with the
single exception of St. Augustine's, is there any
religious agency trying to reach this class of the
unchurched, which includes, of course, the vicious
and criminal element among the Negroes. Probably no section in Boston calls for wise and energetic religious work as does the colored quarter of
the West End. Here the missionary will find, if

not the largest opportunity, at least the most urgent need.

The Church of St. John the Evangelist, with its monastic clergy, holds a unique place among the Episcopal churches of Boston. From the character of its worship and discipline, it appeals to Episcopalians of extreme ritualistic tendencies scattered throughout the city. Thus it is the church of a special class rather than of a particular locality.

The opposite extreme to the elaborate ritualistic worship at St. John the Evangelist's is the service at the Second Reformed Presbyterian, or "Covenanter," Church on Chambers Street. Here the use of a church organ is not tolerated, and only the psalms in a metrical version are sung. Psalm singing, Scripture reading, prayer and a sermon make up the order of worship. The membership of this church is composed of Scotch people from the British Provinces, having their homes for the most part outside the city. The building where they meet was a chapel of the Old South Church when that society worshiped in the historic edifice on Washington Street.

The First Methodist congregation is another example of a fairly prosperous church which touches at only a few points the life of the neighborhood in which it worships. Of its four hundred enrolled members, fully one half live at a distance from the church building, although a somewhat larger proportion of the attendants upon its services come from within a radius of half a mile. The church missionary on her round of calls visits in Forest Hills, Revere, Brookline, Somerville and Charlestown, as well as in the West and North Ends.

In the local work among the white people, three organizations are striving to meet their needs in some direct and systematic way. Bulfinch Place Church, which represents Unitarian effort, antedates by some years the other two, having occupied its present building since 1869, when it removed from Pitts Street. Although its policy has been from the first to retain under its care all who have been numbered among its adherents, even after they have removed from the neighborhood, it is actively engaged also in building up a local constituency. About two hundred families and individuals living in the vicinity are ministered to in some regular way, many of whom are without church affiliation of any kind. Under the leadership of its present pastor, the church has instituted a number of changes in the direction of a social ministry. To a slight extent this unsectarian work touches Jews and Italians.

St. Andrews is a dependency of Trinity Church, and was organized through the efforts of Phillips Brooks in 1876, when its attractive house of worship was built.   It has about one hundred and fifty communicants, and nearly as many members of the Sunday-school, including the officers and teachers. Besides the usual services, prayers are read daily at five o'clock in the afternoon, with an attendance varying from twelve to fifteen persons.   At all of the services the number of children present is noticeable.   A parish house adjoining the church building furnishes convenient quarters for the social activities of the church, which include a medical dispensary for women and girls and a mutual aid society with insurance benefits.   A number of social clubs for boys and girls are formed chiefly though not exclusively out of the membership of the Sunday-school.   Space is provided for a kindergarten in charge of the city, and a playroom is carried on in the summer time.

A unique branch of St. Andrews is a mission for deaf mutes, established in 1892.   Through the minister in charge and lay readers, this mission has carried the gospel to deaf mutes in other Episcopal dioceses of New England, and to-day has congregations in Maine, New Hampshire and Rhode Island.   About thirty communicants are cared for by the original mission.

When St. Andrews began its work twenty-five years ago, the section of the West End in and around Chambers Street was the home of a large number of English-speaking Protestants, — people from the north of Ireland and the British Provinces, interspersed with some Americans. To-day nearly all of these have disappeared, and their places have been taken by the Jews from the North End. This complete change in the character of the population has given an embarrassing check to the work of the church; but it holds many of the results of its effective efforts in the past, and is on the alert for whatever forms of human service the needs of the new situation may demand.

The Tabernacle Baptist Church, like the Bulfinch Place Church, makes special efforts to reach the lodging-house class. In common with the other downtown churches of the city, however, it has a scattered constituency. Hardly more than a fourth of its five hundred members live on Beacon Hill, the remainder having their homes as far away as Somerville, Everett, Chelsea, East Boston or Dorchester. This non-resident portion of the church includes nearly all of the families, while the unattached individuals live in lodging-houses in this general section of the city. Unlike the Bulfinch Place Church and St. Andrews, it engages in few forms of social activity, but is a people's church conducted on distinctively religious lines. If its results in numbers are not large, they are quite substantial.

In that part of the West End where the social outcasts of both sexes congregate, or through which they pass, four rescue missions and a corp of the Salvation Army have established themselves. A large restaurant is carried on in connection with one of the missions, where good food is sold at extremely low prices. The room used for the restaurant purposes is below the line of the sidewalk, and is bare and dingy. There is no attempt at decoration, save a few Scripture mottoes on the wall. The floor is thickly covered with sawdust. The deal tables are without cloths. Cleanliness in the preparation and serving of the food is noticeable, however. As many as eighteen hundred men have been fed here in the course of a single day. Low as the prices are, the place meets its expenses and provides in addition the funds for carrying on the mission, including the rent of the rooms and the salary of the superintendent.

Without doubt these agencies succeed now and then in the reclamation of some man or woman, but their chief service is rather one of witnessing to the existence of a real need than in meeting that need. The Salvation Army ceased long ago to excite opposition, and is fast ceasing to excite even passing interest. Its meetings are attended by comparatively few outside the number of its direct following.

Taking the West End as a whole, therefore, it is quite clear that Protestantism is passing. From the North End, to all intents and purposes, Protestantism has already passed. The religious issue, in all its depth of meaning to personal and public welfare and progress, so far as it concerns the actual constituent life of these two districts, lies with the Roman Catholic and Jewish systems.

Five Roman Catholic churches have their places of worship in the North End and one in the West End, — three Irish, two Italian and one Portuguese. St. Mary's, an Irish church, is the oldest as well as the largest of them all, and the second church of the Roman Catholic faith established in Boston. The site of its house of worship on Endicott Street was purchased by the Roman Catholics for a church building as early as 1834, and two years later a completed structure was dedicated. The present building, erected about twenty-five years ago, is an imposing edifice with a seating capacity of about eighteen hundred. Since 1847 the church has been in charge of the Jesuit order, which has two other churches in the city.

St. Mary's is a mission; hence, though serving as a parish church, its ministry is not restricted to those living within its parochial bounds. Visual evidence of this is given by the throngs that pour through the doors of its sacred edifice after a Sunday morning mass and scatter to other parts of the city. The procession of these returning worshipers going over the new Charlestown bridge presents a truly impressive sight, extending from one end of the bridge to the other, a compact moving column, and occupying a considerable time in passing. Indeed, the non-resident following of St. Mary's offsets more or less the shrinkage in its local constituency caused by the removal of the Irish from the North End. Fully five thousand people still attend its various Sunday services. After a recent mission, forty-four hundred came to its confessional, and there were many attendants besides who visited the confessionals of other churches. In addition to its ministrations to its own congregation, St. Mary's maintains chapels at the city penal and pauper institutions on the harbor islands.

St. Stephen's, which shares with St. Mary's the spiritual care of the Irish Roman Catholics in the North End, is a parish church merely. Hence it has been affected much more than St. Mary's by the moving away of the older and more prosperous

Irish families. Nevertheless it is still a large and important church. As the distinctive and influential parish church of the North End, it has a special attraction for local politicians who wish to use its social and charitable organizations as so many additional means of advancing their interests with the public.

St. Joseph's, on Chambers Street, cares for the Irish Roman Catholics at the West End, with the exception of those who attend the mission church of St. Mary's. Formerly its number of communicants was so great that on special occasions the spacious building could not hold all who came, and the broad steps leading up to the doors, and even the sidewalk itself, would be crowded with kneeling worshipers. To-day no congregation that comes is too large for the accommodations, so greatly has the Irish population at the West End fallen off.

These churches, like nearly all Roman Catholic churches, include among their organizations sodalities of adult members for religious instruction and the promotion of a stricter observance of the sacraments, and a conference of the Society of St. Vincent de Paul, to care for the poor of the parish. In common with the Roman Catholic Church in general, they seem to be realizing the demoralization caused by drink among their people, and are increasingly aggressive against it. St. Mary's and St. Stephen's provide some opportunity for secular culture in a Reading Circle. Each has also in its parish building a spacious hall for social and other purposes. St. Mary's Hall is equipped with stage and scenery for dramatic performances. St. Stephen's, aside from its parish interests, is taking an active part in promoting the general welfare of the North End. Under its leadership an organization of prominent citizens, including Protestants and Jews, has been formed to coöperate with the police and other departments of the city government in securing better conditions throughout the district.

The Italian Roman Catholics have had a place of worship on Prince Street since 1874. Their present church home consists of an older part dedicated in 1890, and a newer part recently added. The church is known as the Church of St. Leonard of Port Maurice, and from the first has been in the charge of the Brotherhood of St. Francis. Its interior adornment includes some beautiful work done and contributed by parishioners. Peculiar interest attaches to St. Leonard's because of its shrine of St. Anthony. Roman Catholics from all parts of Boston, irrespective of race or social condition, visit this shrine to make some request, usually for physical healing, in behalf of themselves or their friends. Tuesday evening a special service is held for the visitors, when a relic of the saint is shown. At this service the scene around the altar suggests what one might see on a larger scale at St. Anne de Beaupré, or even at Lourdes, — a motley crowd of young and old, of poor and apparently well-to-do, of " the lame, halt and blind," pressing forward to kiss the relic and receive the blessing of St. Anthony. The church derives a good part of its income from the gifts of these visitors and from the sale of small articles relating to St. Anthony.

Dissatisfaction on the part of some communicants with the Franciscans' management of St. Leonard's led to the establishment of a second Italian Roman Catholic church in 1895. Those who came out of the Prince Street church bought, of their own initiative, a building on North Square for the use of the new society. This edifice had been the scene of a religious and social work among sailors conducted by " Father " Taylor, well known as an eloquent Methodist preacher. The title to the property is still held in the name of a committee of the church, although the church itself is under the direction and authority of the diocese. A situation as unusual as this, from a Roman

Catholic point of view, was brought about only by a special concession from Rome, and has but one or two parallels in this country.

The Church of the Sacred Heart is the name given to this second congregation. Within its house of worship an interesting scene is presented whenever a service is going on. At the farther end of the audience room, presenting a brilliant contrast to the dingy walls and rough woodwork of the rest of the place, rises a richly adorned altar, the lofty reredos of which fills the entire space between the galleries. Kneeling figures of angels, one on the right and one on the left, keep guard over the altar, while a shrine occupies either corner under the galleries, before which burn great clusters of candles. Every seat on the floor and in the gallery is taken, and all available standing room is crowded almost to the point of suffocation. The dark eyes and swarthy complexions of the worshipers, the gayly colored head coverings of the women, their large gold or brass ear-rings, and, indeed, the whole aspect of the place, might easily lead one to believe that he had wandered into a chapel in the outskirts of Genoa or Naples.

The Roman Catholic Sunday-schools are largely attended, but seem to be of no great value. They are not much inferior, however, to the Sunday-schools connected with most of the Protestant centres of these districts. In the case of the Catholics, insufficient care about religious training in the Sunday-school is abundantly made up in the parochial school. At St. Mary's and St. Stephen's, where alone in the North and West Ends, until recently, parochial education was provided, the schools gather in practically all the children of those parishes. The parochial school at St. Mary's is the oldest in the city. It was established as the result of an incident which occurred in 1859, when a boy of the parish was punished by a public-school teacher for refusing to read a passage from the Protestant Bible. This present year, both Italian churches have opened parochial schools for their own children.

The Irish and Italian Roman Catholics differ one from the other in certain broad respects, arising from differences in the religious traditions, as well as in the temperaments, of the two races. The Vatican's hostility to Italian unity has created a conviction more or less widespread among the Italians that the church is the enemy of the people's liberties. Wherever this exists, there is an accompanying feeling of estrangement from the church, for the Italians are " patriots first and churchmen after." A considerable number of the immigrants retain a sincere piety, especially those from districts where the priests' authority is still unchallenged, but the majority are indifferent to their inherited faith. Some entertain toward it a feeling of actual hostility.

The Irish, on the other hand, have found the church the very bulwark of their liberties. Through it they have maintained such nationality as they possess, and to be included within its fold gives them dignity in their own eyes and in the eyes of the world. Religious feeling, also, is much stronger in this people than in the Italians. Hence, generally speaking, the Irish are far more devoted to their church than the Italians, and submit much more fully to its authority. But this difference does not show itself in the matter of mere church attendance. Indeed, it would be hard to say which race goes to public worship more generally, the Irish or the Italian. In the motive of church going, however, the difference appears. The Irish go to church more especially for reasons of devotion ; the Italians for social reasons. Of course there are many exceptions among both races ; all the devout Roman Catholics are not Irish, nor are all the indifferent ones Italians. Both kinds of motives run off more or less into superstition. The extent of this cannot be traced in either nationality, but it is safe to say that among the Italians its influence is the more general.

The social atmosphere which the Italians cast about public worship appears in the scenes in Prince Street and North Square on Sunday morning. Those coming out from mass, or waiting until the hour for the next mass, congregate in large numbers, filling street and sidewalk alike, all talking and gesticulating. This open-air conclave has become so great an institution that those working at a distance return whenever possible in order to be present at it.

The Portuguese Roman Catholics differ little from the Italians. They have, however, a deeper, perhaps more superstitious, regard for their church, and very generally attend religious services. But the corrective and restraining influence of the church on their lives is certainly no more powerful than in the case of the Italians. The strength of Roman Catholicism in the North End is in the Irish rather than in the Latin churches. It is not too much to say that St. Mary's, from the character of its ministry and the loyalty of its followers, is the most important agency for righteousness in this part of Boston.[1]

[1] For some estimate of the influence of the Roman Catholic

Nearly all of the Jews living in the North and West Ends are, or recently have been, of the orthodox faith. Their chief and largest house of worship, which is the headquarters of orthodox Judaism in Boston, stands in Baldwin Place, off Salem Street. This structure, built originally by the Second Baptist Society, has been occupied by the Jews for about twelve years. Next to this in size and interest is a building erected quite recently on a site adjoining Baldwin Place. A third important meeting-place is in Smith's Court, off Joy Street, on the north slope of Beacon Hill, in a building which was relinquished a year or two ago by St. Paul's Church, the oldest congregation of colored people in Boston. The change in the ownership of this building within so recent a time registers the curious social displacement that is coming about in that part of the West End.

Besides the congregations worshiping at these three centres, there are smaller congregations meeting in various halls. A number of families from the same province or city in Europe unite to form a synagogue, to which in many instances they give the name of the place from which they come. These smaller or " neighborhood " synagogues usu-

Church on the personal and family life of its people, the reader is referred to *The City Wilderness*, pp. 202, 221, sq.

ally combine the functions of religious worship with those of a benefit order to provide against sickness and death. The rooms in which they meet are used also, to a certain extent, for social purposes. Connected with each synagogue, and maintained by it, is a school for instructing the children in the Hebrew language. Additional schools are supported by the synagogues in common, especially for the poorer children.

Between the older and the younger Jews there is a marked difference as regards loyalty to the faith. The grandparents, and among the later immigrants the middle aged, cling to the old customs and traditions with passionate tenacity, while each succeeding generation is more noticeably breaking away from them. One of the men of the Jewish colony told the whole story of the growing infidelity among his people when he said, " My father prays every day; I pray once a week; my son never prays." But the attendance at religious services is probably, on the average, as great as among Protestants. Unlike that of the Protestants, it is predominantly of men, for according to the Jewish system the women are not under the same obligation as the men to be present at the worship of the synagogue.

Their more important religious festivals are still

very generally observed, even by those who pay little regard to the ordinary round of religious duties. The Day of Atonement, especially, is a rallying time for the indifferent and devout alike, ushering in the most solemn period in the Jewish year, — the period when, according to the Jewish belief, the good or ill fortune of each one is fixed for the next twelve months, and the lists are made up of those appointed to die and of the souls destined to be born. Therefore it is a period to be observed with fasting and prayer, with attendance upon the services of the synagogue, and, during certain of the eight days of its continuance, with abstinence from all secular employment.

As the hour of sunset draws near on the evening which marks the beginning of the festival, all the Jewish places of business are closed. Throngs of Jews of all ages and both sexes fill the streets on their way to the various places of worship; for he would be an apostate, indeed, who voluntarily absented himself from the synagogue on that evening. Evidence that large numbers of the Jews seldom if ever attend public worship throughout the rest of the year is furnished by the fact that during the Atonement season the usual synagogues cannot begin to accommodate the crowds, and additional halls and rooms are brought into use.

Within the Baldwin Place synagogue the scene is strange and impressive. The entire floor of the place is a solid mass of men and boys, while the galleries are crowded with women and girls. All heads are covered, and in addition every male has over his shoulders a " prayer shawl," — a scarf of silk or linen with curiously knotted fringe at the ends. The older men are clad also in long garments of white linen, the robes of their burial. Upon a raised platform around the reading-desk are grouped the readers who have been called up from the congregation, the cantor in his raiment of white and gold, and the members of the choir, wearing black robes and turbans. At the right and left of the " ark," in the "chief seats," sit the president and other officials, or " rulers," of the synagogue. An ever-burning lamp, symbol of Jehovah's presence, hangs high over all.

As the service proceeds, the sacred books from which one reader after another has read, or rather chanted, in a high pitched voice, are rolled up and returned to the " ark " in solemn procession. At a given signal the whole congregation rises and breaks into some repetition, in the Hebrew tongue, uttering the words with great rapidity and swaying their bodies back and forward in rhythmical accompaniment, the more venerable the worshiper the greater his earnestness. The confusion of sounds subsides, and the cantor takes up the service, his voice swelling out in lamentation or dying away in a sob; now rising in a shout of triumph, now sinking down to a whisper that seems to be the utterance of hope and peace. At frequent intervals the choir chimes in with strong, well-trained voices, singing the words to some melody that has come down from the remote past.

Next to the Day of Atonement in importance and in the generality of its observance is the Feast of the Passover. This substitutes rejoicing for humiliation and confession. The scene of the supper itself is the home, not the synagogue. It is, indeed, the patriotic and home festival of the Jewish year, a combination of the American Fourth of July and Thanksgiving.

Sabbath observance is fast becoming confined to the older people. Each year fewer stores and workshops in the Salem Street neighborhood are closed on the seventh day. When, a year or two ago, by a special police concession the places of business in this particular section that were closed on Saturday could be kept open on Sunday, many of the Jewish proprietors saw in this only an opportunity to gain an additional business day. While shutting the doors and drawing down the shades of

their places of business on Saturday, they would
remain near for any chance customer. This abuse
of the concession led finally to its withdrawal.
Such incidents would seem to mark a serious departure from the standards of Sabbath observance
in the stronghold of orthodox Judaism.

It is a striking fact of Judaism that it remains a race bond even for those who have lost its
spiritual impulse. Nationality is still a mould in
which their scheme of the moral life is cast. The
patriarchal elder sighs for a handful of the sacred
soil of Palestine on which to rest his dying head,
and even many emancipated youth look with devotion to the Holy Land.

Zionism as found in these districts is not identified with extreme orthodoxy, but includes among
its advocates many who are far from strict ob-
servers of their religion. There is quite a general
agreement that its aim and motive is to establish
a refuge in Palestine for the persecuted of their
race. In fact, here as elsewhere it has more " the
character of an enthusiasm than of a reasoned
policy." Five or six societies of Zionists have
their headquarters in this part of the city. Here
they meet for social purposes, and maintain a
forum for the discussion of current events. The
ardor of many of the members of these societies

carries their thoughts beyond the bounds of a mere racial utopia and makes them socialists.

At the North and West Ends, Roman Catholicism and Judaism, existing side by side, present a sharp and dramatic contrast to each other. Never is this more apparent than when, as sometimes happens, the season of Easter and that of the Passover are coincident. While the Roman Catholics are thronging their churches in sorrow and penitence because of a betrayed, crucified and buried Saviour, the Jews, gathered in family groups about the Passover supper, joyously recite the story of Israel's deliverance from Egyptian bondage, and renew their faith in the coming of another deliverer, one who will be greater than Moses. In the Roman Catholic churches, the figures on the altars are shrouded in token of the dead Christ; in the Jewish home the door stands open for Elijah, the herald of the Messiah, and the cup of wine is ready for the longed-for guest. On Easter Day the Roman Catholics have removed the emblems of mourning from their altars, and are rejoicing with the rest of Christendom over the resurrection of Christ from the dead; but the Jews have sadly closed the door opened in vain, and poured the wine from the untasted cup.

During this period, if ever, it is natural to suppose that the two religious elements would clash ; but strange as it may seem, aside from the cry of "Christ-killer," with which a Roman Catholic child now and then greets his Jewish fellow, few expressions of bigotry are to be heard on either side. In common with the Jew, the Roman Catholic is constantly experiencing some disadvantage on account of his religion, and this makes him more or less tolerant of his Jewish neighbor. The Jew, on his part, has learned patience and long-suffering through ages of oppression. In too many cases on both sides, however, this forbearance arises from lack of religious earnestness. In one very curious way they are actually brought together by their religious difference, for many Roman Catholic boys make a business of lighting and caring for the fires in Jewish homes on the days when the Jews are enjoined by their religion from engaging in manual labor of any kind. "Fire, fire!" is the cry that may be heard throughout the Jewish quarter on the morning of such days, as the "fire-lighters" go about seeking customers. While these boys render a needed service, they are, nevertheless, held in contempt by their employers. Indeed, the ignorance and stupidity of the "fire-lighters" has passed into a proverb among the Jews.

The Italians make the saints' and other church days occasions for out-of-door decorations and pageantry as well as of church going. In the morning, mass is very generally attended, and in the evening, after the lanterns are lighted, a procession is formed which, headed by a native band, parades through the principal streets of the North End.

The Jews confine their religious celebrations to the synagogue or to the privacy of their own homes. Indeed, one might walk through the Jewish quarter on the Day of Atonement or of the Passover and, aside from the number of Jews going to and from their places of worship, fail to detect any sign that a festival is in progress.

The Jewish religious system intensifies the family life. Its personal moral code is without doubt the secret of the astonishing vitality of the race. The quality of the affection which exists in the home seems almost enough to atone for the narrow life of the wife and mother, whose range of duty is simply to bring up her children well, keep a kosher house and be kind. The intense inner life of the persecuted has developed in many of the Russian Jews a fine emotional nature. This ingrained type of family and clan religion, however, has tended to prevent friendly feeling for

outsiders. The Jew prides himself upon his
acuteness, upon the high tone of his family life
and upon what he deems the special enlightenment
of his form of faith.   Considering himself superior
to Christians, he is very likely to misjudge and
distrust them.

The Roman Catholic Church exerts a powerful
constraining and disciplinary power among its followers, many of them detached from their social
and even from their domestic moorings.   This is
particularly true of recent immigrants, like the
Italians and Portuguese, in a country utterly
strange and bewildering in thought, speech and
ways of life.   That these nationalities have on the
whole maintained so creditable a morale is largely
owing to the Church's overshadowing presence and
its familiar, insistent appeal to the moral imagination.   What the effect of the new life will be
upon this influence is yet to be determined.

With the Irish, the Roman Catholic Church
has had more time in which to provide for the
new situation.   Its influence in safeguarding the
family is distinct and determined, affording an
indispensable check to the corrupting influences
of the local life.   The Church thus preserves the
force of that enthusiasm which is one of the chief
distinctions of the Irish race, and affords direction

and steadiness to an often mercurial and contradictory temperament.

Roman Catholicism and Judaism, widely separated as they are in all outward aspects, yet fundamentally meet on common ground. Their systems of ethics, coming down out of the long past, have brought with them a large traditionary element which includes prescriptions and observances that once fulfilled moral needs but do not sufficiently lay hold on life in these fast-moving days. All the underlying principles in these great systems have their profound force and meaning, but both put a disproportionate emphasis upon special observance as against daily conduct. In the ghettos and cloisters of the past, religion must needs create a world of its own; but the open world of to-day, with all its new challenge to the souls of men, presents the living issues out of which real religion must grow. In both Roman Catholicism and Judaism, punishment is looked upon as something extraneous to sin, imputed to it by solemn outward decree, rather than like unto it and coming out of its very heart. Roman Catholicism, by placing its awards in an unseen world, to a degree suggests the inward personal quality of the punishment of sin. In Orthodox Judaism the penalties of disobedience are represented as falling mainly in this world, — he who eats bread during the Passover shortens his days.

A system of restrictions whose scope is narrower than the normal contemporary life leaves, as all history shows, the alternative between a mechanical formalism on the one hand and irreligion on the other. Among Roman Catholics skepticism has gained but little ground ; but the artificial character of the attachment of a considerable and increasing proportion of its adherents is hardly open to question. The opportunities of the new life lead the Jew to make short work of his traditions, and throw him out of the pale of religion altogether. The danger is that the very fineness which Judaism has created may only make him the more open to all the subtle undermining influences of city life. In the Roman Catholic Church, the crisis has not yet come in the contest between a negative, protective religious policy and the ever-expanding life of the people. When the crisis does come, there will no doubt appear a new and interesting programme of adaptation to facts on the part of this most flexible of historic institutions.

In any case, there is much hope in the increasing activity among well-disposed men and women of various religious connections toward building up the outer intrenchments of the spiritual life by the improvement of personal, family, neighborhood and municipal conditions. The better understanding which arises between Protestant and Catholic, between Christian and Jew, when they work together thus on common ground, will give that sense of human unity out of which vital forms of religion in the future must come.

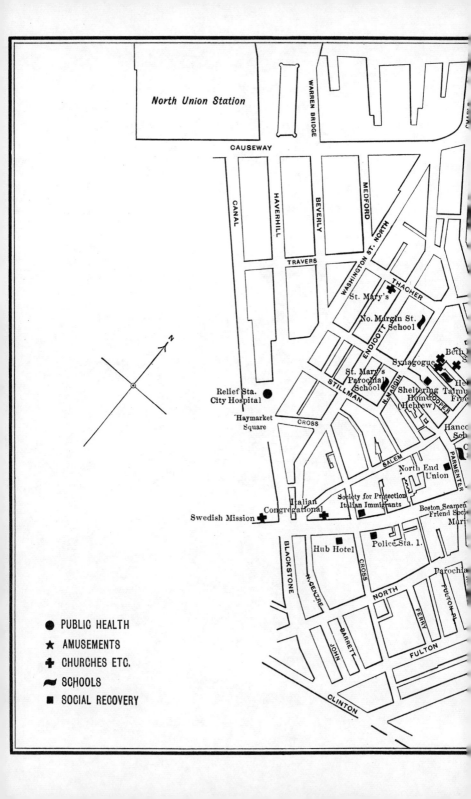

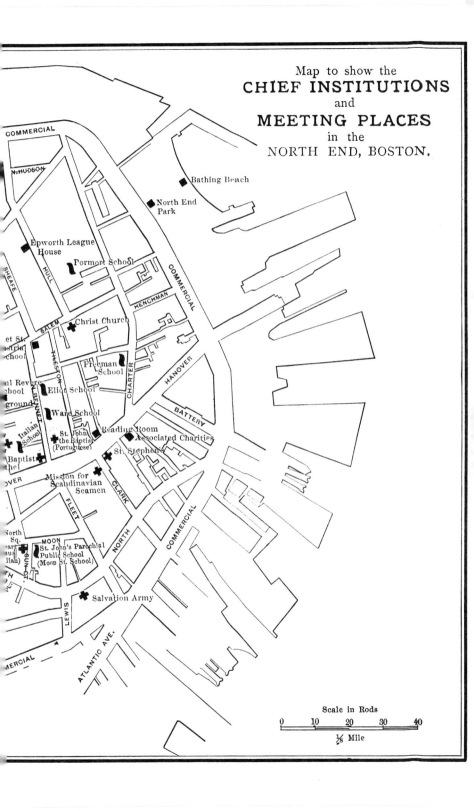

Map to show the
CHIEF INSTITUTIONS
and
MEETING PLACES
in the
NORTH END, BOSTON.

Bathing Beach

North End Park

Epworth League House

Pormort School

COMMERCIAL

N. HUDSON

SHEAFE

HULL

SALEM

FLEETON

N. BENNET

Italian School

MENCHMAN

Christ Church

Freeman School

Eliot School

Ward School

Reading Room

St. John the Baptist (Portuguese)

Associated Charities

St. Stephen's

Mission for Scandinavian Seamen

et St. ...tria ...chool

ul Revere ...chool ...ground

Baptist ...hel

OVER

FLEET

CLARK

NORTH

MOON

SUN CT.

North Sq. ...ear ...us ...lian)

St. John's Parochial Public School (Moon St. School)

Salvation Army

LEWIS

ATLANTIC AVE.

CHARTER

HANOVER

BATTERY

COMMERCIAL

COMMERCIAL

MERCIAL

Scale in Rods

0   10   20   30   40

⅛ Mile

for children chiefly of foreign birth and wholly of foreign parentage. At the North End of Boston, the public schools have to deal with a child population of which more than ninety per cent. is of Hebrew or Italian blood. Certainly half these children were born on foreign soil, while the remainder come from homes scarcely touched by American influences, and where the English language is only imperfectly known.

The universally significant facts among such a school population are only those incidental to the elementary schools, and an attempt to picture the local school life can hardly overstate the importance of these grades, or paint their meaning to the child in too vivid colors. There is no high-school building in the schoolhouse group that lies to the northwest of Hanover Street, nor is there need of one. "From the kindergarten to the master's class" defines the entire school career of a child who, in comparison with his fellows, may be looked upon as having received a thorough education. A sketch of the years included within these limits is practically all that is required in an effort to show the relation between the public school and the immigrant child.

The goal of the master's class, to which comparatively few attain, is reached by two converging paths: by the regular course of promotions, following the kindergarten through nine primary and grammar grades; or by a less well understood period of instruction, known as " ungraded class work." The distinctive peculiarity of school work at the North End is the ungraded class for newly arrived foreign children. This is a characteristic necessity in a district where a master may say of his graduating class, " Twenty-seven out of forty-two were born in Russia; and from three to five years ago not one of those twenty-seven could speak English." Another remark made by the same master shows more fundamentally the need and nature of ungraded work at the North End : " We have five fresh from the steamer to-day. They go into the ungraded classes for special language work, and they will be pushed ahead as fast as possible toward their proper grades."

Pouring constantly into the ungraded classes are European children of the most impressionable age, whose first acquaintance with American life and whose only hope of a good command of the English tongue lie in the public schools. Nearly all of them, of course, have had more or less school training in their native language; but, for a time, they are as speechless, for all practical American purposes, as newly entered pupils in the Horace Mann

School, for deaf mutes, at the other end of the city.

The devotion and skill with which the North End teachers perform their task of making the dumb to speak strengthen the parallel. Their success is astonishing, even with the average child; while the occasional, phenomenal results are almost beyond belief. " Land on Saturday, settle on Sunday, school on Monday, vote on Tuesday" is a proverb among the teachers ; and one is inclined to take the saying literally after conversing with a Russian girl sixteen years of age who, leaving the steamer the first of March without a word of English at her command, is explaining to a visitor by the middle of May that her only real difficulty in seventh grade work is with the text-book of United States history, which seems to her written in another language from the one she is learning to speak.

" And the English these children give us back," says an enthusiastic master, " is our own English." Enthusiasm is found everywhere among the instructors of foreign children, and with it is a corresponding fervor of belief in the ability of their pupils, especially the Hebrews, who are said to " rush through the grades as soon as they get the language."

The process of getting the language is worthy of attention, particularly in its beginning. Side by side in an ungraded class sit little women of seven or eight, miniature European peasants in dress and bearing, and older girls, for whom a fortnight has sufficed almost to eliminate Russian or Italian peculiarities of costume. These children are ungraded as to years, but all are of one grade in speechlessness and in eagerness to learn the strange tongue of the new land. Their progress is suggestive of dawning intelligence in babies, and the surprised happiness of one face after another, as each in her order of quickness catches an idea, is indescribably touching in its almost infantile spontaneity. Over and over, in quiet pleasant tones, the teacher repeats every-day words and simple sentences, accompanying them by explanatory gestures, until at last " Rise " and " File " and " Put your pencil *in* your desk " and " Put your pencil *on* your desk " have accomplished their purpose, and the class is ready for more abstract ideas.

It is not language alone that these new little citizens acquire in the early days of public-school life. Not the least important result of the speedy transition from ship to school may be traced to the fact that the schoolhouse steps lead to a practical knowledge of law as well as letters. " Fresh from the steamer " is no figure of speech, and the short time that elapses before the immigrant child becomes a registered member of the school world gives him little opportunity to fall into the lawlessness that naturally attends a change of environment. The school's neighborhood representative, the truant officer, does much, directly and indirectly, to bring about this speedy enrollment in the blue book of the school ; yet he is not always obliged to take the initiative. The parents' own preconceived idea, that America means education, is usually aided by the quickly volunteered information of more experienced neighbors that the place for children is in school. An interesting sight in the office of a North End school is a flock of frightened little foreigners under the kindly guardianship of an Americanized relative ; or, more pathetic still, shepherded by an equally frightened, speechless mother, who can make known only by signs that she wishes her offspring started upon the right road. Probably neither children nor parents have any idea how stringent and far-reaching is the jurisdiction under which they are now coming. By means of teachers and truant officer, the school practically dictates the conduct of the child during his waking hours. The precision with which the complicated school machinery moves, in a district where its obstacles are of the most unique and baffling description, is a tribute to the imagination, as well as to the diligence, of the executive force. Not a child shall be lost seems to be the motto, — and it is a practically accomplished ideal. Chevan Panhasky, as occasionally happens, in her enthusiasm for things American, may elect between terms to be known henceforth as Celia Smith. The school does not dispute her right even while deploring her taste. Her disappearance must be accounted for, however, though it mean weeks of effort, and until Celia Smith has explained her identity, search for the missing Panhasky is not given over.

Such is the beginning of school life for a large part of the children who will quickly be the English-speaking, and therefore the influential, residents of the North End, — the more disciplined, and therefore the controlling, members of the community. As a general result of these years of training, there is an ability on the part of the children to speak a fairly pure English tongue and to understand a purer one ; to comprehend the penalty of broken law, if not to feel the beauty of law preserved. A glance at the dialect of some realistic novel whose scene is laid in an East London slum gives a vivid idea of the difference it might make, to both state and individual, were these

same little foreign people left to acquire a street
vernacular and limited for life to such a feeble,
squalid vehicle as that; while only a slight observation of any crowded immigrant quarter brings a
menacing conception of what a future generation
would be were it bred in American freedom without American law.

At the other end of the path, to which many
find their way through the ungraded class, is the
master's class, with its hope of the grammar school
diploma. This, as has been suggested, is the definite educational goal of the children of this quarter of the city. To attain it is to " graduate," an
achievement which ranks here, in popular regard,
with graduation from the high school in another
district, or the obtaining of a college degree in yet
more favored circles, — though neither high school
nor college is entirely unknown or unsought.
Each September, indeed, a surprisingly large
number of boys, and a handful of girls, go up to
the high schools at the South End, carrying their
grammar school diplomas as certificates of admission. Not infrequently the boys have in view
college or professional training. That the girls
never have, and that the proportion going further
than the grammar school is so small, is due, not
to lack of ability or inclination, and not wholly

to straitened means, but to the custom of early marriage, which is particularly strong among the Hebrews.

It seems truly unfortunate that girls who show both talent and desire should be denied the privilege of higher studies; but the more serious evil is that so few children, boys or girls, should have the training of the entire nine grades of the elementary schools. These high school candidates are favored representatives of an already picked corps, and their existence does not detract from the statement that the facts incidental to the elementary schools are the only ones of universal significance. The graduating class of a grammar school is a small part of the children who entered some six years before. The law requires that children between seven and fourteen years of age shall be in school; but at every stage in the course these immigrant children, so unevenly started, are attaining their sad majority. Where two hundred enter, only about fifty graduate. The master's class ranks in school nomenclature as ninth grade. Between it and the grade below there is no appreciable diminution in numbers; but between the seventh and eighth grades the difference is pitifully great. Only about half the children who leave the seventh grade in June reappear after the long vacation to enter the

eighth grade. The reports of the schools composed
largely of the children of immigrants show approximately that seventy-five per cent. of the pupils
never reach the eighth grade ; that a fraction of
this seventy-five per cent., moreover, are unable
to keep up in the regular course, and are given
instruction in what English educators call " special
difficulty classes " ; and that of those who do complete the nine grades, one half the boys and four
fifths of the girls do not go further. Such statistics bring out clearly the vital meaning of the
elementary schools in districts like the North End,
and the imperative need of a curriculum specifically
adapted to children who must get all the educational training they will ever get in the public
schools and before their fifteenth year.

Pupils leave school for a variety of reasons. A
broad division of these reasons might be made
under the heads of *poverty* and *lack of interest.*
Instances of the first in the cases of pupils of
unquestionable ability are many and touching.
To alter this is a hope of the future. The immediate concern is to secure a school curriculum
that will remedy the second condition, and at the
same time give to those to whom the first applies
the best training the few years admit ; to make
school life so practical and attractive that an effort

to keep the children in school will be made by the parents and will not be resisted by the boys and girls. The necessary routine of language, geography and arithmetic is a heavy burden for children who cannot in any way connect these studies with their home lives. Something is needed to help float the load, — something that will both enliven school hours and bring them more closely into relation with the homes and every-day experiences. Various expedients are tried, and most hopeful among them is industrial training of different sorts. In this work the children are happy; the parents understand and approve it; and observant teachers state concerning it that the actual working power of the pupils seems increased by the relaxation and pleasure of the change. The special importance of industrial training in the immigrant districts is emphasized by a glance at a list of parents' employments, taken from the records of an ungraded class, — 27 laborers, 1 clerk in bar-room, 3 barbers, 1 dressmaker, 3 tailors, 4 peddlers, 1 housekeeper, 4 organ grinders, 1 stone cutter, 1 harness maker, 1 rag picker, 1 rabbi, 2 shoemakers, 1 undertaker, 1 clerk, 2 fishermen, 2 bricklayers, 1 blacksmith, 1 baker, 1 painter, 1 gravedigger, 1 fruit vender.

"I am weary," says Ruskin, "of seeing the

subject of education treated as if education meant only teaching children to write and cipher. The real education, the only education which should be compulsory, means nothing of the kind ; it means teaching children to be clean, active, honest and useful." Out of twenty-five school hours a week, the time devoted to pursuits specifically in line with the great man's ideal is given as follows in the Course of Study for the Boston Grammar Schools published in 1899 : —

Moral training, one half hour a week.

Physical training and recesses, three hours a week.

Manual training, two hours a week.

To this should be added, in a discussion of the North End, the time allowed in the Paul Revere School for a weekly bath.

The new building of this school is a marked result of the increasing responsibility the city feels towards its child population and their special, local needs. The school's spacious basement is lighted by electricity and furnished with shower baths. Here six hundred little children are bathed each week; and by one who knows anything of North End tenement houses the question of the necessity of public bathing facilities will not be raised. Not long since a kindergarten teacher had occasion to remove a child's frock for the purpose of trying on a garment. The child was found to be completely encased in woolen rags sewed securely around its body. Upon the teacher's applying the scissors to some of the stitches, the child screamed: " Don't do that, my mamma's got me sewed up for all winter ! " From the standpoint of the foreign mother there was nothing reprehensible in this, but it is plain that the convenient sewing-up system must vanish before the introduction of the public bath. It is close by the Paul Revere school that the city has reserved a lot of land for one of its public playgrounds, and in some of the neighboring school buildings the plan of leaving schoolyards open for the children's use is also being tried.

The North End schools are fortunate in being in close connection with two philanthropic enterprises, the North End Union and the North Bennet Street Industrial School, and the buildings of both are so near as practically to form a part of the great public schoolhouse group. Both these institutions supplement the training of the schools by clubs and free classes. In the day of its founding, the North Bennet Street Industrial School had no parallel among the public schools of the city in its methods. That industrial training is now given throughout the city is largely due to its founder, Mrs. Quincy Shaw, and the noble example she set in its establishment. The Eliot Grammar School has not yet facilities for manual training, but once a week its boys are sent down the street to the Industrial School, where, through Mrs. Shaw's liberality, they receive more varied and extensive training than is given by the city. A choice is offered between modeling, carpentering, printing and leather-work, and the boys are divided about equally in their tastes. One of the results of both these institutions is that pupils once in the day classes are likely to follow up their work after business hours in the evening classes.

The industrial training given in the grammar school is received with intelligent appreciation by the boys and girls of the three upper grades. For the girls the term implies instruction in sewing and cooking. The latter is perhaps the more popular occupation, and the girls regret so keenly being obliged to give it up upon entering the master's class that a special arrangement has been made in the Hancock School by which the pupils of the ninth grade are given an opportunity several times during the year to prepare and serve a dinner for the teachers. The work that goes on in the charming upstairs kitchen of the Hancock School really should be dignified by the name Domestic Science. That it implies something far more serious than even the important art of cooking will be granted when it is understood that there are some among the girls of each successive class who, from religious scruples, never taste what they painstakingly and happily prepare; and there are many others who will eat only a limited number of dishes. It is the ways of healthful, happy homes that the girls catch a glimpse of during the two hours a week that for two years of their school life they spend in the upstairs kitchen. A woman who comes into unusually sympathetic relations with the daughters of immigrants says, as a result of her years of experience, that she is convinced that it is not the acquisition of facts but cultivation that the foreign girls need for their future happiness and usefulness, — correct ideas of life, and freedom from superstition, rather than definite knowledge about trade winds and syntax. Within two or three years of leaving school, sometimes sooner, these girls are wives and mothers. If the object of education is to fit for life, it seems hardly an open question whether industrial training under skilled, cultivated direction does not contribute as much to the desired end as the more academic branches. One far-reaching, desirable function it certainly fulfills, — that of a connecting link between school and home. The girls can discuss sewing and cooking with their mothers when they have no language to discuss trade winds and syntax; and they constantly demonstrate the material results of their training in a fashion highly acceptable to the whole family. It does not seem improbable that marriage might be delayed a year or two if fathers and mothers could see that a further school course would mean definite training for the life that is to them the only life a girl should look forward to. The question of difference in ideals has an important bearing upon any discussion of the early training that best fits for life. The daughters of Russian and Italian immigrants do not look upon teaching, bookkeeping, stenography or shop-tending as aims of life. They simply and openly desire a sound mind, so far as they understand it, within a sound body, that they may make good wives and present their husbands with healthy sons.

The mere fact of graduation is urged strenuously by the teachers, even when there is no hope of the high school for pupils, because of their belief of the important effect it has upon the children's after-life. A grammar school diploma, framed and hanging upon the wall, confers academic dig-

nity upon a home. The possession of it entitles
the owner to various social privileges. One advantage that comes from graduation is the right of
membership in the old graduates' associations.
There are a number of these at the North and
West Ends. Thus far they have been composed
largely of those who made their homes in the district in its more prosperous days. Recent graduates are becoming eager to join as soon as they are
so circumstanced as to afford the entrance fee.
The associations hold occasional reunions in addition to their business meetings, and they show their
love for the old school in various practical ways.
One society supports a library in the school building, and in addition to this pleasant aid to school
work, it has recently added a fine stereopticon, which
is in constant use. Each school building is a social
centre in the chance which its " public days "
afford for reunions, and it is the pupils who have
achieved graduation who are apt to come back,
feeling sure of welcome and recognition from the
teachers. Graduates' clubs, made up of members
of individual classes, are well-known features of
the neighborhood. In their organization and functions they are a credit to their schools, and they
show the force of a master's statement that the
ninth grade illustrates the survival of the fittest.

A study of these yearly survivors, their conditions and their victory over conditions would be intensely interesting were there time for such an examination. The members of the graduating class and the grade below it hold their places, as a rule, through ability and force of character, and not infrequently, it should be noted, as a result of great sacrifice on the part of their parents. It is no easy matter for fathers and mothers limited as to language and educational traditions, and forever under the galling conditions of precarious employment, to allow a boy or girl capable of adding to the family income to spend five hours a day in school and one or more in home study. The wonder is that it is ever done; for while the attainment of a grammar school diploma is an honor, failure to attain it is not looked upon as a disgrace. To be without it, in the eyes of the parents, is hardly a deprivation. The children themselves show independence and business enterprise in the struggle. In the Eliot School alone three hundred and fifty boys are licensed newsboys and bootblacks. But it is still likely that the lists of graduates would diminish in the face of such obstacles were it not for the encouragement of the teachers and their interest in individual pupils. If children show ability they are pushed through the grades as fast as can be done conscientiously. This is in order that they may reach the eighth grade at least before the age limit is attained; for at the eighth grade begins a sort of home stretch where children and parents have caught their second breath, and become able to endure to the end.

The meaning of school life to some of those who have been thus hurried on may be read in the stirring autobiographies that the graduating class of one school is each year asked to write. Refugees from Russian persecution tell in eloquent, well-chosen words personal experiences holding all the elements of tragic drama, and they picture vividly the contrast between the conditions of their European homes and the school privileges of America. The intelligent appreciation and the frequent literary merit of these records are among the things that place the foreign poor and their possibilities in an entirely new light, and arouse the devotion and enthusiasm of those who come in contact with them in the schools. In a survey of the immigrant quarter of the city, where the combination of foreign habits and extreme poverty results in such deplorable conditions, it must not be forgotten that dwelling in the midst of these conditions there are those capable of rising above them, not only from sporadic ability, but also by reason of naturally inherited powers. The determination that has kept Judea a name for two thousand years, the fire that made Italy one and free, are in our North End schools being developed and directed by what the City provides. Side by side with sluggish Sicily sits eloquent, ambitious Lombardy; while among the Hebrew children are the sons and daughters of men of learning, whom only a foreign tongue keeps in such narrow circumstances. Thus it is not surprising that there is real ability among the holders of the grammar school diplomas, and it seems beyond question that their after-lives justify the effort of the attainment. " The Jewish boys will take from a third to a half of our prizes right along," writes an English High School teacher. " Out of thirty Franklin medals awarded in 1897, 1898, 1899, five were awarded to boys from the Eliot School at the North End. The results of the awarding of Franklin medals in June, 1900, show that five of the ten were given to Jewish boys from the North and West Ends." The prize winners do not all stop here. On the rolls of the law and medical schools of Boston and Cambridge are increasingly recorded Russian and Italian names; while already in the city there are men of foreign birth and North End breeding who have made their way through high school and university, and are now practising their professions close by the schools from which they received their first diplomas.

From such statements as these, and from a visit to the schools, one might be led to suppose that the shifting of population has left the district entirely Continental in its racial character. This is not quite true. Though the Irish race is being pushed out of its old home by the new immigrants, the change has not taken place as entirely as the appearance of the public schools would indicate. Some twelve hundred children, of whom the larger part are of Irish birth or descent, are cared for by the parochial school system of the Roman Catholic Church. St. Mary's School, in the old armory building on Endicott Street, numbers 630 pupils; St. Stephen's School has 550. The schools accommodate both boys and girls, though they are not coeducational in their plan. The instructors are all women. The lady in charge, and the teachers under whom the girls are placed, are sisters of a religious order. The boys are in charge of lay teachers, graduates of church schools. In both these schools the preference is given to Irish children. St. Stephen's school is still almost exclusively Celtic, but St. Mary's is feeling the change in population, and dark Italian faces are

thickly sprinkled among the fairer children of
the earlier inhabitants.   Each parochial school includes the regulation nine primary and grammar
grades, and a " receiving class " somewhat corresponding to the public kindergarten.   For ungraded classes they have as yet no need.   St.
Stephen's school has an additional three years'
course of high school work for girls.   The graduating class of the grammar school consists of about
fifteen boys and girls.

The grade work of the parochial schools is very
similar to that of the public schools, though from
lack of funds it is necessarily limited to bare essentials.   The diplomas of both schools admit boys
to Boston College, a Jesuit institution, but not
to the public high schools.   Boys who intend to go
further are preparing for the most part to enter
the former institution, at which St. Mary's school
has four scholarships.   Alike as the public schools
and the church schools are in many ways, their
dissimilarities are yet marked and interesting.
Church symbols and ecclesiastical uniform, in the
parochial schools, everywhere lend their own subtle
charm and influence to the modern schoolroom
atmosphere.   In the daily work, certainly as much
time as the public schools allow for their nature study
and industrial work — both of which the parochial

school is obliged to forego — is taken up in the
lines that specially distinguish the parochial school
system, — religious exercises and instruction. One
half hour of religious instruction is given each
day. School sessions open and close with devo-
tional exercises. Every half hour, at St. Mary's
school, little heads are dropped for a moment of
prayer. The books used are partly those of the
public schools; but some are, of course, special in
their nature. The school reader is markedly ecclesiastical in its tone.

One aspect of the public school system of the
North End is too interesting to be passed over,
though it has little connection with the child life
of the district, — and that is the work of the evening classes. Very few children attend. The six
hundred pupils who meet in the Eliot School for five
months in the year are mostly men over eighteen
years of age, recent immigrants who come to school
to learn the language. The plan is practically that
of the ungraded classes already described. The
Italians are the predominating race; next to them
come the Russian Jews. Between the adult pupils
of these two races there exists the most childish
and unreasonable antagonism, which at times becomes so violent in its expression that it is not
feasible for them to mix in class work. Offense

is taken upon the slightest occasion. The oppro-
brious epithets of "Dago" and "Sheeny" are
apparently the earliest and easiest of English
words. A class of Italians is said, not long since,
to have got into such an uproar that the presence of the head master was necessary to quell
the incipient riot. The teacher, a man of German
extraction, proved unequal to the emergency, and
was ignorant of the origin of the outbreak. When
quiet had been restored, and inquiries were being
made, the class insisted, in the face of the German's protestations, that he had called them
"Dagos." After much discussion the mystery
was cleared up. The teacher, in course of instruction, had repeated the familiar conjugation of
"to go." His Teutonic accent had transformed the
innocent plural into the unfortunate sounds of
"We go, you go, *Dago*," and his class, to a man,
had furiously resented the insult.

As in the case of the children of the day
schools, the Hebrews are far cleverer with books
than the Italians, and do more advanced work.
With either race considerable determination is
required to face the discomforts attendant upon
evening school instruction. The session begins
at 7.30. Most of the men come direct from
work, thus going without their suppers till half

past nine. The rooms are close and crowded; the teaching force, though of excellent quality, is inadequate as to numbers; and the men, sometimes gray-headed, and as often as not middle-aged, are painfully squeezed between seats and desks planned for children anywhere from nine to fifteen years of age.

Quite the most interesting class in the building is a roomful of Greeks, — strong, good-looking young fellows, most of whom have received a fair education in their own country. Some among them are university graduates. Two years ago the Greek class chanced to be made up of fifty young Spartans. Now the membership is from various parts of Greece. The distinction of the class lies in its teacher, — a young Greek who has been several years in this country and has volunteered his services to his countrymen as instructor in the language in which he has become fluent himself. The class is conducted in good modern Greek, used as a medium of instruction in English. Most of these men are fruit venders and, except for a few months in the winter, are roaming about the country in various capacities connected with the fruit trade.

The importance of making still further use of ample school buildings, situated in such a densely inhabited district, has for a long time been keenly felt by the North End teachers.   One master, with a number of his assistants, has formed a corps of instruction, serving without pay, to meet in the evening the more advanced day school pupils and assist them with the preparation of their lessons and in other ways.   Pupils who wish only to come and read by themselves are encouraged to do so.   During the latter part of last winter the North End was one of the two sections of the city in which the School Board began a new and admirable experiment in the way of making the schoolhouse a centre for evening instruction in certain interesting forms of handicraft as well as for popular lectures and various forms of social recreation.[1]

The possible significance of an ideal school life perfectly adapted to the needs of a locality cannot be overestimated ; the actual significance of any school life is great and, with rare exceptions, implies happiness and growth.   These are general truths, and their force is increased when applied to children for whom school is not simply the most important interest, but usually the only daily interest representing high ideals and development. It is too much to expect of youth that it will fully appreciate its privileges.   Yet it is clear to a care-

[1] The board has also begun to provide vacation schools.

ful observer that school life is on the whole enjoyed, notwithstanding much adult misapprehension,
which too often expresses itself in undiscriminating
and sweeping criticism. Just as all life has its
dreary spots, so school life is not exempt. A comparison of the mere creature comforts of the
schoolroom with the average home of the poorer
districts, an acquaintance with the attractive devices used by teachers to lighten the burden of the
elementary studies, and especially an intelligent
appreciation of the spirit and skill of the instructors, must bring any fair mind to the conviction that the public school, with all its defects, is
the happiest, most hopeful part of child existence
in the North End. The discouraging statements
of truancy may be urged against this position.
The question of truancy, however, has many sides.
The line between culpable and excusable absence
is hard to draw, and often confirmed truancy is a
habit resulting from repeated discouragements that
lie neither at the door of the school nor at that of
the pupil. A drunken mother, a dying baby sister,
a chance for work compelling both parents to be
away from home and throwing the care of some
half dozen younger children upon the shoulders of
a boy or girl of twelve, — these are conditions,
reported by the truant officer, that force a teacher

into reluctant charity for even such flagrant offenders as truants, and cause her to feel that too
harsh reproof may be outraging a child's finest
instincts.

Children of the school age are profoundly affected by imagination and ambition. The school
appeals to both these qualities, though more successfully, as yet, to the latter. The spirit of emulation is strong in the public schools, and while
it occasionally may be forced to excess, its general
results are good and productive of sound growth.
Children value the visible symbol of success, and the
ingenious teacher takes advantage of this feeling.
The position of monitor, even though the duty im-
plied be nothing more than sharpening pencils;
the possession of the little flag, loaned to the line
that goes through the gymnastic exercises with the
most military precision, — such distinctions as these
are stimulating in possibility and give much joy
when attained. To be head boy of the fourth or
fifth grade is an honor as keenly appreciated as
municipal preferment of a later day. To hold
two hundred fellow pupils spellbound while one
thunders the speech of John Adams from the platform, with only a suggestion of Italy in one's ac-
cents, is perhaps as intoxicating as any success of
after life. Moreover, it is an incentive to manly

bearing to file in and out, upstairs and down, a big brick building several times a day feeling that the eyes of great men are upon you, as master and assistants watch your progress and note your possible forgetfulness to doff your cap.

Such influences as these are calculated to work toward manliness and patriotism, though just here lurks a possible defect of public school education — one that must be recognized to be averted. " You taught me language," mocks Caliban at his master, " and my profit on't is, I know how to curse." The patriot is preceded by " Young America" in the little citizen's development. It will depend much upon the work of the elementary schools whether Americanism stops with unprincipled partisanship and bombastic jingoism, as embodied in ward politics, or develops into genuine, intelligent love of country. Certainly the change which comes over the children is a swift and apparently spontaneous one. A little girl of foreign birth and stammering tongue, in one of the lower grades, tells an English visitor that the beautiful portrait of the Father of his Country, hanging upon the schoolroom wall, is Buffalo Bill. This is the beginning. A few grades higher a group of boys of foreign birth are celebrating Washington's birthday. In mimic scene they reproduce the proceedings of the last Continental Congress, statesman after statesman answering as his name is called. The gentleman from Virginia delivers himself of his great utterances, hardly able to await his turn; the gentleman from Pennsylvania protests in vain; all at last agree vehemently to hang together or to hang separately, and they affix their names to an imaginary Declaration of Independence, their audience cheering the while with excitement and joining with the patriots later in singing fervently and unquestioningly "Land where our fathers died."

It is deliberate choice on the part of both boys and girls to ignore their foreign origin. They are American, and at times disappointingly American. Their very names become unlovely to their Anglicized ears, and the result is often a bewildering change that asks neither the advice of elders nor the consent of the law. Their taste in amusements undergoes a similar change. Should the student of comparative folk-lore pursue his researches in the North End, he would be met by the familiar strains of "Sally Waters," and he would find the polyglot Russian boys preferring to discuss "craps" in English, rather than to conduct some European game in their inherited Yiddish or Slavic tongues. If a dramatic club is formed, the children choose American plays; and in all entertainments their national airs give way to the street songs of the city and the patriotic hymns of the school. The Hebrews have had no country; the Italians have found a better one; the new land is large enough for both: and while Hebrews affiliate with Hebrews and Italians with Italians, there seems to be no recognized antagonism between them more serious than a strong feeling of class superiority on the part of each race.

Such a state of things during school life is bound to have its influence upon future conditions, the more so because the direct influence of the elementary schools is not soon outgrown. Even to the boys and girls who go higher, the grammar school remains the most tangible object of affectionate loyalty. Children cannot spend from five to ten years in one locality, with one set of interests, under leaders better known and of more immediate importance than the President and his Cabinet, without strong ties being formed; and these ties, as the school course nears its end, are made closer by charming devices. The story of the master's class is a tale by itself. Boys and girls who reach that stage of advancement, who go through the impressive ceremonies of graduation, who leave the big brick schoolhouse carrying

a grammar school diploma, take out into the world
not only the sense of dignity that comes from
attainment, and from possession of the rudiments
of knowledge, but also sentiments, memories and
traditions, enriched by a consciousness of warm
and enduring friendship with masters and teachers,
which deepen as the years go by.

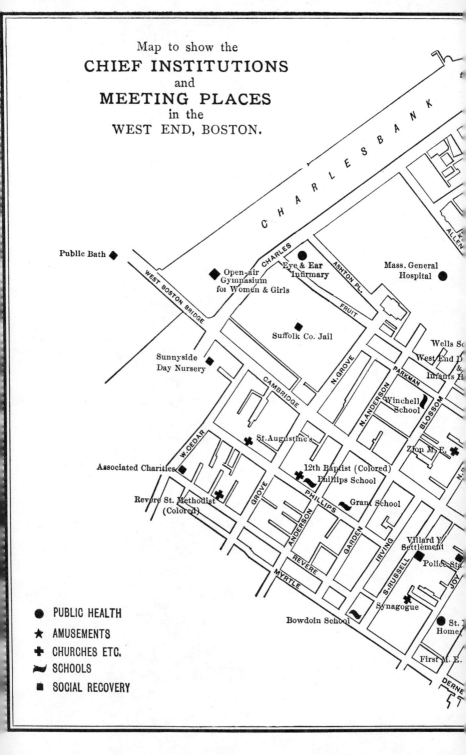

Map to show the
CHIEF INSTITUTIONS
and
MEETING PLACES
in the
WEST END, BOSTON.

CHARLESBANK

Public Bath

Open-air Gymnasium for Women & Girls

Eye & Ear Infirmary

Mass. General Hospital

WEST BOSTON BRIDGE

CHARLES

ASHTON PL.

FRUIT

Suffolk Co. Jail

Sunnyside Day Nursery

Wells Sc

West End D &
Infants H

N. GROVE

N. ANDERSON

PARKMAN

CAMBRIDGE

Winchell School

BLOSSOM

W. CEDAR

St. Augustine's

Zion M. E.

Associated Charities

12th Baptist (Colored)
Phillips School

GROVE

Revere St. Methodist (Colored)

PHILLIPS

Grant School

ANDERSON

GARDEN

IRVING

Villard Y
Settlement

Police Sta

REVERE

S. RUSSELL

JOY

MYRTLE

Synagogue

Bowdoin School

St.
Home

First M. E.

DERNE

● PUBLIC HEALTH
★ AMUSEMENTS
✚ CHURCHES ETC.
〰 SCHOOLS
■ SOCIAL RECOVERY

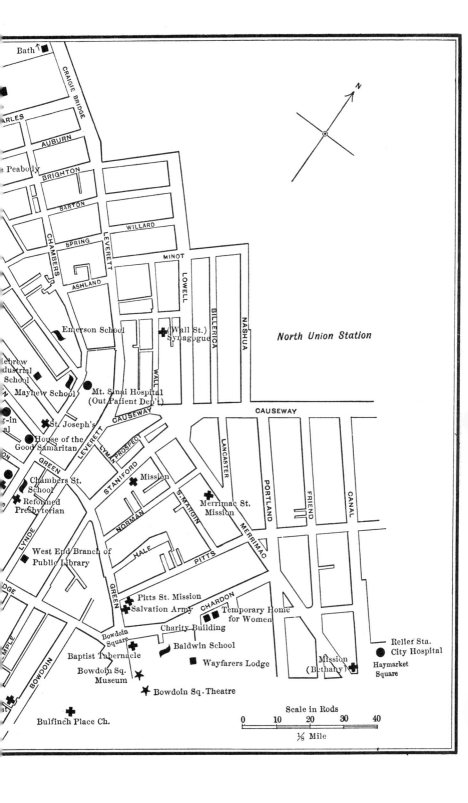

Bath

CRAIGIE BRIDGE

ARLES

AUBURN

Peabody

BRIGHTON

CHAMBERS

BARTON

SPRING

WILLARD

LEVERETT

MINOT

ASHLAND

LOWELL

BILLERICA

NASHUA

North Union Station

Emerson School

(Wall St.) Synagogue

Hebrew Industrial School

WALL

Mayhew School

Mt. Sinai Hospital (Out Patient Dep't)

CAUSEWAY

CAUSEWAY

St. Joseph's

LEVERETT

LYMAN

PROSPECT

House of the Good Samaritan

GREEN

STANIFORD

Mission

LANCASTER

PORTLAND

FRIEND

CANAL

ing-in al

Chambers St. School

NORMAN

S. MARGIN

Merrimac St. Mission

Reformed Presbyterian

HALE

PITTS

MERRIMAC

LYNDE

West End Branch of Public Library

GREEN

Pitts St. Mission

CHARDON

Salvation Army

Temporary Home for Women

BOWDOIN

DGE

Bowdoin Square

Charity Building

Baldwin School

Reller Sta.

City Hospital

MPLE

Baptist Tabernacle

Wayfarers Lodge

Mission (Bethany)

Haymarket Square

Bowdoin Sq. Museum

Bowdoin Sq. Theatre

Bulfinch Place Ch.

Scale in Rods

0   10   20   30   40

⅛ Mile

CHAPTER XI

PHILANTHROPY, as it is now understood, must work with rather than for those whom it would help. Defective parts of human society can never be repaired from without like parts of a broken machine; they must share actively in working out their own salvation. On the other hand, any part of society that needs regeneration is little likely to accomplish the task by itself. Social reform, to be in the highest degree sound and permanent, must spring from the coöperation of all classes. Yet nearly all efforts at social reform lean to one side or the other. They are predominantly either exertions of certain public-spirited individuals in behalf of others, or else spontaneous unaided efforts of the mass in its own interest. In a few cases — and here lie the greatest possibilities — the two elements are combined more equally.

Enterprises designed to secure and maintain the indispensable conditions of a wholesome life, without which a person can hardly be expected to stand

on his own feet, are almost inevitably of the first sort
— efforts for people. They may fairly be called
remedial, in that they strive for a state of social
health in which all individuals shall be capable of
self-direction and self-support. Not only the ordinary material relief agencies, but those providing
medical aid, care of children and proper housing
conditions are of this kind.

The spontaneous form is seen in the effort to
satisfy sometimes widespread desires, sometimes
merely private, local wants. Such are trade unions,
social clubs, patriotic orders among the Italians,
benefit orders and Zionism among the Jews.

The third form, the coöperative, finding its opportunity after the remedial has supplied the absolute essentials, and reaching out with intelligent
sympathy to all sorts of popular association, endeavors to lead to higher levels of thought and life.
It includes, therefore, the church, the school, privately established educational experiments and the
social settlement with its varied programme of local
improvement.

This classification implies no judgment. The
three classes are not three levels, one above another; they simply represent different kinds of
work demanded by different circumstances. An
enterprise in any one of the three divisions may

do really constructive work in the sense of achieving some fresh adaptation of the community's means to its needs, of making some distinct gain, more or less permanent, in guiding social energy toward the accomplishment of useful social ends. Nevertheless, the most effective philanthropic work is that directed by disinterested intelligence which seeks the coöperation of those to be helped.

In districts like the North and West Ends, where a large proportion of the population is foreign in habits of life and thought, even when not in birth, and quite unacquainted with the ideas of modern democracy, it is to be expected that most of the social effort should come from without. The immigrant from Russia or Italy, accustomed to the tyranny of the Czar's police or to the exactions of the tax-gatherer, naturally devotes all his energies toward making some place for himself and his family in the whirl of new life into which he has plunged. Had he the aptitude for concern about the common welfare, he lacks the time. Furthermore, the idea of his having any influence upon the conduct of public affairs is bewilderingly novel; the possibility, too, of combining with his neighbors even for purely private purposes is a privilege not at once appreciated. Remedial agencies, therefore — effort of outsiders for the district — have the most imposing equipment and present the greatest array of activities. Since the needs to which they minister are for the most part concrete and easily distinguished, the methods of dealing with them are correspondingly well reasoned out and highly developed.

It happens that in a single building in the West End most of the large relief-giving organizations of the city, both public and private, have their headquarters. The Charity Building on Chardon Street, under the management of the Overseers of the Poor, furnishes offices to some fifteen charitable societies, rent free, except that they share the running expenses of the building.

The municipal provision for poor relief is in the hands of two boards, — the Overseers of the Poor, who have charge of outdoor relief [1] and temporary lodging and meals, and the Pauper Institutions Trustees, controlling the two almshouses. The outdoor relief of the Overseers is intended only to furnish partial support; the entirely dependent are cared for by the Pauper Institutions. In the last twenty-five years, though there has been a slight increase in the total amount of outdoor relief, the number of families aided has been reduced

[1] Outdoor relief is aid furnished to families in their homes, in distinction from the indoor relief of the almshouses.

by one half, thus doubling the average amount per family. The inference is that each family receives more effective treatment than formerly. The Overseers also have the administration of private trust funds for various designated purposes, amounting to three quarters of a million dollars. Under the direction of the Overseers, too, the Temporary Home on Chardon Street and the Wayfarers' Lodge on Hawkins Street furnish for short periods shelter and food, — the one to women and children, the other to men. The women perform the household duties of the Home, while the men work in a woodyard. It is upwards of twenty years ago that Boston did away with the old system of giving temporary lodging in police stations. At that time some 60,000 men sought such lodging in the course of a year; now, owing to the increasingly strict rules of the Lodge in the matter of cleanliness and sanitation, and its steady insistence on the work equivalent for lodging and meals, the number of tramps has greatly diminished. A fair proportion of those who come to the Lodge are young or middle-aged able-bodied men, neither professionally vagrant nor vicious, but moderately able workmen. Industrial disturbances over a wide area are felt in the fluctuation of numbers at the Lodge.

If all the private relief agencies including the city in their scope were to be enumerated in these pages, this chapter would be converted into a directory; for more nearly than any other American city, Boston resembles London in inheriting from the past a legacy of charitable societies. Out of the long list a few accomplish the most of what is done, especially in the North and West Ends : the Associated Charities and the Provident Association, the Federation of Jewish Charities, the St. Vincent de Paul, and several smaller societies which devote themselves to the needy of a particular race or creed. Some of these aim to be more than relief dispensers, and endeavor, by getting at the main causes of need, to effect a permanent remedy.

The Associated Charities organization, which now has twenty-five years of activity behind it, declares its main objects to be " to raise the needy above the need of relief, prevent begging and imposition and diminish pauperism." To further these ends it strives " to secure the concurrent and harmonious action of the different charities in Boston," and " to encourage thrift, self-dependence and industry through friendly intercourse, advice and sympathy." In effect, the society is a clearing-house, referring cases to the appropriate special agency or, if none such is available, itself assuming charge. As an organization it furnishes no direct relief, but procures it, when necessary, from others. Its mechanism is well known: the city is divided into districts, each of which is cared for by a paid agent in coöperation with a group of people willing to do what they can in the way of personal service. The agent does most of the investigating and executive work, while the volunteers undertake the friendly visiting. The negative objects at which the society aims are of course less difficult of accomplishment than the positive: it is much easier to " prevent begging and imposition " and, to a less extent, to prevent the duplication of effort than " to raise the needy above the need of relief " and " to diminish pauperism." Accordingly, the society has been the more conspicuously successful in the former tasks. Four of its conferences share the responsibility of the North and West Ends. Conference VI. cares for the territory lying north of Prince Street and east of Salem and Hanover streets. Hence its work is largely among the Italians. Conferences VII. and VIII. include within their districts those parts of the North and West Ends which constitute the Jewish quarter, and Conference IX. presides over the section where is congregated practically all the Negro population of the West End.

The Society of St. Vincent de Paul is the great Roman Catholic relief-giving agency. It is represented at the North End by conferences at St. Mary's, St. Stephen's and the Sacred Heart of Jesus, and at the West End by a conference at St. Joseph's. Like the Associated Charities, this organization lays considerable stress on friendly visiting.

The Federation of Jewish Charities includes the Hebrew Benevolent Association, the Leopold Morse Home, a free employment bureau and several other societies with special objects. For newly arrived Jewish immigrants the Baron de Hirsch fund makes provision. This fund may be devoted to trade instruction, establishing men in business, forwarding families to friends or to where employment may be secured, or, in case of incapacity for self-support, to returning them to Europe. A home on Cooper Street affords temporary shelter. The Hebrew Benevolent Society aids those who have been in this country for more than a year. Perhaps three fourths of its work is done in the North and West Ends, and most of the remainder in the South End. As compared with the Associated Charities, it is more of a relief-giving organization. Its policy may be described as that of giving relief in such a way as to prevent further necessity for relief ; it provides for whatever subsidy may set breadwinners upon their feet, — temporary removal of children, temporary relief or transportation to another place where work is to be obtained, — while the Associated Charities lays the stress upon personal influence.

The remainder of the agencies make it their chief business to dispense material relief, for the most part visiting only enough to guard against fraud. The various churches, of course, also carry on more or less desultory work of this kind.

Among the larger organizations there is considerable combined effort and division of labor. The Overseers care for those in chronic poverty ; the Associated Charities for those who show some prospect of getting upon their own feet ; the Provident, the Hebrew Benevolent and others, often at the request of the Associated Charities, supply temporary support ; the Jewish Federation and St. Vincent's Society, as far as they can, care for their special constituencies. The information possessed by each is at the service of the others.

The experience of these societies in dealing with the conditions that confront them throughout the city leads one to look to them for certain facts which indicate the part taken by the North and West Ends in the city's problem of poverty. No complete statement can be made, but from the few available records of the leading societies some hints may be gleaned.

Together the two sections contain about 11 per cent. of Boston's population. From them the Long Island Almshouse, which has six sevenths of the city's indoor paupers, draws 18 per cent. of its inmates ; of the persons aided by the Society of St. Vincent de Paul, 12 per cent. live in these districts and receive 13 per cent. of the relief ; the Provident Association distributes 16 per cent. of its coal and groceries here ; and the Associated Charities for five or more years has found 30 per cent. of its cases in this section. These districts appear, therefore, to be receiving aid in proportion greater than that of their population, yet perhaps not in such excess as might be imagined. With an increase of 20 per cent. in the population of the district between 1895 and 1900, the percentage of coal and groceries received by it from the Provident since 1890 has fallen off from 28 to 16. In the same period, the number of persons in the entire city receiving aid from the Society of St. Vincent de Paul has increased 50 per cent., while in these districts the increase has been slight. Parallel with this there has been for the whole city a small increase in the amount of relief; for the

North and West Ends, a slight decrease. These figures, so far as they go, indicate that the districts are at least not increasingly dependent.

To this result the Jews contribute not a little. Through their Federation, they succeed in providing for the bulk of their poor, very few of whom fall to the care of the Overseers. In the North End, as nearly as can be ascertained, out of about 120 families aided by the Overseers in 1901, perhaps a dozen were Jewish, and half of these were aided only temporarily. The conference of the Associated Charities which deals most with them has not over twenty-five per cent. of its cases from that race. That is to say, the addition of the Jews to the population of Boston has resulted in little permanent direct increase of demand upon the city's relief resources. Indirectly, of course, their mere presence has contributed to the industrial pressure which has forced others to apply for aid.

Among the Italians there are one or two relief societies, which, however, are in the main mutual insurance orders, paying sickness and death benefits. Their general charitable work, limited as it is to their surplus funds, is necessarily of small extent. In many cases where Italians ask for aid it is because sickness has exhausted the little hoard accumulated in the summer for maintenance during the idle winter months. When they obtain aid from the Overseers, work is required at the Wayfarers' Lodge, where they often believe themselves on a " City job." Most of the aid given them is temporary. Out of the 120 families already mentioned as being aided by the Overseers of the Poor at the North End, about 25 were Italian, and only 7 of these have received continuous relief. The Associated Charities last year, on the other hand, found three quarters of its 279 North End cases, of which 103 were new cases, among the Italians.

Though the total number of cases relieved through Conference IX. of the Associated Charities was 309, the number of colored families receiving assistance was but 35. This is accounted for not so much by prosperity — for there is much poverty among the Negroes — as by the forms of mutual aid that exist among the people of this race. Nearly every respectable Negro belongs to a sick benefit association, which he values, when in health, for its social opportunities, and turns to for aid in time of need.

By elimination we come to a conclusion, also verified by positive experience, that the Irish race furnishes the bulk of the dependents in the North and West Ends. Of the families in the North End aided by the Overseers, sixty per cent. are Irish or Irish-American ; of the admissions to the Long Island Almshouse from that district, half are Irish or Irish-American. And ordinarily it is not the lately arrived immigrant that falls back on charity, — it is either those who have been in this country a long while or an American-born generation.

So far, then, as the North and West Ends are dependent districts, immigration is not immediately and directly responsible. The newcomers, while many are poor enough, are usually here in order to better themselves ; most have not lived in large cities, nor have they an extensive acquaintance with charity. It is rather the stragglers left behind by the earlier immigrants that are unequal to the task of self-support. Years of residence in a poor, crowded quarter, association chiefly with their own countrymen and contact with American life only at isolated and often the least salutary points undermine their self-respect and make them liable to become alms receivers.

Systematic care of children necessarily works in intimate association with other kinds of organized effort. The specific work of this nature in Boston is divided between the City and several private societies. The City conducts all juvenile work through the Children's Institutions Department, which takes in charge not only dependent and neglected children, but also truants and juvenile lawbreakers. Boy criminals are sent to the House of Reformation at Rainsford Island; the truants are sent to the Parental School at West Roxbury; while the dependent and neglected children are placed out in selected homes in various parts of New England. In the placing-out work, the children are assigned to families of the same religious faith as the parents. On February 1, 1902, the end of the recording year, 860 children were in charge of the Placing-Out Division, of which number 319 were boarding and 320 in free homes; the remainder were in institutions, chiefly the Massachusetts School for the Feeble-Minded.

It is the policy of the Children's Institutions Department not to admit children to its care if any private agency is available. The most extensive of these agencies is the Boston Children's Aid Society, which does comprehensive and thorough-going work with both destitute and wayward children. Its methods are, in brief: first, investigation and, if likely to prove sufficient, advice; if further treatment is required, it refers the case whenever possible to some other and special agency; when this is not feasible, it retains supervision itself. Its work in all three ways is elastic and personal. The Bureau of Information and Counsel, although less conspicuous than the other departments, is especially valuable because its work is so largely preventive; its importance will appear somewhat from the fact that it rendered service in over 750 instances during the past year, — a larger number than was credited to any other department. The Placing-Out Department has under its supervision at any one time an average of over 250 children, scattered over New England in private homes.

Destitute and abandoned children are also cared for through the Society of St. Vincent de Paul. For the most part, this society does not continue a systematic supervision, but places the children in Roman Catholic institutions. Out of 368 variously placed last year, 293 were consigned to such institutions and 69 to private families.

The Society for the Prevention of Cruelty to Children protects neglected or abused children, chiefly by legal means. It effects this in the homes of the children if possible; otherwise, it removes the children.

The day nurseries, of which there are two — one at the North and one at the West End — not only provide during the day better care for young children than they are likely to receive at home, but allow mothers opportunity for work or for recovery from sickness. In connection with the North Ben-

net Street Day Nursery, at the North End, older
girls are taught cooking, table work and care of
children, mothers' meetings are held, and entertainments are given for both fathers and mothers.
The matron visits in the families of the children,
and by suggestion and encouragement tries to increase the sense of responsibility in the mothers,
and to help toward healthy, prudent home life.
This nursery is entirely free; at the West End,
the payment of five cents a day is required.

At the North and West Ends, as in the city at
large, resources for medical aid are comparatively
abundant. Perhaps no form of charity is given or
received with more satisfaction. Given, it meets
an evident need; received, it produces little of
the demoralization often consequent upon material
relief, although not even medical aid, of course,
escapes being imposed upon. In the West End
there is particularly easy access to such resources,
as it contains the Massachusetts General Hospital; the Boston Lying-in Hospital; and the House
of the Good Samaritan, where care and medical
treatment are provided for white women and girls,
and for young boys; the West End Nursery and Infants' Hospital; St. Monica's Home, a hospital for
colored women and girls; the Vincent Memorial
Hospital, for wage-earning women and girls; the

Massachusetts Charitable Eye and Ear Infirmary; the New England Eye and Ear Hospital; and in Haymarket Square, the Relief Station of the Boston City Hospital. A branch of the Mount Sinai Hospital has recently been erected by the Jews for the better accommodation of the patients of that race. Eight or more prominent hospitals situated elsewhere in Boston are open also to the sick of these districts. The House of the Good Samaritan, the out-patient departments of the other hospitals, and the Relief Station are entirely free, but with these exceptions the hospitals make some charge whenever the patients are able to pay.

Dispensaries are connected with nearly all of these hospitals, and a number of independent dispensaries are to be found here and there in this part of the city. In connection with one of the latter a hospital is maintained at the South End. The Epworth League maintains a medical mission in the North End. Two doctors and two nurses are kept busy answering the calls of the neighborhood, chiefly among the Jews and the Italians. A small fee is charged for prescriptions, and a moderate charge is made for visits to the homes.

In the North and West Ends, though not to the same extent as in the South End, the sign " Dispensary " is occasionally hung out to attract practice for a quack doctor, or is applied to what poses as a charitable institution in the announcements of "benefit" performances, while it more than covers expenses by its charges for medicine.

Under the classification made at the beginning of this chapter, a few enterprises stand on the border line between the remedial and the coöperative. They furnish a much needed form of charitable aid, but it is their purpose to use business methods as far as possible. The Industrial Aid Society, the remainder of whose corporate name reads " for the Prevention of Pauperism," is a free employment office for both men and women. It makes special efforts to secure situations in the country. Of its applicants at present about one half of the men and one third of the women — these often with children — are sent to be employed out of town. Nearly twice as many positions are found for women as for men. " The men and women," says a late report, "for whom we seek and find work are very largely drawn from that class of the community who are helped by private charity, and are liable at any moment to become recipients of public aid and thereby become veritable paupers." This society has for some time attempted to coöperate with the City's Wayfarers' Lodge and Temporary Home, in the case of the latter with more success than in that of the former. The men interviewed by the society's agent at the Lodge, while they appeared "temporarily out of a place and willing to work if work could be found for them," proved in many instances to be "wholly indifferent to their own welfare, caring only to obtain a shelter for the night and something to eat." For a number of women from the Home, places have been provided by the society.

Another small private charity of similar nature is a society which is connected with Conference VII. of the Associated Charities. This society gives out plain sewing to women, and sells the completed garments at a reasonable rate to the poor. It is intended to be educational in its influence, helping the women to a permanent trade.

From the density and character of the population in the North and West Ends, one would suppose that here, if anywhere in the city, is the place for efforts at model housing. The only organized attempt of the kind, however, is that of the Boston Coöperative Building Company, two of whose five estates are in these districts. Neither building was erected by the company, though a new addition was made to one of them. The tenements are kept in a sanitary and not overcrowded condition, and proper moral standards are insisted upon. The limited extent of this company's effort in the North and West Ends is due to the law which requires that a house containing more than three families shall be thoroughly fireproof. A recent report of this company declares: " Careful estimates of the cost of model tenements make it clear that such a house cannot be expected to make a good return upon the investment. . . . It is clear that as far as the North End is concerned it will not much longer be a residential district. The encroachments of business, especially since the building of the new Union Stations, have raised the price of land to such a point that it becomes impossible for us to supply good new tenements at low rentals." In the West End the colored people are being crowded out by " the Jews, for whom we need not build, as their own people supply all necessary accommodations." The upshot is that this company is locating its new buildings on the edge of Roxbury.

By individual initiative, however, a few additional attempts in this direction have been made. Among the houses privately owned or leased and conducted upon improved methods may be mentioned several on Chardon Street and others on Norman Street and Church Place.

Jewish landlords, as the report of the Boston Coöperative Building Company points out, are building tenement houses, but the accommodations which they furnish comply with the law by the narrowest possible margin. Such structures tend to throw the burden of maintaining tolerable housing conditions upon the Building Department of the City and the inspectors of the Board of Health.

Extensive as is the equipment and organization of all these remedial agencies, and imposing as is the array of their activities, all combined they succeed in accomplishing little more than enabling the community to hold its own in the struggle for social health. Their work is negative; it strives merely to prevent the weaker parts of the community from succumbing to forces too strong for them. So far as it is successful, it gives people the bare opportunity to make what they can of themselves, but does little to aid them in the process.

Of the spontaneous efforts at self-improvement, the trade union, one of the most familiar, seems to be of less importance in the life of the North and West Ends than elsewhere, at any rate among the more recent immigrants. In trades like the garment-makers, the Jews form the majority of the union membership; the Jewish bakers are organized separately ; in a few trades there are some Italians. In the Jews the racial combination of the communistic and individualist tempers, now one, now the other uppermost, prevents effectual coöperation. Often ready enough to organize, they with equal readiness break up on a division of interests. The Italians commonly do the most unskilled sort of work ; this, in addition to the jealousy felt toward each other by natives of the different sections of Italy, renders concerted action difficult. Both Jews and Italians, being unaccustomed to liberty, are at a loss how to use it. The Irish of the district, on the contrary, are natural organizers, and have been in this country longer than either of the Continental peoples. Probably a fairly large proportion of them belong to unions. But these represent mostly unskilled trades, demanding no very high grade of ability ; and the organizations, being no more stable than the members composing them, form on the whole no influential part of the trade-union world, on which, indeed, they sometimes bring discredit by hasty, ill-considered action.

There are many Socialists among the Jews, and a few among the Italians. At present they are not to any great extent banded together in active organizations. No doubt good times largely account for the absence of aggressive social unrest. In any case, extreme types of Socialism, imported from amid Continental proletarian conditions, soon become much modified by American influences.

The form of organization which seems to have struck the fancy of the Jews is the benefit order. Some of these are exclusively of Jewish membership, like the Brith Abraham and the Sons of Benjamin, which extend throughout the country; others — and these seem to be in even higher favor — are lodges of familiar American orders, such as the Knights of Pythias. The social features of these societies constitute, of course, no small part of their attractiveness.

The Italians have a number of benefit orders. Some of these are lodges of national organizations like the Foresters and the Knights of Columbus. They also have several military societies. They belong in greatest numbers to the religious societies connected with the various churches. Demanding little from members in the way of dues or duties, appealing to traditional sentiment in the perpetuated celebration of festival days, and providing social intercourse in many ways, the religious societies have, especially among the Southern Italians, a well-nigh universal following.

Among both Jews and Italians there are small local clubs for purely social purposes. These are apt to be rather short-lived, springing up among groups of young people that happen to be thrown together, and dying out when their interests begin to diverge. The masters of the North End schools are encouraging the formation of associations among their graduates, in an attempt to make social intercourse more permanent and to have it centre around educational influences.

The importance of the spontaneous efforts often lies not so much in the external, concrete effect they succeed in producing as in their disclosure of real wants. It often happens that the more necessary a reform is, the less able are those in need of it to carry it out. But wherever there is a persistent endeavor for a certain object, no matter whether or not the endeavor succeeds, there exists a want which the best intelligence of the community must reckon with sooner or later. Here is the point at which social energy put forth will count for most, because at this point it will meet with most coöperation.

In the enterprises which we have termed in the broadest sense coöperative, we find the desire to improve met half-way by the desire to help. In them the community's best intelligence is set to guide aspirations to their fulfillment, — the ideal form of social service. Its greatest embodiments are the church and the school, which are, in spite of their imperfections, the most powerful institutions in human society aside from the family. There must be a continual readjustment of professional methods, but this form will always remain the ideal, — the expert in the service of the many.

Perhaps the most conspicuous example of this sort of organization in the districts under review is the North Bennet Street Industrial School. The name designates a group of very effective enterprises more or less independent of one another, but housed in one building. Founded some twenty years ago as a mission, before long it began to be definitely educational in purpose. Its workers became convinced that the greatest need of the district was training in industry, and accordingly they began experiments, the success of which did much to force that training into the public schools. For fifteen years classes have been sent from the public schools to its different departments; its present public school classes, some fifteen in number and comprising about nine hundred pupils, are instructed in modeling, sloyd, leather work and printing. In addition it has its own evening classes in millinery, dressmaking, cooking and sewing, together with gymnastics for both girls and boys.

Besides the Industrial School proper, and en-

tirely unconnected with it, there is in the same
building the day nursery already mentioned and a
kindergarten, from which a number of clubs have
grown up. By intimate acquaintance with the
families, it aims to coöperate with them in the
training of the children; at the same time it is
careful not to diminish the parents' responsibility.
Bearing only indirectly upon the local life, there
is a normal training school in sloyd, of whose graduates about one hundred and fifty are now teaching
in various parts of the country. A branch of the
Public Library in the building does much to stimulate and supply a local desire for good reading,
especially among the children. Its quarters, however, are really inadequate; there should at least
be separate rooms for adults and children. This
group of enterprises is an example of intelligent
adaptation of means to needs. Discarding several
departments — an employment office, a relief station and others — when they proved ill advised, it
has progressively met the wants of its district. A
reading-room on Hanover Street, while not connected directly with the North Bennet Street Industrial School, derives its support and direction
from the same general source. This pleasant resort, which is for men only, is open afternoon and
evening. Representatives of many nationalities

and types of employment avail themselves of its privileges.

Generally similar in character to the industrial department of the North Bennet Street School, although designed specifically for a single race, is the Hebrew Industrial School on Allen Street. Here the work is chiefly among girls and young women, who are taught cooking, sewing, the care of the home and other kindred branches. The aim is less to train them to become wage earners than to fit them for the duties of domestic life. A single club of boys, numbering twenty-five or more, engage in the study of history and in debates upon current questions, to the end that they may take an intelligent part in public affairs and become good citizens. The school follows the best Jewish ideals.

Two other agencies for social improvement are at work chiefly among a single nationality. The Society for the Protection of Italian Immigrants aims to insure new arrivals from Italy against deception and villainy, and also to instruct them in the English language and to give them some knowledge of the institutions of this country. Educational classes are held at its headquarters on Hanover Street. Like the Hebrew Industrial School, this society is conducted by representatives of the same race as that of its constituency.

They both include among their supporters numerous public-spirited citizens of Boston birth and traditions.　The Civic Service House, on Salem Street, is a settlement having Jewish young men for its residents, some of whom have grown up in the North End.　It is intended primarily for Jews, but includes Italians also within the scope of its efforts.　Political enlightenment is the underlying purpose of its clubs, classes and courses of lectures.　Hence it reaches chiefly boys and young men.　Its financial support is from non-Jewish sources.

The oldest of the settlements established at the North and West Ends is the Epworth League House, to whose medical work reference has already been made.　Next in importance to this kind of service is its effort in the interest of advanced education.　Two literary clubs, one of young men, the other of young women, Jews and Italians, have been carried on for a number of years with signal success.　Several members of the young men's club have taken partial or complete college courses, and some have entered professional careers. These received not only encouragement but much of their actual instruction from residents of the Epworth League House.　There is a distinctively religious atmosphere about all the work of this settlement. A Sunday-school has a regular place on its programme. No aggressive attempt is made at proselytism however.

The North End Union, under the direction of the Benevolent Fraternity of Churches, is hardly a settlement in the full sense. During the school year it rents much of its room to the city for school and kindergarten purposes. In two trades, printing and plumbing, a sort of trade school is carried on ; only those, however, already engaged at the trade may attend. The school aims to supplement the practical knowledge gained by daily work, not to teach beginners. Its classes are recruited from the city at large. In other ways the Union touches more nearly the life of the neighborhood. A gymnasium and a bath are at the service of all on simple conditions, and a reading and recreation room is open to boys certain hours of the day and evening. There is also a Sunday afternoon school broadly ethical in its aims. A flower mission is an important part of the summer work. For the accommodation of the children, a separate house is provided a few doors away. Here sewing and other classes for girls are held.

There are two settlements in the West End, both having women residents only. The work of the Elizabeth Peabody House centres about the kindergarten and the influence upon home life which may grow out of it. The House is situated in one of the most thoroughly foreign spots in the West End, where the homes stand in great need of the domestic standards inculcated by the residents. The Willard Y. Settlement makes a special point of the provision of quarters for working girls, although it also devotes considerable attention to the children of the neighborhood. Connected with this settlement is a summer playground for children.

Very much in the spirit of the settlements are the home libraries of the Children's Aid Society, scattered throughout the district to the number of twenty. Since the first of these libraries was established fifteen years ago, the plan has won wide recognition, and has been adopted in many other cities. The system, which is now familiar, consists in placing a small library in some home, with one of the children as custodian, and with a volunteer visitor in charge. The library group, ten in number, meet the volunteer director once a week in the home, talk over the books which they have read, play games or plan for any activities which the group may carry on. From this centre influences branch out in all directions, and the possibilities are limited only by the personal resources and capacity of the leader. The children belonging to these libraries are usually under fifteen years of age.

The Stamp Savings or Home Savings Society affords a natural introduction to a neighborhood. It at once gives the collector an occupation with which he may be identified in the minds of his public, and puts in his way many opportunities for friendly service. There are collecting stations at the North End Union, the Epworth League and Elizabeth Peabody Houses and St. Andrew's. A number of independent collectors have lists of families whose savings they call for at weekly intervals.

Aside from its work through such agencies as its Building Department, Board of Health and Street Cleaning Division, the City contributes to the health and enjoyment of people in its crowded quarters through its public baths, gymnasiums and playgrounds. The North End Park, which lies along the water-front at the foot of Copp's Hill, combines a beach bath with a general pleasure resort. Here on either side is a solidly constructed building containing dressing quarters, one of the houses being for men and boys, the other for women and girls. A double recreation pier extends well out into the water, affording a delightful view of the harbor. A portion of the beach is reserved for girls and young children, where swings, see-saws and piles of sand are provided. Space is furnished also for quoits, hand ball and other games in which the boys like to engage. The play, as well as the bathing, is in charge of attendants and instructors in the pay of the City. Band concerts are occasionally given, and the season ends with a water carnival, at which prizes are offered for proficiency in swimming. Everything is entirely free with the exception that a small fee is charged for the use of bathing suits and towels. In the case of children, even this charge may be remitted. The popularity of this park may be inferred from the number of bathers during a single summer. In 1901 this amounted to 280,000, the larger part of whom were from the immediate vicinity. The North End Park is in charge of the Department of Public Baths.

At the West End, similar opportunities for health and recreation are provided in the Charlesbank, a park extending along the river-front the whole distance between the Craigie and West Boston bridges. This park is under the direction of the Municipal Park Commission. There are no out-of-door bathing facilities, but hot and cold baths are furnished the year round, the two sexes occupying separate buildings. An open-air gymnasium adjoins each of these bathing establishments ; and the women may continue athletic exercises through the winter in a gymnasium under the same roof with their bath. The women's gymnasium, as well as a spacious playground for children, is in charge of the Massachusetts Emergency and Hygiene Association. The Charlesbank includes a pleasant resort with shaded walks and seats and an attractive view of the river.

In the West End Branch of the Public Library, the City has made local provision for needs of another character. The stately old West Church building was purchased in 1894 for the purpose, and has been admirably adapted to its new uses. Here three hundred or more reference books may be consulted, and selections may be made from twelve thousand other volumes for reading on the premises or for use at home. In addition, the two reading-rooms, one for adults and one for children, are well supplied with periodical literature. Each year sees a marked increase in the number of people availing themselves of these privileges. In 1900, 131,522 books were taken out for reading at home; in 1901, 137,713. The reading-rooms, with a combined seating capacity of 350, are often crowded, especially on Sunday. Among this great number of patrons, the Jews are the most largely represented; the Irish come next, and there is a considerable proportion of Negroes.

Very recently a combination of interests has been formed with the general improvement of the North End as its object. Its significance lies in the fact that it undertakes to be an alliance of all citizens in sympathy with its object, and includes Roman Catholic clergy, local politicians and settlement workers. The churches were the prime movers, driven to such exertions by the menacing fact that the better members of their congregations are leaving the district for more desirable residential quarters. Already something has been accomplished in the way of securing cleaner streets and better order. It is through concrete effort based on familiarity with the detailed facts that this attempt promises to be effective.

Slight as this enterprise is, it represents a sufficient conjunction of forces to rouse the hope of distinct and permanent gains in social conditions at the North End. It is carrying toward a logical conclusion the motive in which the best type of social service, as seen in these districts, is undertaken. By means of allied action on the part of all their centres of influence, whether of a normal or an exceptional character, the great bulk of the population of each district could be drawn into a common loyalty and trained to a collective initiative. Every helpful agency would be enabled to make its full contribution to the local well-being with only a minimum of loss on account of isolation or cross-purposes. Each would have its standing as a recognized constituent factor in the total life of its district. The best inherent possibilities of the people would be brought to light by such developments of mutual aid. It would then be easy to secure from the municipality further large measures designed to meet district needs. In general, through the growth of district public spirit, the North and West Ends, as compact units, would be enabled to draw far more deeply upon the vast resources of the city's civilization.

CHAPTER XII

ASSIMILATION : A TWO-EDGED SWORD

THERE is somewhere a parable that narrates how a dread disease appeared in the lodge of a great estate. The manor-house was far in through winding lanes. Yet one day the scourge, spreading this way and that, leaped over the distance, smiting the firstborn and future master. Thus was it burned into the souls of those in the great house and those in the cottage that there is one human family.

At the city's gateway lie two communities stricken with the evils attendant on toil and deprivation, and kept aloof by alien birth as well as by poverty from prosperous, indigenous citizenship. In the simpler round of domestic life and friendly intercourse, the people are to a surprising degree without reproach ; but the larger social life tends to drift as it will. There is a measure of vicarious public spirit sustained for these districts by men and women whose sphere of influence would ordinarily lie elsewhere. These persons also strive to broaden and strengthen character among the people against the strain of an untried, distracting existence. The ultimate issue for individual and common well-being lies in the counter-currents which are bringing these communities into the full vital circulation of the city's existence.

The North and West Ends, along several important lines, provide a large share of the labor force required for the city. They are also rapidly opening avenues of small trade auxiliary to some of the city's principal business enterprises. The development of skilled workers is slow and needs encouragement. Not so with the shopkeepers. Indeed within a comparatively short time many of them will be found in the ranks of the downtown merchants, while their children are even now forcing their way upward into the professions.

Yet the path of success is blocked to many of those who feel in themselves the capacity for better things. To them America has represented great hopes. Democracy meant a breaking down of the barriers that confined them ; but they discover this to be true only as affecting the technical framework of democracy, — the administration of government. Baffled in other directions, men with initiative and mental grasp give rein to their power and ambition in the field of politics. These leaders develop an unscrupulous system of control over local interests, public and private. The spread of this system to all similar districts has made it to a large extent dominant in the public administration of the city. The prosperous classes have begun to find that a demoralizing political régime, bred in the midst of an alien, ill-favored way of life, is getting its hold upon the affairs of their pleasant residential districts, and even at times threatens important downtown business interests.

Here begins the application of the parable. Among the most respectable suburban population to be found within the boundaries of the city there is a startling instance of political contagion. A man holding great political power, formerly in high office, determined to hold still higher, stands practically convicted of misappropriation of public funds. Notwithstanding this fact, it is only by the most earnest and persistent efforts of high-minded citizens that he is kept from full political control of the district. What is the secret of his mysterious power? This man, a Republican, of New England origin, now living in the same fashion as his suburban neighbors, began his political career not many years ago as a resident of the West End, under the tutelage of the

Democratic boss of that district. The West End
Democratic boss secured his nomination and election as a Republican to the State legislature. This
same boss assisted him to an important appointive
office under a Republican mayor. On removing to
the suburbs he at once proceeded to put in force
the policy of his master, adapted somewhat to different local conditions. The two men continue to
maintain an offensive and defensive alliance, with
utter disregard of party lines. It is as if in the
Civil War there had been two bands of guerrillas,
ostensibly on opposite sides in the contest but
really acting in unison, caring nothing for the
issue at stake, and only for booty. In the City
Council it is now and then possible to see this alliance in actual operation. There are times when
some disgraceful scheme has been so thoroughly
exposed as to draw off all members who have any
healthy fear of public opinion. At such moments,
when the smoke of conflict clears, a group of the
West End type of Democrats and certain Dorchester Republicans are often found standing together,
held by the honor which obtains among such.

This combination greatly aids the boss of the
West End in postponing the effects of the incur-
sion of an alien race into his ward. The North
End leader has been studying how he too, under

similar stress, may make to himself friends of the suburban mammon of unrighteousness. He is, in a different way, proceeding to lay a long base line for general municipal operations. He has decided to give up his home in the country and establish himself as resident boss in one of the Dorchester wards, just beyond South Boston, whose leader died recently. This ward presents a promising future to him, as it is fast becoming Democratic. His brother will remain as regent in the North End. The North End ward and this Dorchester ward, in the near future, will be found acting in rigid unison. They will exercise a combined leverage at City Hall equal to that of three or four wards acting separately. Supposing the present political working unity between the North and West Ends to continue, the two districts pictured forth in this book, each with its surburban satrapy, will determine the public policy of the city of Boston.

Political conditions in districts like the North and West Ends are the occasion of much of the corrupting influence which certain corporations exert upon the City Council and the State legislature, though the blame of the corporations is not less but greater on that account. The bosses of these two districts are frequently mentioned in such connections. There is striking evidence that corporation leaders accept, use and fortify the ward machine system. A recent flagrant case before the legislature, involving a matter profoundly and obviously affecting the well-being of the congested masses of the people, was at last disposed of satisfactorily only by a powerful veto message from the governor. At every stage the representatives of the North and West Ends voted like automata in support of extortionate corporation demands. The explanation is, of course, that so many corporation jobs and other favors have been dispensed in those districts that their representatives were completely in the power of the corporation. If a prominent corporation leader aspires to the governorship, with its saving veto power, the ease with which he secures control of the political resources of Wards 6 and 8, and similar districts, is the prime element of strength in his candidacy.

The time must come when the honest citizens of Dorchester, who find themselves hard put to it to crush the viper in their bosom, shall open their eyes to the fact that the political problem of Dorchester cannot be disposed of except by including the North and West Ends in a combined attack. Back Bay citizens with some of the old-time Boston public spirit, who are amazed to discover college mates

and fellow club members confronting them in their
reasonable efforts to protect the public interest,
must begin to devote an important part of their
attention to the enemy's base of supply for aldermanic and legislative votes in Wards 6 and 8 and
similar little known sections of the city. Sagacious business men, demanding that the legislature
shall treat corporation franchises precisely as a
business firm would, must not only scrutinize the
propositions which the corporations set before the
legislature, but must deal with those determining
factors in the background, where legislators from
the crowded districts have their walk and conver-
sation with their constituents, which prevent their
making a good bargain for the public and cause
them so easily to acquiesce in arrogant corporation
demands.

It may be doubted whether evil communications are much worse than no communications at
all. There is a strange, ever-increasing reaction
upon the life of affairs and upon social morality in
Boston as a result of the rift in society between
the native and immigrant stocks. In affairs the
distinction, speaking roughly, is that between business and politics. The successful business classes
are filled with contempt for the entire political
personnel. Membership in the City Council im-

pairs a man's business credit if he has any. It is literally true that among business men an apology seems to be called for when one is seen in City Hall. In Athens it was the mark of the aristocracy that they governed the city, while the newly enfranchised class attended to its provisioning. In this latter-day democratic city, the situation is precisely reversed. This means that the large majority of those men in Boston who are making the fullest use of American economic opportunities are fast dismissing from their minds the civic responsibilities which form the just and essential balance to those opportunities. Considering the serious nature of our municipal needs, the question may fairly be raised whether the average business man in Boston is any worthier pillar of a democratic municipality than is the average politician.

On the moral side, the working classes, strikingly illustrated by the two districts under review in this volume, are not held together with the established and comfortable classes in a single great spiritual communion standing ever for common humanity. The two sections of society are in separate and opposing religious bodies. The force of these divergent loyalties is distinctly anti-social. Religious cleavage, coinciding very closely with racial and industrial lines of distinction, tends to make the old-established Protestantism of the city a mere middle-class religion. To Protestantism, and to Protestants as such, this means exclusion from the most essential moral function of the church in a democracy, and ultimate apathy and atrophy in the face of public moral needs.

So far as informal social intercourse goes, the native part of the city's population has been constituted a separated aristocracy, in spite of itself, by the coming of the immigrants. There is sometimes a saving human relation between classes where they have the same blood and the same traditions, as in Scotland. Here, on the contrary, the favored class, except by special exertion, has little if any common experience upon which to base common understanding with those who make up the city's industrial population. Even when persons from one side come in contact with persons from the other, there are special obstacles to that by-play of acquaintance which softens and uplifts the motives of life, and serves particularly as an antidote to the temptations of the prosperous. It even begins to appear that the absence of the means of social intercommunication is a serious hindrance in the conduct of business. To the employer, the ease of coming to terms and keeping on terms with his labor force is an increasingly important factor in his

success. Many thoughtful business men are conscious of the fact that the character of the growth
of the city's population has left them particularly
at a loss in this respect.

It is clear, therefore, that the problems of the
North and West Ends cannot be considered alone.
In the more obvious point of view, the needs of
these districts, in themselves, are so great as to
call upon the whole city for remedy. When the
situation is looked into more deeply, the reflex
influence of these communities upon the city as an
entirety is so pervasive as to challenge the collective efforts of citizens and the corporate action of
the municipality and the commonwealth.

There has already been governmental procedure
against unsanitary dwellings, against a degrading
form of industry, against base amusements, which
has lifted the whole material and moral scale of
living. Steps toward the public supply of positive
social opportunity are now being taken. The two
waterside playgrounds for summer sports are soon
to have their complement in two public indoor gymnasiums with baths, one for each district. This,
with the provision of baths in the new school buildings, will furnish satisfactory public facilities for
cleanliness and physical exercise. A beginning has
been made in the public use of school buildings, out

of regular hours, for special forms of education and recreation; this movement will, without doubt, be rapidly extended. At no distant date there must be in each of these districts a kind of local town hall which shall serve as a highly attractive centre for technical and artistic training, for the popular ministry of good music, good books and good pictures, and for every sort of friendly gathering that includes large numbers of different racial types of the people. Such an institution may, without hesitation, be said to be a necessity to the Americanization and general progress of such communities.

Along with new forms of municipal enterprise, there is still need of further penetrating action in the better care of the streets, in the establishment of a still higher standard for the condemnation of unsanitary dwellings and in further restrictions upon the alteration of old houses into flats and tenements. It is much to be hoped, in the interest of the North End population, that the day may soon come when the business of the city will require the opening of new streets which shall cut through some of its congested areas to connect the North and South Stations.

The development of a far-sighted, human municipal policy will add greatly to the health and happiness of North and West End people. It will have an indirect result which will be hardly less important. Such municipal action, coming close to the needs of the people, will create among them a realistic civic sense. It will give them some actual experience and training in the privileges of democracy. It will constantly illustrate to them, in such ways that they will themselves feel the distinction, the relative effects of good and bad administration. While such a programme will not destroy boss power, it is certain that abstract reform is impotent to produce that result in these districts. What may be hoped for is the gradual rise of a higher type of political leader, one who will seek popular support through the promotion of such public services as have been mentioned, rather than through various dubious forms of patronage.

A quite unideal politician of this more progressive type may well have the coöperation of those who are seeking the next step, not the ultimate height, in municipal and social improvement. Politicians who persist in turning their eyes away from the light, who show no sense of their public responsibility, and no purpose to raise the condition of the entire mass of the people in their districts, must be pilloried as public enemies. Here again there must be a general movement throughout the city if actual results are to be achieved. The power of all the local politicians is, to a large extent, sustained and increased by combinations formed in the Board of Aldermen. The total number of responsible citizens throughout the city could assert their will if the aldermen were nominated and elected at large, and the records of all candidates for the board placed under the scrutiny of the whole city.[1] The Public School Association, after a few years of determined effort, has been able to change the character of the School Board. Having won in this preliminary skirmish, municipal reform must now proceed to the far more serious task of providing the city with a responsible group, if not majority, of men in its chief legislative chamber. The high standard which has been kept for the mayoralty would thus be made much more secure ; but, what is especially to the present point, the possibility of drawing upon public resources and wielding public influence as material of ward machine transactions would be greatly restricted.

---

[1] Recent legislation looking toward the abolition of nominating conventions makes the chance of success in this matter much greater than it has been at any time before. These conventions are often used to defeat the popular will.

In support of this attack, front and rear, in City Hall and among the tenement houses, against the worst phases of municipal corruption, there is urgent need of action on the part of business organizations, on the one hand, and the church, on the other. The commercial and moral welfare of the city is certainly deeply involved. But aside from politics, the situation in the North and West Ends, and other similar districts, calls for large enterprise on the part of these interests, each acting within its own sphere.

There are ways of economic service for the sake of the city and the nation amid such populations, affecting their housing, their food, their industry, their recreation, in which there is urgent need of the best business method and the best business skill. Young men in commercial callings, who under different circumstances would aspire to fulfill some honorable official public duty, may thus find opportunities which to the discerning mind are quite as interesting and rewarding.

As to the churches of the well-to-do, — which, speaking broadly, means the Protestant churches, — it has been made clear that in their formal doctrinal capacity, they can touch only the fringe of the situation set forth in these chapters. Not far from one third of all the people of Boston fall into the same general category as the inhabitants of the North and West Ends, — heavily handicapped by material conditions in every struggle for character and the more abundant life, held in religious associations chiefly made up of themselves, and therefore impotent to lift the load. Numerous forerunners have indeed gone forth out of the resourceful, separated churches of the prosperous city districts ; but there must come out of these comfortable congregations a large, free, adventurous movement which in the name of the one God and a common humanity shall address itself to this greatest of all the city's spiritual needs. It is a melancholy reflection that when any serious moral crisis arises in the thick of the Boston working classes, the old-established religious life of the city is almost utterly without authority or power among them in shaping the issue. Yet there are a thousand human ways, aside from the region of sectarian strife, in which such moral influence can be established.

For the larger work of social uplift among the people of the North and West Ends, the foregoing studies indicate the main lines of action. The population may be broadly separated into three different strata, each having needs quite different from those of the others. There is the residuum at the bottom,

characterized by some chronic form of dependence
or degeneracy. There is the aristocracy of labor at
the top, those who are likely to rise out of working-class life altogether, including all who are born
with special capacity, whatever their surroundings
may be. Between the two levels is a great middle
class of labor, the working class proper, made up
of those who will neither rise nor fall out of their
grade, and most of whose children will not pass
above it.

Among those who make up the residuum, much
more thoroughgoing methods are needed than those
now in force. The tramps, or roving paupers, who
are very common in these districts, especially in
winter, ought to encounter in Boston a work test
that would be sternly reinforced by the police and
by an awakened public sentiment. The Board of
Overseers, by a daring, determined policy in connection with the Wayfarers' Lodge, could effectually remove Boston from the tramps' road map,
and thus abolish the roving pauper so far as Boston is concerned. The early stages of resident
pauperism, drunkenness, prostitution and crime
should be met by patient counteracting treatment;
but their more advanced phases ought all to be
dealt with after the manner of the cumulative
sentence leading up to permanent seclusion. By

removing these specially difficult factors from the poverty equation, it would be much easier to conduct forms of relief for those who have honorably fallen out of the struggle for subsistence, temporarily or permanently. There would be free scope for broadly devised private, coöperative and municipal measures of assistance to families overcome by some domestic catastrophe, to workmen forced into the ranks of the unemployed and to industrial veterans who have worthily ended their term of service. All such effort, since early Christian days, has had its dignity from the side of human compassion. Modern economic science has given added meaning to it by showing the importance of saving the wastes of labor force, and of shielding the superior grades of labor from the disastrous competition of those who, for one reason or another, are driven to a desperate fight for bare existence.

For those who stand contrasted with the stragglers of the industrial army, whose native capacities mark them out for the higher levels of work and an appreciation of the finer things of life, it is of the greatest public importance that a cramping environment should not be permitted to shut them off from opportunities on the plane of their talents. One of the most serious obstacles that

confronts the ambitious youth from the North and
West Ends takes the form of certain racial dislikes
felt by men of power in the city's business affairs.
Whatever ground there may be for such feelings,
they are comparatively groundless as affecting the
rising generation. An attitude of this sort, where
there ought to be opened up to the bright young
Jew the full range of industry, is condemning
him, somewhat as in the Middle Ages, to certain
narrow lines of trade. It leaves to enterprising
young Irish-Americans little recourse aside from
the ever open path into corrupt politics. Frequently they go into ward politics in order to get
a start in business or the law, and are held for life
by its lucrative but ignoble inducements. The
Italians cannot be kept from entering a very wide
range of occupations, but their rise in their callings is often hindered by that caution on the part
of employers which is akin to prejudice. There
must be a wider entrance for the children of the
newcomers into the great constructive activities of
the city. This is a matter of serious moment to
the commercial progress of the city, as well as to
the young men of the immigrant nationalities.

The waste of ability and genius — one of the
sadly prominent phenomena of North and West
End existence — is coming to be recognized as a

dangerous form of public profligacy.[1] The productive capacity of a nation or a city is the fundamental source of its wealth. In the city of Boston, three brilliant races are bringing forth a new brood. The Irish, for the first time in their history, are having a just opportunity to work out their destiny, held by emulation of the Anglo-Saxons, but no longer driven to the wall by their sheer aggressive force. The Jewish race has an immemorial record as the prolific mother of genius. The Italian strain has historically outstripped all others by being thrice — once politically, once religiously, once intellectually — the dominating power of the world. Yet it is almost a matter of haphazard whether children of these races among us, who may be born with the highest order of capacity, do not have the spirit within them quenched by a childhood spent in dismal, degrading streets. Even after such capacity has begun distinctly to manifest itself, we are content often to throw it away by not making unfailing provision for necessary training and apprenticeship. In England and France it is now publicly recognized as essential to the general advancement in wealth and welfare that the education of specially capable boys and girls should not be hindered by

[1] Marshall: *Principles of Economics*, Vol. I, 2d. ed., p. 272.

such an adventitious circumstance as the poverty or ignorance of the parents. There could hardly be a more profitable investment of public funds than by the establishment of scholarships under which the successful grammar school pupil, otherwise kept by poverty from going farther, should have the opportunity of continuing his education along academical or technical lines, until he had received the best development and training which his talents justified and the community could supply.

For the vast majority of the people in the North and West Ends, between the submerged grades at the bottom and the aristocracy of labor at the top, the sound policy is to encourage and mould every helpful form of association. They are not, on the one hand, goaded by necessity, nor on the other incited by ambition. They constitute the working class proper. They are collectivists ; and loyalties of various kinds are the determining forces among them. Indeed the whole movement of present-day society makes it essential that they should cling together. It is of vital consequence to all concerned, however, that such forms of attachment should be tempered by intelligence, and by tolerance toward other types of people in the community.

Trade unionism is indispensable to a fair standard of life in such a population. Organization for the protection of wages is a step to which the more recent bodies of immigrants may well be urged. This would prevent them from establishing for themselves and tending to fix for others a scale of living which is deleterious to the interests and prospects of the city and the nation. A compact and enlightened form of political organization among the more recent immigrants will be the means of securing them such individual consideration as they need from public authorities, and will teach them the more advantageous as well as nobler way of seeking the general bettering of the local life rather than joining in a scramble for patronage and spoils.

In stimulating such organized action, as well as leavening with better purposes the whole local scheme of mutual aid in the home and of friendly intercourse in the neighborhood, the settlements and other similar centres play an increasingly important part.[1] The Roman Catholic churches, which

---

[1] The public value of such work is beginning to be capable of statistical demonstration. The report of the Institutions Registration Department for 1901–2 shows a falling off in juvenile arrests of from twelve to twenty per cent. throughout the city during the past ten years. The cause of this improvement is ascribed tentatively to the better provision for special cases of

until recently have kept to their one great task of direct appeal to the inner personal nature, are catching something of the same spirit. Too high praise cannot be given to the plan of the newly formed North End Improvement Association, which was organized at the instance of some of their clergy, and includes representatives of all the leading agencies for social improvement in the district.

In the training of the mass of the children, with their average abilities, there is profound need of instruction directed specifically toward their best future usefulness. It is a curious anomaly that the public school should send its pupils forth into the world presumably to earn their livelihood, but with no training for any sort of vocation. Manual training for boys and domestic instruction for girls are being introduced under the stimulus of private philanthropic enterprise. It is to be hoped that they will take up much more space in the public school curriculum, even if a much shorter list of studies should be made necessary as a result.

The importance of industrial education is, however, coming to be felt by all observant persons. The vital question of moral education remains

neglected and dependent children, and to "the manifold individual and associate efforts to improve the environment of children and to direct their youthful energy within law-abiding channels."

strangely in abeyance. It cannot long remain so; it must soon become a burning issue. The Roman Catholic Church stands alone in its proper insistence upon such education; but by maintaining separate schools it serves to keep alive prejudices in its own and other followings which injure the cause of religion as well as the cause of patriotism. The time must come when the public school authorities must make it possible for different religious persuasions to provide their different types of instruction in harmonious relation with the public school system. In this way the values which the Roman Catholic is rightly intent upon would be secured, while the dangers which the Protestant rightly fears from any connection of Church and State would be reduced to a minimum.

Among the different racial types found in the North and West Ends, there are two which present problems that are exceptionally difficult, though hardly at all involved with any question of foreign immigration. The Negro in the Northern cities may, in time, present difficulties comparable to those which he stands for in some of the agricultural regions of the South. So far as the slum is to be a permanency in Boston, it will exist in a chain of black neighborhoods, each having a penumbra formed by mixture with the offscouring of other races. There is much encouragement to be found in the advance made by many colored people ; but for a considerable proportion of them, as against the barriers of almost ineradicable race prejudice, there is little hopeful prospect.

The lodging-house population, an increasing mass of men and women of American or nearly related origin, without the restraint of family ties, ground in the highly organized machinery of great business establishments, the men's wages lowered by the competition of the women, and the women hoping to marry the men whose incomes they have unwittingly undermined, constitute a situation that seems to epitomize the industrial and moral complications of city life. Some slight efforts are being made to make good the peculiar social deprivations of these people ; such efforts must be greatly increased. The state of things is likely, however, to be worse before it is better ; and real improvement must await certain changes in the underlying causes which produce it. The sentiments of people generally must be altered with regard to the desirability of mercantile employment as against skilled manual work ; and there must be a less regard for appearance in the establishment of home life.

The time has hardly yet arrived for any safe estimate of the psychological traits which the different immigrant nationalities will contribute to the future type of Boston citizen. Amalgamation has hardly yet begun. It is clear enough, however, that they are, each in its different way, making valuable contributions to the city's economic and moral welfare.

The Irish, holding to Celtic clan traditions, advance in a body. Their progress is slow, but quite general. The North and West Ends contain a considerable number of them who have proved incapable of rising, but throughout the city their steady ascent in the scale of well-being is one of the obvious facts of the city's life. It is true that as voters many of the Irish can hardly be said as yet to be Americanized. To an observer situated so as to measure subtle changes in their social standards, a higher type of public spirit is clearly seen to be spreading among them. Such progress will be more rapid when public spirit among the native population inclines to seek the coöperation of the best leaders among the Irish in making the city government more fully serve the local public needs of the more congested wards. In the matter of liquor drinking, the past few years have witnessed a distinct veering of sentiment on the part of many Irish citizens, and the Irish clergy in Boston are fast coming into line for organized opposition to the saloon. The beneficial results of such a change of attitude among the leaders of the Irish population will be inconceivably great.

In the North and West Ends, within a few years the last signs of the supremacy of the Irish must pass away, and there will be only degraded remnants of them left stranded in odd nooks and corners. The North End, so far as the encroachments of trade allow it to continue as a place of abode, is to be an Italian stronghold. The West End will pass quite fully into the possession of the Jews. The more progressive members of both nationalities will gradually leave these colonies and scatter themselves throughout the city and suburbs. Thus bereft, and not being so much under the observation of people of other types, there will be danger in both colonies of a relapse. The baser sort among the Italians will feel themselves under less restraint against deeds of disorder and violence. Many of the Jews will inclose themselves in an inhuman sordidness. The violence is no greater evil than the sordidness; there will be need of penetrating measures against both. It is impossible to doubt, however, that each colony in its characteristic way will maintain a predominantly worthy character. In both there will be a high degree of industry, sobriety and domestic peace.

In one the goal of effort will be prosperity ; in the other the simple joys of life. There is already ground for hope that many of the enterprising spirits, who leave their immigrant neighborhoods for the larger theatre of the city's activity, will find satisfaction in seeking the welfare and progress of the local communities in which they and their countrymen were introduced to the ways of American citizenship.

The immigrant nationalities are already adding variety and fresh impulse to the city's industrial and social interests. It is essential that the established civilization of Boston should much more fully lay hold upon the body of feelings and traditions which are represented at the North and West Ends. The motive should be to have them affected by the American spirit, but also to have the American spirit affected by what is real in them. The loyal American, honoring and seeking to preserve much in the genius of each nationality, will thus stimulate each racial type to seek for what is worthy in all the others.

There is a growing conviction that democracy is not merely a political system, but an ethical philosophy. In either view it requires for its existence a large measure of social coherence. This must not be of the nature of a formless solidarity, but must provide for the perspective that comes of having genuine identity in every type of mind and character, and in every form of association which men make on the basis of their heredity, their work, their recreation, their moral ideals. The political framework of the country is a federal union, established in sacrifice, preserved at an appalling cost. In an equally profound sense, the better social order in which the American life of the future will be gathered up must be a federal union also.

INDEX

ADAMS, SAMUEL, 26.
Agricultural work, 118.
Aldermen, Board of, 169.
Alleys. *See* Streets and alleys.
Almshouse, City. *See* Boston, Pauper Trustees.
Americanization, 50, 61 ff., 253 ; of children 291 f., 317 ff. *See* Nationalities, Immigration.
Americans, 42 f.
Amusements, Chap. viii. *See* Nationalities.
Ann Pollard, 12.
Arrests, North End, 190 ff., 196, 202 f. ; West End, 211 f., 220 f. *See* Crime, Police.
Art galleries, 236.
Artisans and mechanics, Colonial, 14, 16, 17, 27, 29 ; Irish, 121 ; Italian, 117 ; Jewish, 117 ; Portuguese, 122 ; statistics of. *See* Assessors' list.
Assessors' list, 135 f.
Associated Charities, 326 f., 329 ff.

Banks and bankers, 111, 119 f.
Barbers, 122 f.
Baron de Hirsch Fund. *See* Jewish Charities.
Baths, at North End Union, 349 ; public, 365 ; school, 300.
Beacon Hill, 13.
Better Dwellings Society, 86.
Blackstone, first settler, 11, 22. *See* Streets.
Boarding houses, 38 f., 140. *See* Lodging houses.
Bootblacks, 118.
Boss, political, 151 ff., 171, 177, 359 f. *See* Political types.
Boston, Almshouse, 127, 330 ; Common, 1, 37 ; Coöperative Building Co., 81, 339 f. ; Health Act, 82 ; House of Correction, 127 ;

incorporation of, 73 ; Island of Boston, 12, 35.
Bowdoin Square, 21, 28, 36.
Bowling Green. *See* Bowdoin Square.
British-Americans, political temper of, 65.
Building Company, Boston Coöperative. *See* Boston.
Buildings. *See* Legislation, Tenements.
Burglary. *See* Crime.

Carpet-baggers, 162, 166.
Catholicism, compared with Judaism, 282 ff. ; Irish and Italian compared, 273 ff. ; Portuguese, 275 ; methods of, 376.
Caucus, methods, 165 ff. ; nomination papers, 163. *See* Parties, Politics.
Cellars, 78, 82, 84 f., 98 f.
Census. *See* Population.
Charity, Chap. xi. *See* Philanthropy.
Charlesbank. *See* Parks and Playgrounds.
Child Labor, 118, 125 f., 306.
Children, Chap. x. ; training of, industrial, 299 ff., 377 ; moral, 300, 377 f. *See* Child labor, Philanthropy.
Children's Aid Society, 334 f. ; Home libraries, 350.
Churches, Catholic, Chap. ix. : North End, St. Mary's, 267 ff. ; St. Stephen's, 268 ff. ; Sacred Heart, 271 f. ; St. Leonard's, 270 f. ; West End, St. Joseph's, 269. *See* Catholicism, Religious work.
Churches, Jewish, Baldwin Place, 276 ; Smith's Court, 276.
Churches, Protestant, Chap. ix. :

The Riverside Press

Electrotyped and printed by H. O. Houghton & Co.
Cambridge, Mass., U. S. A.